Literary Coteries and the Irish Women Writers' Club (1933–1958)

LIVERPOOL ENGLISH TEXTS AND STUDIES 87

LITERARY COTERIES AND THE IRISH WOMEN WRITERS' CLUB (1933–1958)

DEIRDRE F. BRADY

LIVERPOOL UNIVERSITY PRESS

First published 2021 by
Liverpool University Press
4 Cambridge Street
Liverpool
L69 7ZU

This paperback edition published 2024

Copyright © 2024 Deirdre F. Brady

Deirdre F. Brady has asserted the right to be identified as the author of this book in accordance with the Copyright, Designs and Patents Act 1988.

All rights reserved. No part of this book may be reproduced, stored in a retrieval system, or transmitted, in any form or by any means, electronic, mechanical, photocopying, recording, or otherwise, without the prior written permission of the publisher.

British Library Cataloguing-in-Publication data
A British Library CIP record is available

ISBN 978-1-78962-246-1 (hardback)
ISBN 978-1-80207-367-6 (paperback)

Typeset by Carnegie Book Production, Lancaster

Contents

Acknowledgments	vii
List of Figures	ix
Introduction	1
1 Intellectual Fraternities? Dublin United Arts Club, the Irish Academy of Letters and the Irish PEN	15
2 Coterie Culture and the Women Writers' Club, 1933–1958	53
3 "A Wild Field to a Later Generation": The Book of the Year Award	77
4 Women Writers in Irish Print Culture, 1930–1960	127
5 Coterie Culture and Modernist Presses: The Gayfield Press	149
Conclusion	167
Bibliography	173
Index	187

Acknowledgments

I would like to thank Dr Caoilfhionn Ní Bheacháin and Dr Kathryn Laing for their unfailing support throughout the process of writing this book. Their enthusiasm and encouragement sustained me throughout the project. I would also like to thank Professor Gerardine Meaney who was the first to prompt the conversation about the Women Writers' Club. Thanks also to Professor Margaret Harper and Dr Maureen O'Connor for their stimulating discussions about women writers, and to Dr Breda Gray for initiating the research project. The guidance and support from those who work in the libraries of the National Library of Ireland, Trinity College Dublin, the University of Limerick and University College Dublin was invaluable. I would also like to thank those who granted permission to quote from the archival material, including Naoise Deevy, Anthony Shanahan, the Sheehy Skeffington family and Aoife Clarke.

On a personal note, my journey as a writer was inspired by many wonderful women including my mother Patricia, my aunt Marie, my sisters Anne and Teresa, and my lovely daughters, Elaine, Rachel and Gemma. Finally, thank you to my husband, Stephen, for his love and support and unfailing patience.

Figures

1 Photograph of playwright Teresa Deevy receiving her "Book of the Year" award from the Women Writers' Club in 1949. Also pictured are Kyle and Reenie Deevy, along with guests for the Annual Banquet. Picture courtesy of Naomi Deevy from a private family collection.

2 Advertisement for the PEN Anthology of Poetry: *Concord of Harp: An Irish PEN Anthology of Poetry* (Dublin: Talbot Press Ltd, 1953). *Irish Independent*, June 10, 1953.

3 Detail from photograph of Women Writers' Club Dinner. February, 1938. Press Photographs of Eamon de Valera (1882–1975). P150/PH/3664/4.

4 Newspaper cutting of Ena Dargan (left) and Kate O'Brien (middle) at the Women Writers' Club Dinner in the Hibernian Hotel in 1950. *Irish Press*, December 19, 1950.

5 Letter from Blanaid Salkeld to Hanna Sheehy Skeffington, February 12, 1936. MS 47, Sheehy Skeffington Papers, MS 33,607/13, February 12, 1936. Thanks to the Sheehy Skeffington family for permission to use this material.

6 *Fisherman's Wake* (Dublin: Talbot Press, 1940), collection of poetry by Temple Lane.

7 Frontispiece of Maura Laverty's *Cookery Book* (1946), with a section on diet by Sybil le Brocquy and decorations by Louis le Broquy.

8   Newspaper cutting of Ethel Mannin (middle) with Lorna Reynolds (right) at the Women Writers' Club Dinner, circa 1948.

9   Leaflet announcing Extraordinary General Meeting of the Women Writers' Club, 1958.

10 Photograph of "The Inca King: Folk-play at Oruro Carnival". Photographer: Ena Dargan. From: Ena Dargan, *The Road To Cuzco: A Journey from Argentina to Peru* (London: Andrew Melrose, 1950).

11 Cover of ... *the engine is left running* (1937), first publication of the Gayfield Press.

12 Illustration by Cecil ffrench Salkeld for children's book *Once Upon a Time ... Being Stories about a fierce Ogre and a small Boy, and a little Princess and a tiny Bird* (circa 1938), published by the Gayfield Press.

13 Illustration by Cecil ffrench Salkeld for Ewart Milne's poem "Oboe for Yeats" in the Gayfield publication *Forty North Fifty West* (1938).

14 Letter from Blanaid Salkeld to Austin Clarke regarding the Gayfield Press's series of broadsheets, May 18, 1939. Thanks to Aoife Clarke, granddaughter of Austin Clarke, for permission to use this material.

15 Roy McFadden's poem "Russian Summer", published in 1941 by the Gayfield Press for their series of broadsheets, with illustrations by Leslie Owen Baxter.

16 Photograph of the interior of the restaurant Jammet with waiters in attendance. Postcard (2012). *Restaurant Jammet*. 9. https://arrow.tudublin.ie/jamres/9.

17 Frontispiece from Helen Waddell's book, *The Desert Fathers* (London: Constable, 1936).

Figure 1: Photograph of playwright Teresa Deevy receiving her "Book of the Year" award from the Women Writers' Club in 1949. Also pictured are Kyle and Reenie Deevy, along with guests for the Annual Banquet. Picture courtesy of Naomi Deevy from a private family collection.

Introduction

The literary scene of mid-twentieth-century Ireland is often identified as culturally isolated and out of touch with wider European ideas and intellectual networks. This book refutes this perception by presenting the original insights of the highly engaged and interactive community of professional Irish women writers who were directly connected to international writers' networks, feminist activist movements and modern European ideas. By examining the print culture of the period through a coterie lens, this book sets out to recuperate the lesser-known history of women writers of the period. More specifically, using the Women Writers' Club as the primary focus of intellectual thought between 1933 and 1958, the book delves both into the complexities and conflicts that arose between writing groups of the period, and the spirit of collegiality and egalitarianism of this forward-thinking and internationally engaged literati. This study therefore covers social events, reading committees, literary prizes, publishing histories, private printing presses and the various political philosophies shared by members of the Club, and reveals how professional women writers deployed their networks and influence to carve out a space for their writing in the cultural marketplace and mingled with other artistic groups to fight for creative freedoms and the right to earn a living by the pen.

This book begins by redrawing the literary map to include the significant contribution of professional women writers to Irish print culture. Spatial geographies are critical to this investigation in terms of the publishers, writers, actors, writers and like-minded male and female intellectuals who congregated in shared social spaces to promote the development of their arts. The history of the Women Writers' Club is intrinsic to the flourishing counterculture milieu that operated at the margins of conventional literary society, and is integral to any authentic discussion of the literary life of Ireland at this time. As a movement, the Club represented a set of progressive ideas and cultural practices that left an indelible mark on print culture and facilitated the movement for equal rights that anticipated the demands of second-wave feminism. Embracing the new ideas of professionalism fostered through their national and international networks and connections, the Women Writers' Club became a dominant force in shaping a new professional class for women writers. Given its literary prominence and cultural significance, it is astonishing, then, that it has received little academic attention.[1] This book aims to redress this imbalance by interrogating the role of the Club in Irish literary life as a community that supported professional women writers, reviewers, translators and publishers as equal actors in the literary realm.

The historical period in which the Women Writers' Club was founded was one of immense change; socially, politically and legislatively. Artistic expression underwent a seismic shift from the radical clubs and "little theatre movement" of the 1920s to formal subscription-based clubs with official executive memberships and authoritative bureaucratic records. As a writers group, the Women Writers' Club aimed to create what Lorna Reynolds described as "a wild field to a later generation" to build on the work of their predecessors and create a heritage of their own.[2] Collectively, they sought to transform the literary field into a more democratic space where the focus lay not on gender power relationships but rather on practical issues such as censorship and the promotion of Irish books. As a seedbed for dissident texts, coterie culture provided the support system for individual writers to flourish within the collective. Prominent members had roots in political movements, including Cumann na mBan and Inghinidhe na hÉireann, and for some, politics and art were indistinguishable. Notwithstanding, many of these women writers moved beyond post-revolutionary politics to write about something different; thereby advancing universal ideas around the

---

1 One exception is Gerardine Meaney, who has called for more historical research into the Club, noting "the longevity and invisibility of the Club in literary records is equally striking". Gerardine Meaney, "Regendering Modernism: The Woman Artist in Irish Women's Fiction", *Women: A Cultural Review*, 15.1 (2004), p.73. Hereafter Meaney, "Regendering Modernism".
2 Lorna Reynolds, "Thirty Years of Irish Letters", *Studies: An Irish Quarterly Review*, 40.160 (1951). Hereafter Reynolds, "Thirty Years of Irish Letters".

right to individual freedom of expression and the experiential realities of women's lives, and the forging of liberal values through the medium of the book.

"How do books come into being? How do they reach readers? What do readers make of them?"[3] These questions posed by Robert Darnton in his view of the role of the book within society are instructive for this study. Darnton's "circuit of communication" demonstrates how the disciplines of history, literature, economics, sociology and bibliography are incorporated into one multifaceted methodology, which dictates that author, publisher, printer, shipper, bookseller and reader operate in a consistent and related way. While it is beyond the scope of this book to provide an in-depth examination of each separate element, it will offer a more holistic history of coterie culture by considering the social relationships between these categories and the various intellectual, social, political and commercial elements that affect textual production, since by "unearthing these circuits, historians can show that books do not merely recount history; they make it".[4] Such models of communication build on essential theories of twentieth-century print culture, including that of bibliographer Donald McKenzie, who commends book history methodology as a reliable approach through which more complex aspects of book production may be assessed:

> [The history of the book] permits the resurrection of the most marginal texts and their makers (the documents and writers who have always been excluded from the merely literary canon) and thereby the study of all who were kept from the centers of power by reason of their sex, race, religion, provincial or colonial status. In that, it opens up the possibility of a far more comprehensive reconstruction of cultural history.[5]

The Women Writers' Club is examined through the prism of book history and includes a broad range of actors. Using McKenzie's paradigm as a framework for this investigation, those beyond book writers are also included; namely, the academics, artists, journalists, radio presenters,

---

[3] Robert Darnton, "What is the History of Books? Revisited", *Modern Intellectual History*, 4.3 (2007).

[4] Robert Darnton, "What is the History of Books", in D. Finkelstein and A. McCleery (eds), *The Book History Reader*, 2nd ed. (London: Routledge 2006), p.22.

[5] Donald F. McKenzie, "History of the Book", in P. Davison (ed.), *The Book Encompassed: Studies in Twentieth Century Bibliography* (Cambridge: Cambridge University Press, 1992), p.296. Hereafter McKenzie, "History of the Book".

publishers and other bohemian consumers involved in the promotion and/or dissemination of their art. In recognizing the Women Writers' Club's role as a vehicle for the production, distribution and reception of ideas, and their texts as the material artifacts through which female intellectual ideas flowed, a new and more comprehensive perspective of Irish feminist literary history is gleaned.

Communication theory is key to understanding the trajectory of the book and the reciprocal connections among those involved in the book trade. Trysh Travis's notion of the "alternative communication circuit" provides a useful matrix for much of the discussion.[6] The establishment of an exclusively female professional coterie captures Travis's concept of a female-centric "network of readers and writers, editors, printers, publishers, distributors and retailers through which ideas, objects, and practices flowed in a continuous and dynamic loop".[7] Indeed, the female-centric networks of the Women Writers' Club, the celebration of female experiences through their books and their response to the reception of their works epitomize the Club's conscientious commitment to creating conditions where female writing could flourish, free from patriarchal control.

This book is based on extensive archival research from historical records, both published and unpublished. As such, it includes private letters, diaries, committee reports, government documents, newspaper reports, postcards, personal letters, promotional leaflets, invitations, business correspondence, editorials, membership lists, headed notepaper, photographs, essays and bibliography lists. Over one hundred and twenty articles from digital newspaper archives are cited in this study: some ninety from the Irish Times Digital Archive.[8] The remainder are sourced from the digital sources of other national newspapers such as *The Irish Press* and *The Irish Independent*. While the overall construction of this study is somewhat hampered by the fragmentary nature of women's archives, the absence of certain documentary records such as committee reports, and the lack of book trade statistics in terms of sales and readership trends, the abundance of private correspondence, letterheads and official documentation to be found in the rich archives of the National Library of Ireland, afford a wealth

---

6 Trysh Travis, "The Women in Print Movement: History and Implications", *Book History*, 11 (2008), p.276. Hereafter Travis, "The Women in Print Movement".
7 Travis, "The Women in Print Movement", p.276.
8 Irish Times Digital Archive, available at www.irishtimes.com/archive.

of relevant details underlying analytical bibliographies. Private papers have also yielded a rich argosy of material. Relevant sources include the Sheehy Skeffington Papers,[9] Papers of Rosamond Jacob (1878–1960),[10] Papers of Patricia Lynch and R. M. Fox,[11] le Brocquy Papers,[12] Austin Clarke Papers, Sheila Wingfield Papers,[13] and Edward MacLysath's unpublished memoir, "Master of None",[14] among others. The wealth of such material is extensive; yet more must be done to shed light on what Anne Fogarty refers to as the "mute status of texts that remain outside literary history".[15] My function in this book is to give voice to the cadre of female writers involved in the Women Writers' Club, to prominent figures within the Club and to various literary networks in order to articulate a vivid and unique account of literary life in Ireland during these times. Insights into meeting places, dates, agenda items, campaigns and literary events are elicited through a range of correspondence. Important information concerning guest attendees, Club membership figures, committee breakdowns, the structure of the Club, and discussions held at private "at home" gatherings are revealed through contemporary newspaper reports. Biographies, committee reports from writing clubs including the Irish PEN, and the Irish Academy of Letters, correspondence with feminist groups in Ireland and Britain, and society pages in women's magazines yield further

---

9 MS 47, Sheehy Skeffington Papers, MSS 33,603–33,635, National Library of Ireland; and MS 82, Sheehy Skeffington Papers (Additional), MSS 40,46040,563; 41,176–41,245, National Library of Ireland. Hereafter MS 47, Sheehy Skeffington Papers, and MS 82, Sheehy Skeffington Papers, respectively.
10 MS 30, Papers of Rosamond Jacob (1878–1960) MSS 33,107–MS 33,146: MS 32,582, National Library of Ireland. Hereafter Papers of Rosamond Jacob.
11 MS 79, Papers of Patricia Lynch and R. M. Fox, MSS 34,923–34,931; 40,248–40,419, National Library of Ireland. Hereafter Papers of Patricia Lynch and R. M. Fox.
12 Le Brocquy Papers, MS 24,232, National Library of Ireland. Hereafter Le Brocquy Papers.
13 MS 83, Austin Clarke Papers, MSS 38,651–38,708, National Library of Ireland. Hereafter Austin Clarke Papers. MS 107, Sheila Wingfield Papers, MSS 29,047–29,062; 25,559–25,616, National Library of Ireland. Hereafter Sheila Wingfield Papers.
14 Edward MacLysaght's unpublished memoirs "Master of None", MS 41,750, National Library of Ireland. Hereafter MacLysaght, "Master of None".
15 Anne Fogarty, "'The Influence of Absences': Eavan Boland the Silenced History of Irish Women's Poetry", *Colby Quarterly*, 35.4 (1999), p.258. Hereafter Fogarty, "The Influence of Absences".

fascinating accounts of the period and add to the growing interest in book history scholarship.[16]

This study builds on exciting new scholarship in the history of the book and Irish studies. Critical works such as *Reading the Irish Woman: Studies in Cultural Encounters and Exchange, 1714–1960* by Gerardine Meaney, Mary O'Dowd and Bernadette Whelan shed much needed light on the reading practices of Irish women from the eighteenth to the mid-twentieth century.[17] Studies such as *The Oxford History of the Irish Book, Volume V: The Irish Book in English, 1891–2000* (2011), edited by Clare Hutton and Patrick Walsh, provide illuminating background information on publishing histories and cultural practices during the twentieth century.[18] Recent work on Irish women's literature, including Heather Ingman and Clíona Ó Gallchoir's *A History of Modern Irish Women's Literature* (2018), have opened up the debates about women in Irish print culture.[19] Biographies are also vital in this regard. Leeann Lane's portraits of prominent Club members Rosamond Jacob and Dorothy Macardle in *Rosamond Jacob: Third Person Singular* (2010) and *Dorothy Macardle* (2019) offer intimate insights into the lives of these dynamic women and the cultural practices of the period. Likewise, Lucy Collins's edited anthology, *Poetry by Women in Ireland: A Critical Anthology 1870–1970* (2012), recuperates the works of such regularly overlooked poets as Blanaid Salkeld, Winifred M. Letts (Mrs Verschoyle), Sheila Wingfield and others too numerous to list here

---

16 The history of Irish PEN is constituted from a variety of material that consists of 205 handwritten and typed committee meetings, held in the depositories of the National Library of Ireland, alongside sixty-one newspaper articles predominantly from *The Irish Times*. Irish P.E.N. Papers, 1935–2004, National Library of Ireland, Dublin PEN Centre minute books, 1935–2004, MSS 49,143–49,144. Hereafter "Minutes Irish PEN" and date. For the purposes of this book, the acronym PEN will be denoted as PEN, and to distinguish International PEN from Irish PEN, the latter will be denoted as PEN or Irish PEN only.

17 For more on this, see Gerardine Meaney, Mary O'Dowd, and Bernadette Whelan, *Reading the Irish Woman: Studies in Cultural Encounter and Exchange, 1714–1960* (Liverpool: Liverpool University Press 2013), pp 183–185. Hereafter Meaney et al., *Reading the Irish Woman*.

18 Clare Hutton and Patrick Walsh (eds), *The Oxford History of the Irish Book, Volume V: The Irish Book in English, 1891–2000* (Oxford: Oxford University Press 2011).

19 Heather Ingman and Clíona Ó Gallchoir (eds), *A History of Modern Irish Women's Literature* (Cambridge: Cambridge University Press 2018). Hereafter Ingman and Ó Gallchoir (eds), *A History of Modern Irish Women's Literature*.

but cited throughout this book.[20] Digital databases have also been integral to this study as rich sources of reference for biographical, spatial and publishing data. These include the Modernist Archive Publishing Project (MAPP), Irish Women's Writing (1880–1920) Network, Women in Modern Irish Culture Database (WIMIC), Ricorsco: A Knowledge of Irish Literature, Centre for Cultural Analytics (UCD), and various digital newspaper archives including The Irish Times Archive.[21] These sources serve to bridge the gaps between the fragmentary quality of archival resources and historical realities.

Certain terms used in this book require elaboration. My conceptualization of "coterie(s)" is derived from the Oxford English Dictionary definition. As such it obtains to "a small group of people with shared interests or tastes, especially one that is exclusive of other people".[22] Print culture is here understood as a body of knowledge linked to the printed word and image and known as "publishing history", "textual bibliography" and "book history". For the purposes of this venture, print culture also refers to production, distribution, reading, reception and social relationships, and along with books per se also includes discussions of magazines, newspapers, theatrical plays, periodicals, book illustrations and broadsheets. This expanded interpretation also accommodates analysis of printing presses, commercial documents and book production. While the layout, illustrations, fonts, bindings, covers and other bibliographic codes are also considered, film, phonograph and/or other art technologies of the period are omitted.

The story of the Women Writers' Club may be traced to 1933 when a group of women attended an inaugural meeting at 43 Morehampton Road; home of the renowned poet and *salonnière* Blanaid Salkeld. The impressive membership list, which included notable writers such as

---

20 Lucy Collins, *Poetry by Women in Ireland: A Critical Anthology 1870–1970* (Liverpool: Liverpool University Press, 2012). Hereafter Collins, *Poetry by Women in Ireland*.

21 See Bruce Stewart, "Ricorso, A Knowledge of Irish Literature", Ulster University, www.ricorsco.net (hereafter Stewart, "Ricorso"); Caoilfhionn Ní Bheacháin, *The Dun Emer Press*, Modernist Archive Publishing Project (MAPP), available at www.modernistarchives.com/business/the-dun-emer--press (hereafter Ní Bheacháin, *The Dun Emer Press*); Women in Modern Irish Culture database, https://warwick.ac.uk/fac/arts/history/irishwomenwriters/database/#!/people/-340794009, AHRC/University College Dublin/University of Warwick.

22 Oxford English Dictionary (2019), Definition of *coterie* in English, available at https://en.oxforddictionaries.com/d'finition/coterie.

Elizabeth Bowen, Helen Waddell, Kate O'Brien, Maura Laverty, Dorothy Macardle, Patricia Lynch, Blanaid Salkeld, Temple Lane, Hanna Sheehy Skeffington, Rosamond Jacob, Nora Connolly O'Brien, Lorna Reynolds, Christine Longford (Countess of Longford) and Teresa Deevy, boasted published works across a diversity of genres, including fiction, children's stories, history texts, historical fiction, modernist poetry and plays. In fact, the texts in question extensively showcase the lived realities of contemporary and historical figures in Irish life and the issues that concerned them. While certain members were prolific internationally celebrated novelists, others were minor or sporadic writers who were little known outside Ireland, or indeed their immediate literary circle. Yet all were committed to the development of women's writing. They understood the power of the written word in continuing the tradition of their bluestocking foremothers to foster what Bridget G. MacCarthy, academic and member of the Club, championed as "the tattered banner of the female pen".[23]

Chapter One explores the broader cultural context that gave rise to the Women Writers' Club. It provides an account of the dominant literary clubs of the period and the politics of writing groups such as the Academy of Letters and the Irish PEN; and examines the Club's ethos, activities, membership lists and qualification procedures. It also charts the meeting places of these groups and considers the importance of spatial geography in constructing author identity and accessing centers of influence. These collegial networks were somewhat disrupted in 1932, when W. B. Yeats founded the Irish Academy of Letters in partial response to the Censorship Act of 1929. Membership was strictly by invitation to those Irish writers deemed worthy by Yeats and his executive enclave. The ensuing membership selections, characterized by the omission of women writers (with certain notable exceptions), offer a persuasive rationale for the establishment of the Women Writers' Club just one year later.

The history of Irish PEN delineated in this chapter unsettles the notion that Irish intellectuals were isolated and cut off from contemporary thought in post-war Europe. On the contrary, the PEN was supported by a vast global network of PEN centers, and from the outset, regular communication between the Irish PEN, Belfast PEN and London PEN fostered cordial inter-club relationships. The influence of PEN was wide-ranging. Indeed, Irish writers and Irish literature were promoted

---

[23] Ingman and Ó Gallchoir (eds), *A History of Modern Irish Women's Literature*, p.1, and Chapter Three for further details.

INTRODUCTION

on the national and international stage, to the extent that the Irish PEN was chosen as host for the International PEN Congress of 1953. Their role as mediator between rival PEN factions also played a critical role in opening up the Irish nation to an international audience in the post-war era. Their scale of reference for membership included a broad range of writers and artists; many were also members of other writing groups, including prominent members of the Women Writers' Club.

Chapter Two engages specifically with the aims, activities, and professional and personal relationships of the Women Writers' Club, and the social and political context in which it operated. The picture that emerges from this period is one of a united and highly politicized body of female writers with clearly demarcated agendas. The close connections between like-minded intellectuals and the development of social relations in the public sphere highlight the progressive nature of this Club. Unlike other writing groups, they welcomed non-Irish writers, women of letters, radio presenters and journalists. The inclusion of journalists meant that influential activists, such as Hanna Sheehy Skeffington and Maud Gonne MacBride, formed part of this cultural milieu, and brought with them a vast array of influential contacts in international feminist groups and a penchant for challenging the establishment. As the new Irish state evolved, repressive statutes such as sex-specific legislation and censorship were introduced, which threatened to, and occasionally succeeded in, silencing women's voices. The way in which the Club organized and responded to these challenges forms a central theme of this chapter. Newspaper articles, editorials, letters to government officials and personal delegations were among the Club's strategies employed to protest against perceived attempts to relegate women to secondary social status and weaken their right to "earn a living". At every level, they resisted all such efforts to diminish their rights as citizens, using their collective transnational feminist grassroots as support for their campaigns.

Chapter Three elucidates the literary production of these women by examining the body of works awarded the prestigious Book of the Year literary prize. For the purposes of this study, the significance of this prize rests in affirming women's agency and proficiency in advancing the philosophical ideas and ethos of this innovative Club. Thus, it focuses on what was new and valuable about this literary prize and the choices of the reading committee. Over the course of twenty-five years, fifteen prizewinning books were chosen from a diverse range of genres, including fiction, history, plays, poetry, children's fiction and travel writing. The body of works produced and awarded the Book of the Year are thematically categorized here as "An Experimental Form of Literature", "A Broader Republican Identity", and "Censorship and Women Writers: Ethel Mannin, Maura Laverty and Teresa Deevy". The first category explores the thematic concerns of the winning texts, and examines the works of Christine Longford, Kate O'Brien, Blanaid Salkeld, Helen Waddell and others. The next category considers books that sought to promote the role of women in the struggle for independence: writers such as Dorothy Macardle, Rosamond Jacob and Edna Fitzhenry, who not only rehearsed the histories of well-known republican heroes, but also questioned the polarity of contemporary male-oriented narratives. The final category traces the delimiting complications of censorship as it impinged on the writer's reputation and freedom to express the realities of female life. Over a period of twenty-odd years, the award came to symbolize an alternative oeuvre of female literary production.

Chapter Four focuses on the interaction between publisher and writer (or reader), the role of women writers in Irish print culture in the first half of the twentieth century, and how ideas are formed, exchanged and circulated to shape the literary landscape. Thomas Adams and Nicholas Barker suggest that "ideas for books, whether for printing something new or reprinting something old, spring from the intellectual climate of the time and influence the decision to publish".[24] In light of this, Chapter Four also explores the new editions and reprints of the main publishing houses of the time, such as Maunsel and the Talbot Press, and their ability to promote and market their writings in the domestic market, particularly during difficult economic circumstances. The impact of the first Irish Book Fair in 1941 is also examined. Sean O'Faolain, a founding member of the newly established Friends of the Academy of Letters, led this four-day event with the expressed purpose of promoting "Books of Irish Interest", and books "the scene of which is laid in Ireland", extending the exhibition to English writers with Irish themes.[25]

Supported by members of the Women Writers' Club and PEN as well as many publishers, booksellers and celebrated writers such as George Bernard Shaw, Elizabeth Bowen, Ethel Mannin and Lennox Robinson,

---

24 Thomas Adams and Nicolas Barker, "A New Model for the Study of the Book", in D. Finkelstein and A. McCleery (eds), *The Book History Reader*, 2nd edn (London: Routledge 2006). Hereafter Adams and Barker, "A New Model for the Study of the Book".

25 *The Irish Times*, March 15, 1941.

their mission was to "keep alive a distinctive literature" and a cultural context that fostered Irish writing books.²⁶ Periodicals, too, emerged as a central forum for informing Irish readers of cultural debates and political issues and became an essential medium through which women's voices could be heard. What is less well-known is the link between the members of Irish Women Writers' Club and "little magazines", as illustrated through a discussion of the publishing histories of key members. The importance of readers as textual agents is an integral part of this discussion. For instance, examining the reading patterns of Rosamond Jacob mined from the personal diaries of 1941 advances a better understanding of the reading practices of the period, censorship issues, the easy availability of banned books, and the impact of reading on the overall craft of writing. Moreover, it yields rich insights into the intellectual attitudes of the period: attitudes, it must be said, that often clashed with the conservative reading practices of the general public.

Modernist literary salons arguably created the conditions for women's art to flourish.²⁷ However, since obstacles to publishing and/or turbulent economic conditions continued to impede the success of literary women in the male-dominated publishing industry, private printing presses offered one vehicle through which women could regain control over their work. Ownership of a press conferred power and intellectual freedom, and the establishment of a private printing press created literary freedom: as the familiar maxim goes, "freedom of the press belongs to those who own one".²⁸ This freedom was exercised by women such as Harriet Weaver with her magazine *The Egoist*, Winifred Ellerman Bryher's publishing company, Brendin Publishing, and Virginia and Leonard's Woolf's Hogarth Press. Their endeavors laid the groundwork for others to follow, and were supported by international feminist ideals, which encouraged more women to enter the professions.

Blanaid Salkeld's foray into the world of publishing mirrored these ideals, and the case of the Gayfield Press, as the subjects of Chapter Five, explore the first instance of a publishing enterprise that was

---

26 *The Irish Press*, March 4, 1941.
27 Gerardine Meaney, "Fiction, 1922–1960", in H. Ingman and C. Ó Gallchoir (eds), *A History of Modern Irish Women's Literature* (Cambridge: Cambridge University Press 2018), p.187. Hereafter Meaney, "Fiction, 1922–1960".
28 This point is also made by Simone Murray in her analysis of the Women's Press: Simone Murray, "'Books of Integrity': The Women's Press, Kitchen Table Press and Dilemmas of Feminist Publishing", *European Journal of Women's Studies*, 5 (1988).

established, owned and led by a woman in Ireland in the first half of the twentieth century. The founding of the Gayfield Press suggests the presence of a vibrant modernist project that was alive in Ireland as late as 1937, and for this particular enterprise, a continuation of the project until 1946. The press's comparatively subversive content in the form of the feminist poetry of Salkeld, the incisive modernist drawings of her artist son, Cecil ffrench Salkeld, and the anti-war writings of the socialist Ewart Milne, reflect the dissident counterculture at work during this historical period. In this chapter, the aesthetic philosophy of this modernist press is further explored to reveal new insights into writers of the period, including the overt engagement with Russian modernism and experimental literature.

Like many presses of the early twentieth century, Salkeld concentrated mainly on writers within her circle; yet she broke from these to engage in a high-risk strategy of publishing unknown poets including Ewart Milne, as well as young emerging poets such as Sheila Wingfield, Donagh McDonagh and Roy McFadden. To date, any discussion of the Gayfield Press has centered on the activities of Cecil ffrench Salkeld. This study revisits the narrative to excavate a more accurate and telling interpretation of the situation, and examines the conditions around publishing in terms of business models, complexities of daily publishing activities, context of censorship and political leanings and affiliations. Furthermore, it critically assesses the aesthetic vision of the press through a systematic analysis of the books produced and the broadsheet project, and also weighs the social and political coding within these texts. In so doing, it aims to reclaim agency for the autonomous individual in the history of book publication and the influence of the collective on the individual.

The Conclusion evaluates the legacy of the Women Writers' Club. While the literary culture of the period was undoubtedly dynamic and forward-looking, it was also contingent and contradictory. By the end of 1958, at its Jubilee and final meeting, women writers had become significant players in the literary realm; yet their professional struggles persisted. While it is not my intention to cast these women writers as a marginal or oppressed group, it is important to acknowledge the very real constraints that prevailed. Among other things, the experiences of women as professional writers differed greatly from those of their male counterparts in terms of access to the public sphere and restrictions on the right to "earn a living". As Hanscombe and Smyers observe, "A woman writer, in the context of mainstream culture, has always been a trespasser in men's territory. And she trespasses at her peril."[29] Indeed, their research on modernist women writers in Britain in the early twentieth century confirms that women writers were derided as "eccentric", "neurotic" and "unsexed". In the same way, their Irish counterparts were lampooned in the national press as "pen money girls" with "their feline snarls at censors".[30] The clear implication was that such "literary dabblers" were unfeminine, or even inhuman. Bridget MacCarthy maintains that privileged women writers from the seventeenth century onwards escaped similar condemnations due to their class and connections. Owing to their elevated social status such women were tolerated as "literary dabblers who wrote polite verse, translated plays and pious treatises".[31] Three hundred years on, entrenched gender mores and customs represented a different set of challenges to the rising tide of professional women writers of the twentieth century. Their effort to be taken seriously was a hard-fought battle.

This is their story.

---

[29] Gillian Hanscombe and Virginia Smyers, *Writing for their Lives: The Modernist Women 1910–1940* (London: The Women's Press, 1987), pp.3–4.

[30] Flann O'Brien, writing his column "The Cruiskeen Lawn", in *The Irish Times*, ridiculed many writers' groups, including Irish PEN (where he was a member), the Academy of Letters and the Women Writers' Club. For example, *The Irish Times*, May 8 and 9, 1944 and July 3, 1945.

[31] Bridget G. MacCarthy, *The Female Pen: Women Writers and Novelists, 1621–1818*, Cork: Cork University Press, 1994), p.5.

CHAPTER ONE

Intellectual Fraternities?

Dublin United Arts Club, the Irish Academy of Letters and the Irish PEN

Dublin city of the 1930s, 1940s and 1950s was a maze of writers' pubs, stylish restaurants, fashionable department stores, cafés with string trios, exclusive hotels and cultural centers, where the arty element that the founder of the Women Writers' Club referred to as "the mixed swarm of painters, playwrights, lesser poets, journalists, sculptors, actors, musicians, critics and causeurs" mingled and held their various private meetings.[1] It is within this context that we can decipher an Irish cosmopolitan milieu who mimicked the sophisticated activities of such European centers as Paris, London and Berlin. Writers, actors, producers and patrons of the theatre congregated in city center venues on the fringes and margins of the conservative new state. However, it was also a period of immense cultural transition as the revolutionary glamour of post-independent Ireland faded, and artistic expression shifted from the radical clubs and "little theatre movement" of the 1920s to formal subscription-based clubs with official executive membership and authoritative bureaucratic records. As official government forged ahead with building the new nation, independent literary groups sprang up across the city and commingled with a number of established writing clubs including the Dublin United Arts Club (Arts Club), the Academy of Letters, the Irish PEN and the Women Writers' Club.

While the coterie and club culture of the mid-twentieth century was dynamic, forward looking and cutting edge, it was also contradictory and complex. For instance, an elite group of bohemian artists, writers

---

1 Blanaid Salkeld, "Footnote on Mutability", *Motley*, 11 (1933). Hereafter Salkeld, "Footnote on Mutability".

and dramatists tended to gather in smoke-filled basement clubs such as Cogley's Studio, where "Poteen in teacups" was served,[2] while their more conservative peers dined in the salubrious surroundings of the United Dublin Arts Club. There, they were free to use a room for painting or composition, or maybe enjoy Percy French's banjo rendition of "Slattery's Mounted Foot".[3] However, the interactions and overlapping memberships of these distinct artistic communities typifies the duality within coterie culture. In fact, writers cultivated important artistic connections through their "at homes", poetry readings, entered literary debates which were published in arthouse magazines such as *Motley* and *Dublin Magazine* and gathered throughout the city to discuss literature.

Analysis of their social spaces reveals an interesting correlation between place and cultural production. The fluid interaction between traditional and avant-garde groups when viewed through a feminist lens unmasks the hidden story of literary life in such city center spaces during the mid-twentieth century.

With their vast array of cafés, restaurants, arts clubs and theatres, museums, libraries and government buildings, cities offered the communal spaces necessary to accommodate and unite communities of writers, artists and activists. Dublin was no exception. One of the most highly favored meeting venues was the Country Store at 23 St Stephen's Green. Registered as the Country Workers, Ltd, the Country Store was both a restaurant and a depot for the sale of country industries.[4] Following its opening in December 1930, it provided a convivial, semi-public consumer-centered space, which situated the literati within a commercialized setting and enhanced their public status as professional artists and writers. Murial Gahan, the founder of the Irish Countrywoman's Association (ICA), and friend of the writers Winifred M. Letts (Mrs Verschoyle) and Agnes O'Farrelly, ran the store, which was conveniently adjacent to government buildings, two universities and city offices.[5] It specialized in crafts and home-produced

---

2 Patricia Boylan, *All Cultivated People: A History of The Arts Club* (Dublin, Buckinghamshire: Colin Smythe, Ltd, 1988), p.16. Hereafter Boylan, *All Cultivated People*.
3 Boylan, *All Cultivated People*, p.18.
4 *Thom's Directory*, 1932.
5 The ICA (formerly the United Irishwomen) was founded in 1910 by a small group of mainly Protestant women in County Waterford, with the aim of improving the standard of life of women in rural Ireland. Murial Gahan was a former pupil of Alexandra College, where Dorothy Macardle taught English

goods, both foreign and Irish-made; fashioning a lifestyle and an image of an elite coterie lifestyle that helped revamp the market for country industries and home-grown materials. The store or "shop" typified the dichotomy between tradition and modernity that characterizes this period. On one hand, the store aligned with the sentimentalized view of the west of Ireland, with "its bales of hand-woven, naturally dyed, Irish tweed, jewel-colored. Its stacks of tweed hats, peaked caps and Aran sweaters, all smelt faintly of turf and smoke."[6] Many nationalist organizations such as the Gaelic League promoted this image of Ireland; a legacy of the arts and craft movement of the early twentieth century that encompassed the support and encouragement of traditional craftsmanship.[7] These romanticized ideals were expressed in the literature of female writers associated with the Women Writers' Club, and in particular, in the stories written by popular children's writer Patricia Lynch and the novels of Maura Laverty.

On the other hand, the physical design of the shop evoked an image of European modernism, replete with austere futuristic rugs and furniture designed by the influential Finnish architect, Alvar Aalto. This minimalist style reflected the growing modernity of the new Irish Free State as a place of consumption and a site of cultural production, which caused Mary Manning to observe: "Ireland is in transition: the nation is finding its soul. New forces are at work; new ideas are crowding in upon us."[8] Here, business people and architects rubbed shoulders with newcomers in modernist art. Progressive artists such as Mainie Jellett, Norah McGuinness, Elizabeth Rivers, Patrick Scott and Mary Swanzy were drawn to the store. Indeed, Jellett designed a range of textiles and stands for the United Irishwomen Exhibition, which was held on the premises.[9] The avant-garde White Stag Group gathered there every

---

and was known as Maccy to her students. Geraldine Mitchell has written about the life and work of Muriel Gahan and her involvement in the Country Store in Geraldine Mitchell, *Deeds Not Words: The Life and Work of Muriel Gahan* (Dublin: Townhouse, 1997).

6 Boylan, *All Cultivated People*, p.179.
7 For more on the craft of bookmaking, see Clare Hutton (ed.), *The Irish Book in the Twentieth Century* (Dublin: Irish Academic Press, 2004), pp.36–46.
8 Mary Manning, untitled article, *Motley*, 1932, p.3.
9 Róisin Kennedy, "'Experimentalism or Mere Chaos?' The White Stag Group and the Reception of Subjective Art in Ireland", in E. Keown and C. Taaffe (eds), *Irish Modernism: Origins, Contexts, Publics* (Oxford: Peter Lang (2010), pp.179–194. Hereafter Kennedy, "Experimentalism or Mere Chaos?"

Saturday, and it was also the preferred meeting place for the monthly meetings of the Women Writers' Club.[10] Judging by the regular keen attendance of "up to twenty diners" reported in a letter from Blanaid Salkeld to Hanna Sheehy Skeffington, the Country Store was clearly a point of intersection between consumerism and art, and a melting pot of diverse commercial, political and intellectual interests.[11]

Just around the corner from the Country Store was Robert's Café. *Thom's Directory* described Robert & Co. Ireland, Ltd, as "Tea and Coffee Merchants, Confectioners, and Café", with premises at 19 Suffolk Street and 44 Grafton Street. In a style characteristic of the London coffee houses of the eighteenth century, Robert's Café nestled in a busy but exclusive shopping district and became a prominent meeting place for the intellectual discussion and debate of the post-revolutionary set. Both Lady Augusta Gregory and Maud Gonne MacBride frequented the café, and it became the regular haunt of the Irish PEN literary meetings from 1935 until 1940.[12] The Academy of Letters, on the other hand convened in the Píl Café at the Abbey Theatre, thereby simultaneously linking writers and playwrights with a theatrical setting and combining work with pleasure in a specific cultural space.[13]

Wealth and influence afforded access to exclusive cliques. Literary groups held glittering balls and dinners throughout the metropolis in select hotels such as the Royal Hibernian, Jury's, the Dolphin, the Savoy and the Gresham. Other stamping grounds of the literary set included the Green Tree on Molesworth Street and Jammet's on Nassau Street. With entrances on both Grafton Street and Nassau Street Jammet's exclusive French restaurant was a particular favorite of politicians and well-heeled artists. International celebrities also dined there while visiting Dublin;[14] and Edward Pakenham (Lord Longford) and his wife, Christine, were

---

10 Kennedy, "Experimentalism or Mere Chaos?"
11 Blanaid Salkeld to Hanna, January 30, 1936, MS 47, Sheehy Skeffington Papers, MS 33,607/13, National Library of Ireland.
12 *The Irish Independent*, December 22, 2011.
13 Irish Academy of Letters, MS 39, MSS 33,745–33,746, National Library of Ireland. Hereafter Irish Academy of Letters.
14 Jammet's French Restaurant was owned and managed by Louis and his artist wife, Yvonne. It was considered one of the finest restaurants in Europe. By the 1950s, it was a favorite for the "international jet-set", which included film stars Elizabeth Taylor, Orson Welles, Deborah Kerr and Rita Hayworth. See Liam Collins, "Jammet's Restaurant: French Revolution", *Sunday Independent*, available at www.independent.ie/life/food-drink/jammets-restaurant-french-revolution-26733154.html. Hereafter Collins, "Jammet's". See also Figure 16.

regularly patrons of the establishment. W. B. Yeats was known to dine there with members of the Academy of Letters, at his preferred table,[15] and when visiting Dublin to collect the 1948 Book of the Year award from the Women Writers' Club,[16] the British novelist Ethel Mannin also visited Jammet's. Such exclusive venues provided the context from which the status of authors emerged, and in turn conferred recognition and prestige within the public sphere.

Formal government buildings were points of contact between different clubs. Examples include the National Library Reading Rooms where Rosamond Jacob researched her historical treatise on Theobald Wolfe Tone, or the Mansion House, which housed numerous social and political events and where the Irish PEN convened their AGMs throughout the 1930s. One of the many benefits of locating in the city was accessibility to cultural centers and meeting points. The chosen base for the Arts Club was Lincoln Chambers in the center of the city. As Patricia Boylan explains:

> Lincoln Chambers was a flat-roofed building beside the Lincoln Gate of Trinity College, opposite the Turkish Baths ... and just around the corner from Westland Row Station. It was also close to the National Gallery, the Museum, the National Library, the Kildare Street Club, the fashionable shopping streets and the opulent Georgian, Merrion and Fitzwilliam Squares, and was excellently sited for the convenience of AE's friends, whose interests constantly brought them to these areas. It was an ideal address from which to launch the United Arts Club.[17]

While progressive feminists such as Rosamond Jacob were involved in a diverse group of organizations, including the Irish PEN Club, the Women Writers' Club, the Women's International League for Peace and Freedom (WILPF) and other reform groups of the period, Jacob's diaries reveal that access to events and meetings was of vital importance, especially for women. Her personal papers list the many meetings

---

15 Collins records a dinner held in 1933 by W. B. Yeats and fellow writers Brinsley MacNamara, James Stephens, Lennox Robinson, Seamus O'Sullivan, Peadar O'Donnell, Francis Stuart, Frank O'Connor, Miss Somerville, J. M. Hone and Walter Starkie. Collins, "Jammet's".

16 Ethel Mannin to Hanna Sheehy Skeffington, August 27, 1942. See MS 47, Sheehy Skeffington Papers, MS 33,608/6, National Library of Ireland.

17 George Russell (Æ) (1867–1935), poet and author, produced the magazine *The Irish Homestead* from Lincoln Chambers, which Patricia Boylan describes as "the ashram of Dublin's intelligentsia". Æ was a devotee to the theosophical teachings of Madame Blavatsky. See Boylan, *All Cultivated People*, p.16.

attended by the writer and her cohort of political and literary friends. The following extract outlines a typical evening, as she moved between various city-based organizations:

> Had to go to Lincoln Chambers in afternoon to meet Lucy & Mrs Nicolls ... to go through the law items re [] allowances etc., that we want Costello T.D. to put in his bill. S.I.F. [Society for Intellectual Freedom] committee in [] too. Deputation to Lorna Meally & Grimley came too. Met PEN Club com. & ask for evening on censorship on Friday.[18]

The mobility of the intelligentsia throughout official spaces underpinned the networks of a community forged through contiguity, family connections, the bonds of friendship and revolutionary ties. Writers and publishers Blanaid Salkeld and Seamus O'Sullivan were Morehampton Road neighbors, while Rosamund Jacob and Dorothy Macardle shared an apartment at 16 Herbert Place in 1925. Other activists lived on the same street, often in the middle-class districts of Rathgar and Rathmines or in the vicinity of Fitzwilliam Square, Merrion Road and government buildings; the salubrious enclave of Dublin's wealthy upper-middle class.[19] Publishing enterprises such as the Talbot Press, *The Dublin Magazine* and the Gayfield Press were located near the city. But if exclusive hotels, fashionable restaurants and civic buildings formed the muster points of the Dublin bourgeoisie, Madame Daisy Bannard Cogley's Club provided the rendezvous for more bohemian tastes of the 1920s. As Blanaid Salkeld recalled:

> Every Saturday evening, the members (of whom I was one) could drift along and soak themselves in a somewhat obvious, but none the less exciting, atmosphere of artiness. The ingredients were there all right in the best days of the cabaret: arty conversation, political mudslinging, strange raiment, minor blasphemies, and a dash of sex to suit the palate of the burdog.[20]

---

18 Brackets [] denote a word that is either missing or cannot be deciphered. Papers of Rosamond Jacob, MS 32,58/98.
19 For example, Sybil le Brocquy lived in the fashionable Kenilworth Square, Rathgar, Dublin and Miss Madeleine Ross (secretary of the WWC) resided at 13 Upper Leeson St, also Dublin. Many single women such as Dorothy Macardle and Rosamond Jacob lived together at different times. Jacob's biographer Leeann Lane recounts the many times Jacob moved within her life, many of which were not very successful arrangements. For a full account of this, see Leeann Lane, *Rosamond Jacob: Third Person Singular* (Dublin: University College Dublin, 2010), pp.281–301. Hereafter Lane, *Rosamond Jacob*.
20 Salkeld, "Footnote on Mutability".

Salkeld's vivid description of a post-independence society reflects both the optimism of a new emerging Irish Free State and the tensions of an Ireland in transition.[21] As an epitome of this alternative lifestyle, Madame Daisy Bennard, known as "Toto", hosted a basement cabaret at 41 Harcourt Street throughout the late 1920s and early 1930s. A central figure in the Dublin Theatre Group, she was a vocal republican, an acquaintance of Macardle and one of the first directors of the Gate Theatre.[22] She repeatedly featured in the social columns of contemporary newspapers and was famously described as a "pocket Parisian Atom Bomb" in *Trinity News*.[23] Writers such as Blanaid Salkeld, Liam O'Flaherty, Con Leventhal (A. J. Leventhal) and Samuel Beckett frequented Cogley's Club, and following her departure for London in the early 1930s, her absence must have created a social vacuum in the lives of the literati.

Patricia Boylan claims that Toto was a key figure in literary circles whose Club exploits were "known and talked about, but kept taboo".[24] The hint of decadence, as expressed by the relationship between Cogley, the Gate Theatre, the Women Writers' Club and avant-garde artists, hint at a dissident intellectual society within the city and suggest "another layer" within Dublin city, a counterculture to an increasingly conservative Ireland and conventional elite clubs such as the Arts Club. As such, her return to Dublin in the early 1940s was particularly momentous for female artists. For instance, it enabled Teresa Deevy's play *Wife of James Whelan* to be premiered in a fifty-two-seat basement theatre on Mount Street following its outright rejection by the Abbey Theatre.[25]

---

21 Nicholas Allen has written extensively about the post-revolutionary artistic culture of the late 1920s as a time of "upset energies" during a period of transition. Allen writes that Dublin city became a hot spot for writers and artists to congregate in public spaces. See Nicholas Allen, "Cabaret, Sex and Independence: Publishing in the Early Free State", in M. Fanning and R. Gillespie (eds), *Print Culture and Intellectual Life in Ireland, 1660–1941* (Dublin: Woodfield Press, 2006), pp.186–205.
22 Anon, "The Studio", *Trinity News*, May 10, 1956.
23 The full quotation read: "Madame, to her actors, 'Toto' to her more intimate friends, is a pocket Parisian Atom Bomb, and though a grandmother of many years standing, is far from obsolete". Anon, "The Studio", *Trinity News*, May 10, 1956.
24 Boylan, *All Cultivated People*, p.234.
25 Anon, "The Studio", *Trinity News*, May 10, 1956.

The Dublin United Arts Club (The Arts Club)

The Arts Club was founded in 1907 by Ellen Duncan when she sent a circular to the artistic community proposing an art club for artists, musicians and writers:

> No institute of the kind exists at present in Dublin as a convenient place of resort in a central locality; where tea can be obtained, letters written and papers and periodicals seen. It is believed that the Club will offer many attractions both to residents in the city and to those living in the country who occasionally come to town; while on the artistic side the programme of the Club will be one all cultivated people should be willing to further whether they themselves practice any art or not. All such persons will be eligible for membership of the Club.[26]

In other words, the Arts Club was conceived as a social space open to both "Ladies and Gentlemen" with an interest in art, music and literature. More specifically, it was not restricted to a Dublin clique. Prominent names on the membership lists of the early 1900s include Casimir and Constance Markiewicz, Beatrice Elvery, Estella Solomon, George Russell (Æ), Lady Augusta Gregory, William Orpen, Lennox Robinson, Hugh Lane and William Orpen, Dermod O'Brien and the Yeats brothers, W. B. Yeats and Jack B. Yeats. By the mid-twentieth century, membership had expanded to include well-known literary names such as Austin Clarke, Padraic Colum, Richard Ellman, Brian Farrell, Francis Hackett, Denis Johnston, Rutherford Mayne and a handful of women writers including Dorothy Macardle, Sybil le Broquey, Christine Longford and Temple Lane.

The Club was promoted and indeed flourished as a center where artists could meet in a friendly atmosphere. Nonetheless, satirist Susan Mitchell, a friend of Yeats and his family and a prominent member of the Arts Club in the early twentieth century, lampooned the pretentions of the Club:

> If you long for things artistic,
> If you revel in the nebulous and mystic,
> If your hair's too long
> And your tie's all wrong
> And your speech is symbolistic;
> If your tastes are democratic

---

26 Boylan, *All Cultivated People*, p.8.

And your mode of life's essentially erratic;
If you seek success
From no fixed address,
But you sleep in someone's attic ...[27]

Despite the implications of Mitchell's poem, however, most members had little in common with the archetypal poverty-stricken artist in the garret. On the contrary, they were far more likely to hail from the social circles of the Vice-regal Lodge in Dublin Castle or the stylish Georgian houses surrounding the opulent Merrion and Fitzwilliam Squares. Qualification for Club entry remained within the remit of an elected committee, which perpetuated gate-keeping and elitist practices. Banned writers were frowned upon. For example, Kate O'Brien's election to the Arts Club was vetoed by a number of unnamed members owing to her notoriety as the author of a banned book.[28]

Oddly enough, such a rebuff was rarely applied to male members, with one remarkable exception. John Ryan, editor of *Envoy*, claimed the Club infamously "black-balled" the poet Patrick Kavanagh.[29] In any event, it is clear that the prevailing sexual mores of the time inscribed different behavioral patterns for women and men. Indeed, the outnumbering of females caused some disquiet in the Club during the 1940s and resulted in the introduction of a motion to safeguard against such imbalances.[30]

For the first half of the twentieth century, the Arts Club remained an integral part of cultural life within the city. It held regular "nine-arts" costume balls, and their cocktail parties and dinners were attended by prominent artistic figures.[31] The significance of this Club as a social space is evidenced by the vast spectrum of writers and artists who sought membership and participated in their social events. Members from the Academy of Letters included W. B. Yeats, George Russell (Æ), Lennox Robinson, Austin Clarke, Padraic Colum, Oliver St John Gogarty, Stephen Gwynn, George Bernard Shaw and others.[32] Key members from the Women Writers' Club included Sybil le Brocquy, who, in 1945, was

---

27 Poet and satirist Susan Mitchell, cited in full in Boylan, *All Cultivated People*, p.20.
28 Boylan, *All Cultivated People*, p.229.
29 John Ryan, *Remembering How We Stood: Bohemian Dublin at the Mid-century* (Dublin: Gill and Macmillan (1975), p.40.
30 Boylan, *All Cultivated People*, p.212.
31 Boylan, *All Cultivated People*, p.183.
32 Boylan, *All Cultivated People*, pp.273–274.

extolled as a "steadying influence" on the Club.[33] Memberships often overlapped. For example, Isa Mac Nie was a member of both clubs, and her influence such that the Women Writers' Club hosted a dinner in her honor on the occasion of her eightieth birthday in 1949:

> Blanaid [Salkeld] presented her [Mac Nie] with a bouquet of flowers and there were many telegrams of congratulations from old friends such as James Stephens, Padraic Colum, Winifred Letts and some from the USA. Fifty guests attended, including Bertie Smyllie, Hugh Kingsmill, Louis le Brocquy, and Charlie Kelly of *Dublin Opinion*.[34]

Such festivities provide ample evidence of the integrated literary and artistic milieu and foreground the interwoven circles of male and female journalists, publishers, artists and writers within the city space. Its enduring legacy is the carving out of a pleasant central space for artists to develop and share ideas that continues to the present day.[35]

In post-revolution Ireland, both Catholics and Protestants moved in the upper echelons of society, attended the same parties and shared social circles and professional expectations. Social spaces therefore served as conduits where writers could establish important links with other literary agents, critics, publishers, institutions and others. Visibility within the public sphere and literary networks were crucial to the professional development of a writer and their commercial success in the cultural marketplace. Consequently, when W. B. Yeats and George Bernard Shaw founded the Irish Academy of Letters in 1932, their exclusion of a significant cohort of female writers had profound implications for professional women writers. In reality, exclusion from the prestigious Academy reinforced entrenched contemporary perceptions of writing as a male profession and closed off the important social networks intrinsic to every writer's commercial and critical endeavors.

The Academy of Letters

The Academy of Letters was "ushered into the world by George Bernard Shaw and Dr. W. B. Yeats before a representative gathering of Old and

---

[33] Boylan, *All Cultivated People*, p.213.
[34] Bertie Smyllie was the editor of *The Irish Times* in 1949. Charlie Kelly was a cartoonist and founder of the magazine *Dublin Opinion*. Boylan, *All Cultivated People*, p.229.
[35] The Dublin United Arts Club is currently located in Upper Fitzwilliam Street, and is the headquarters of the Irish PEN.

New Ireland".³⁶ The inaugural meeting was held in September 1932, but it took a year before formal proceedings got underway.³⁷ In August 1933, the Academy held its first annual general meeting in the Peacock Theatre, where F. R. Higgins proclaimed their manifesto to avid reporters:

> Our membership ... is thoroughly representative of Irish literature: our authority to speak for it cannot be questioned. The Irish Academy of Letters intends to crown merit and to defend it. We have already done something in its defence.³⁸

In fact, certain powerful members of Irish society did indeed question their presumption of authority, most notably the Catholic Church, and later the following month, the Women Writers' Club. Nevertheless, the Academy became an influential cultural institute, particularly in the 1930s. The first evening was presided over by Vice President Yeats, with Shaw elected as President in absentia, and F. R. Higgins as (pro tem) Honorary Secretary.³⁹ Attendees on the night comprised Edith Somerville, Alice Milligan, Seamus O'Sullivan, Brinsley MacNamara, Michael O'Donovan, Sean O'Faolain and F. R. Higgins, while letters of apology were received from T. C. Murray, Lennox Robinson, Shan Bullock, Peadar O'Donnell, Francis Stuart and Forest Reid. Prominent members also included James Stephens, Padraic Colum, George Russell (Æ), Austin Clarke, St John Ervine, Liam O'Flaherty, Oliver St John Gogarty and Frank O'Connor.⁴⁰

The response from the Catholic Church was swift and unequivocal. In a well-attended lecture at the Theatre Royal, Dublin, entitled "The Irish Academy of Letters: Unwelcomed and Un-authorised", the well-known Jesuit priest Fr Gannon questioned the Academy's promotion of elevated literary standards and argued that such literary institutions eroded originality and hampered the development of literature.⁴¹ Gannon's

---

36 Anon, "Processional", *Motley*, 1.5 (1932), pp.6–7.
37 Minutes of the Annual General Meetings are held in the National Library of Ireland. See MS 39, Irish Academy of Letters, MSS 33,745–33,746, National Library of Ireland. Hereafter "Minutes of the Academy of Letters".
38 This was reported in *The Irish Times*, August 30, 1933. In this report, F. R. Higgins protested against the banning of George Bernard Shaw's novel, *The Adventures of a Black Girl in Her Search for God*. Early in May 1933, a deputation from the Academy visited the Minister for Justice, Mr P. J. Ruttledge, to protest against the banning. Their request was unheeded with no reasons given.
39 *The Irish Times*, August 30, 1933.
40 Minutes of the Academy of Letters.
41 *The Irish Times*, November 14, 1932.

central thesis contested the misleading "Irish" auspices of the Academy. According to Gannon, the name "Anglo-Irish Academy of Letters" would more properly reflect the Ascendancy or "Planter Stock" background of its illustrious members.[42] His insistence that the Academy was unrepresentative of true Irish writing or the cultural values of the predominately Roman Catholic nation echoed the Catholic media's denigration of Yeats's Academy as yet "another bulwark of Freemasonry and atheism".[43] Gannon's public denouncement ignited a fiery debate in the media and a ream of angry exchanges within the columns of *The Irish Times*.[44] Gannon's own broadside included a specific attack on Brinsley MacNamara and Liam O'Flaherty:

> It was only the life of Ireland as seen through squinting windows by the eyes of men, who would seem to have dabbled disastrously in the works of that arch-charlatan, Freud. It left whole areas of our life unexplored and unexplained to concentrate upon the sordid, the morbid, the macabre and the unclean.[45]

The reference to Sigmund Freud, infamous at the time for his ideas about human sexuality, reinforced the idea of the writing profession as inherently "indecent and obscene", and further vilified the public image of the Academy.[46] The Catholic Church quickly seized upon this point, ignoring the fact that some of the writers were raised as Catholics.[47] The associations of pagan immorality with the mainly Protestant Ascendancy class was also repeatedly invoked by the *Catholic Bulletin*, an influential publication that waged a sustained campaign against Irish writers throughout the 1920s and 1930s.[48] Brad Kent also notes that conservatives disparaged it as the "Academy of Immorality" in the periodical *The Catholic Mind*; this was a direct reference to the

---

42 *The Irish Times*, November 14, 1932.
43 Roy F. Foster, *W. B. Yeats: A Life* (Oxford: Oxford University Press, 2003), p.452. Hereafter Foster, *W. B. Yeats: A Life*.
44 A synopsis of this newspaper debate is outlined in *The Irish Times*, December 31, 1932.
45 *The Irish Times*, November 4, 1932.
46 Yeats had defended O'Flaherty's book *The Puritan* earlier in 1932. See Foster, *W. B. Yeats: A Life*, p.448.
47 For example, Liam O'Flaherty and Sean O'Faolain were from a Catholic background.
48 It is worth noting that in 1932, after W. B. Yeats won the Nobel Prize for literature, the *Catholic Bulletin* issued a damning indictment of Yeats and his literary milieu. Terence Brown, *Ireland: A Social and Cultural History 1922–2002* (London: Harper Perennial, 2004), p.61. Hereafter Brown, *Ireland*.

banned writers involved in the Academy.[49] The least taint of indecency had implications for the sale of books and the professional and personal lives of writers, and the Academy had a rather substantial list to choose from, including six banned writers and associates.

Yeats and the Academy proved to be formidable adversaries of censorship and from their launch were vocal in their opposition:

> There is in Ireland official censorship possessing and actively exercising, powers of suppression which may at any moment confine an Irish author to the British and American market, and thereby make it impossible for him to live by distinctive Irish literature ... we cannot exercise an influence unless we have an organ through which we can address the public, or appear collectively and unanimously to the Government.[50]

Yeats's stance epitomized the views of Irish writers, many of whom were enraged and hurt by public and private humiliations. Some writers responded by emigrating.[51] According to the writer Benedict Kiely, Francis Hackett "left in indignation" after his book *The Green Lion* was banned in 1936. *Eve's Doctor*, a novel written by his wife, Signe Toksvig, was also banned in 1937.[52] Those who opted to stay began a protracted campaign against censorship, examined later in this chapter, which resulted in the 1942 establishment of the "Council of Action".

Qualification for membership was by invitation only, and selections made by Yeats and Shaw from a list of Irish writers whose work they deemed creative and "important and Irish in character and subject".[53]

---

49 For more on the reaction of the Catholic Church and their condemnation of the Academy of Letters, see Brad Kent, "The Banning of George Bernard Shaw's 'The Adventures of the Black Girl in Her Search for God' and the Decline of the Irish Academy of Letters", *Irish University Review*, 38.2 (2008). Hereafter Kent, "The Banning of George Bernard Shaw".

50 Anon, "Processional", *Motley*, 1.5 (1932), pp.6–7.

51 For a full account of the impact of censorship in Ireland during this period, see Julia Carlson, *Banned in Ireland: Censorship & the Irish Writer* (London: Routledge, 1990), and Liz Pihl, "'A Muzzle Made in Ireland': Irish Censorship and Signe Toksvig", *Studies: An Irish Quarterly Review*, 88.352 (1999).

52 The Hacketts' literary milieu included the poet Sheila Wingfield, well-known surgeon Bethal Solomons (brother of Estella), W. B. Yeats, Oliver St John Gogarty, Sean O'Faolain, James Stephens, Frank O'Connor, Desmond McCarthy and Joseph Hone. They were neighbours of Seamus O'Sullivan and artist wife Estella Solomons and the poet Blanaid Salkeld, on Morehampton Road, Dublin. See also Penny Perrick, *Something to Hide: The Life of Sheila Wingfield, Viscountess Powerscourt* (Dublin: Lilliput Press, 2007), p.42.

53 Minutes of the Academy of Letters.

In the first instance, they issued a circular letter inviting leading writers to join. Those who signed the letter were automatically elected; an assumption that surprised many authors. St John Gogarty recalled "I did not realise when signing the petition for a Friendly Society Academy that I would be ipso facto a Member",[54] while the poet F. R. Higgins was similarly surprised to find himself on the founding members' list after merely signing the circular. Those who fell outside the core category could be invited as associates but had no voting rights.[55] Yeats actively pursued membership from exiles such as Joyce and O'Casey, but was refused by both. According to Roy F. Foster, Joyce's refusal was based on a distrust of academies, while O'Casey's was based on the rejection by the Abbey Theatre of his play *The Silver Tassie*. Leading academics such as Daniel Corkery also declined Yeats's invitation, owing in part to his misgivings about the dubious nature of the Academy, which he described as "so doubtfully Irish".[56] Corkery's conception of "Irishness" mirrored the Roman Catholic nationalist mindset espoused by Fr Gannon.[57] Moreover, Corkery was arguably uninterested in Dublin's literary scene as he also refused an invitation to address a meeting of the Irish PEN in 1936.[58] Douglas Hyde, founder of the Gaelic League, also turned down his invitation due to the predominantly Anglo-Irish membership of the Academy.[59]

The vexed notion of "Irishness" was deeply entangled in questions of residency, birth and Irish blood connections. Foster observes that the new body of the Academy "also faced an endless opportunity for the advancement of protégés and the blocking of undesirables",[60] and Yeats's overtures to writers outside the "Irish" category, was openly challenged by some. P. S. O'Hegarty (not elected to the Academy until 1954) openly criticized this policy in *Motley*, the Dublin Gate Theatre magazine.

---

54 Foster, *W. B. Yeats: A Life*, p.449.
55 Foster, *W. B. Yeats: A Life*, p.448.
56 Daniel Corkery quoted in Gwynn. See Stephen Gwynn, *Irish Literature and Drama in the English Language: A Short History* (London: Thomas Nelson, 1936), p.224. Hereafter Gwynn, *Irish Literature and Drama*.
57 Kelly Matthews, *The Bell Magazine and Representations of Irish Identity* (Dublin: Four Courts Press, Ltd, 2012), p.8.
58 Daniel Corkery was invited to address PEN in December 1936, but he refused. No reason was given. See "Minutes Irish PEN", November 29, 1935, and January 15, 1936.
59 Kent, "The Banning of George Bernard Shaw", p.277.
60 Foster, *W. B. Yeats: A Life*, pp.448–455.

Drawing up an alternative list, O'Hegarty questioned the "Irish" identity of the writers Eugene O'Neill and T. E. Lawrence:

> But what is his [O'Neill's] claim to an *Irish* Academy? I imagine he was born in America, and that his only connection with Ireland is his name. His father was an American actor, his whole career has been in America, and there seems to me to be no case whatever for annexing him.[61]

Certainly, while O'Hegarty was correct in his assumptions about O'Neill, he failed to mention O'Neill's link to Ireland through his grandparents. Robert M. Dowling retells how, when O'Neill received the invitation to join the Academy, he responded, "Anything with Yeats, Shaw, AE, O'Casey, Flaherty, Robinson in it is good enough for me".[62] In fact, when O'Neill won the Nobel Prize for Literature in 1935, he explicitly identified as "Irish", describing the award as "a credit to old Ireland".[63] O'Hegarty also queried the inclusion of T. E. Lawrence or "aircraftsman Shaw", as "a man of action [whose] literary fame is spurious".[64] Stanley Wintraub claims that T. E. Lawrence, the much celebrated "Lawrence of Arabia" and author of *Revolt in the Desert* (1927), had been secretly adopted by Shaw and his wife, and that Yeats was one of the few who were supposedly aware of this at that time. However, O'Hegarty's side-swipe at "aircraftsman Shaw" suggests that the familial relationship was widely known in literary circles. If not, Hegarty's barbed remarks left readers in little doubt about the connection.[65]

The critic Stephen Gwynn was more forceful and ultimately more public in his critique of the Academy. In his influential book, *Irish Literature and Drama in the English Language: A Short History* (1936), Gwynn claimed the Academy was wholly unrepresentative of Irish literature. He was particularly critical of the omissions of Kate O'Brien and Elizabeth Bowen from the executive, arguing that "if the achievements of Irish writers in prose fiction are to be reckoned, it would be wrong to

---

61 P. S. O'Hegarty, untitled article, *Motley*, 2.5 (1932), p.6. Hereafter O'Hegarty, *Motley*.
62 Joe Cleary, "Irish American Modernisms", in J. Cleary (ed.), *Cambridge Companion to Irish Modernism* (Cambridge: Cambridge University Press, 2014), p.174, and Robert M. Dowling, *Eugene O'Neill: A Literary Reference to his Life and Work* (New York: Facts on File Inc., 2009), p.736. Hereafter Dowling, *Eugene O'Neill*.
63 O'Neill's grandparents were first-generation Irish emigrants. Dowling, *Eugene O'Neill*, p.736.
64 O'Hegarty, *Motley*, p.6.
65 Stanley Weintraub, *Shaw's People: Victoria to Churchill* (Pennsylvania: Pennsylvania University Press, 1996), p.113.

regard the Academy's choices as sufficient representation".[66] While the committee questioned the authenticity of Bowen as an "Irish" woman, Gwynn maintains that "Irish also, though, if the word be insisted on, Anglo-Irish, is Elizabeth Bowen, whose brilliant and growing talent is perhaps strongest in sheer literary accomplishment".[67] He judged that as "a study of Ireland in the revolutionary period" Bowen's novel *The Last September* amply qualified her for inclusion as an Academician. Gwynn also decried the absence of Kate O'Brien from the Academy:

> Miss Kate O'Brien, in *Without My Cloak*, has written a novel which has a richness of life, and in certain passages a beauty, that I do not find equalled among the younger Academicians. It has also, what they do not give, a study of normal Irish conditions, drawn from the existence of the richer Catholic merchants and their families. Perhaps, in manning the Academy, too much importance has been given to novels and plays of revolutionary times; and Miss O'Brien is just as Irish in every sense as Peadar O'Donnell.[68]

O'Brien's exclusion suggests a bias in the qualification policy of the Academy. Although a writer of international standing and acclaim, O'Brien's oeuvre was arguably too overtly Catholic and feminist for the predominantly Protestant, male Academy. However, Gwynn's objections were not confined to female writers. He also expressed dismay at the omission of male poets and authors, noting "A name surprisingly absent from this list is that of Monk Gibbon, in his own phrase, 'a dispossessed poet'". Gwynn proposes that Gibbon's eligibility as an "authentic poet" rested on his later work, *The Seals*, which he considered "fit to put beside Synge's on the Aran Island".[69]

While these debates raged on, Yeats set about promoting the Academy abroad; raising funds on what was to become his last American tour, while back in Dublin, Æ developed the rules of the Academy. Yeats's celebrity status ensured financial success, and he succeeded in raising £500 for the Academy.[70] With *The Playboy of the Western World* coincidentally on tour in New York at the time, publicity for Yeats's efforts centered on his credentials as a founder of the Abbey Theatre and as a politician and former Irish senator. At the same time, his lectures

---

66 Gwynn, *Irish Literature and Drama*, p.222.
67 Gwynn, *Irish Literature and Drama*, p.223.
68 Gwynn, *Irish Literature and Drama*, p.223.
69 Gwynn, *Irish Literature and Drama*, p.223.
70 Foster, *W. B. Yeats: A Life*, p.457.

focused on what he called the "New Ireland".[71] Yeats's vocal promotion of anti-censorship policies was somewhat tempered by his broad support of Irish government policy, including the endorsement of newly elected Eamon de Valera. This diplomatic balancing of art and politics paid off in future support for the Academy, as is evidenced by representation at social events by government officials, ambassadors and academics.[72]

Literary awards became a strategic branch of Yeats's promotional endeavors. Using monies donated by sponsors to finance these awards, the Academy presented Irish writers with an array of prizes for works that they deemed of high quality. These included: the Harmsworth Award of £100 for the "best work of imaginative prose"; the Casement Award of £50 for "best work of poetry and drama"; the O'Growney Award for "best work of the imagination published in Gaelic"; and the prestigious [Lady] Gregory Bronze Medal awarded every three years for Irish literature and drama.[73]

The first recipient the Harmsworth prize announced in April 1934 was Lord Dunsany for his work *The Curse of the Wise-woman* (1933). The final adjudication was undertaken by John Masefield, following nomination by a special reading committee from an "extensive list of books, nominated by members and associates of the Academy".[74] In a tribute to the sponsors, Yeats publicly announced the list of annual prizes at the first annual general meeting in the Peacock Theatre in August 1933:

> Owing to the generosity of the Marquis MacDonald we shall be able to give an annual prize of fifty pounds for the best book of poetry or drama, Irish in subject matter, or written by an Irishman, during the year. This prize is to be known as the Casement Prize. By the generosity of the Harmsworth family and the *Sunday Dispatch* we shall be able to give a prize of one hundred pounds for the best work in imaginative prose by an Irishman, or Irish in subject matter, published during the year. According to the wish of the donors, these prizes shall be conferred as far as possible upon young writers, or writers whose reputation is not yet established. Members of the Academy, whether members or associates, are not excluded. It is proposed also to have a medal cast, which can be conferred at stated periods, say every three years,

---

71 Foster, *W. B. Yeats: A Life*, p.454.
72 Minutes of the Academy of Letters.
73 The poet Cecil Day-Lewis was a recipient of £50 for the "best volume of verse published in 1938–39 by an author of Irish birth or decent". Although it is not specifically named, this is likely to have been the Casement Prize. See *The Irish Times*, October 19, 1940.
74 *The Irish Times*, April 21, 1924.

upon the best work of literature written during that period, irrespective of the age of the writer.[75]

Yeats was keenly aware that literary prizes confer cultural prestige. Indeed, the symbolic capital derived from literary prizes, what James English describes as "a means of recognizing an ostensibly higher, uniquely aesthetic form of value", was not lost on a literary set who seized every opportunity to enhance their profile and influence the cultural marketplace. Moreover, the association of the award with the accomplished Poet Laureate ensured widespread public exposure in the national newspapers, and most importantly, recognition of the merit of their works. The glamour of aristocracy and international éclat of the prizes, some of which were donated by "an anonymous American donor of Irish descent", underscore the influential and monied milieu associated with Yeats.[76] Furthermore, the monetary value of the award, substantial at this time, was also reflected in a concerted effort to promote the art of writing as a serious profession.

The degree of Yeats's influence is manifest in the decline of the Academy following his death. With Ireland's foremost literary talent no longer *in situ* to oversee its management, the Academy and its membership receded. By 1940, the O'Growney award had lapsed, and prizes were no longer monetary but represented "recognition of an author's work".[77] The awarding of the prestigious Gregory medal continued over the next twenty years to predominantly male recipients including Lord Dunsany, Cecil Day-Lewis, Francis MacManus, George Bernard Shaw, Æ, Padraic Colum, Stephen Gwynn, Douglas Hyde and Eoin MacNeill.[78]

The ambiguity of women's position within the Academy was problematized by the awarding of several prizes to female writers such as Margaret O'Leary and Peig Sayers. Sayers's cornerstone autobiography won the £50 O'Growney Award in 1938, while O'Leary, a playwright with the Abbey Theatre, received the Harmsworth Prize for her novel *The House I Made* (1935), with a ringing endorsement from Lennox Robinson who compared it to "Turgenev at his best in his Sportsman

---

75 *The Irish Times*, August 10, 1933.
76 *The Irish Times*, October 14, 1940.
77 *The Irish Times*, February 21, 1940.
78 Francis MacManus was not listed in *The Irish Times* but is listed by Sean O'Faolain in his memoir *Vive Moi!* Sean O'Faolain, *Vive Moi!: An Autobiography* (London: Sinclair-Stephenson, 1993), p.276. Hereafter O'Faolain, *Vive Moi!*, and *The Irish Times*, March 25, 1958.

sketches".[79] However, these are conspicuous anomalies in the long list of male recipients, and renowned Irish female authors such as Dorothy Macardle, Teresa Deevy, Blanaid Salkeld and Mary Davenport O'Neill, were overlooked. Moreover, only two women Academicians out of twenty-five members, namely Alice Milligan and Edith Somerville, were listed at the first Annual General Meeting in 1933. Helen Waddell and Elizabeth Bowen were named as associates until 1937 and 1938 respectively, until their election to full members.[80] By the late 1960s, this imbalance hand swung the other way and women members were more prominent. These are listed in the minute books of the Academy as Constantia Maxwell, Teresa Deevy, Christine Longford, and Patricia Lynch.[81] In 1971, Mary Lavin was elected as the first woman President, closely followed by Christine Longford in 1974.

Questions remain about the qualification for membership. It is widely held that Yeats was generally supportive of women writers, and his encouragement of many leading writers of the period, including Katherine Tynan, Lady Augusta Gregory and Dorothy Wellesley, is well documented. Virginia Woolf's claim that "Yeats recognized women artists on a footing of equality"[82] render the exclusion of the leading cohort of Irish women writers from the Academy even more astonishing. Perhaps the truth is closer to that put forward by Elizabeth Butler Cullingford, who sums up Yeats's complicated relationship with women: "Yeats loved, liked, collaborated with, and respected women – most of the time."[83] In any event, the collective response from literary women was swift.

Within one month of the first Annual General Meeting of the Irish Academy of Letters in August 1933, a group of female writers convened in Blanaid Salkeld's home at 43 Morehampton Road for the first meeting of the Women Writers' Club. This meeting was announced in *The Irish Times* with a thinly veiled jibe at the Academy: "Those who seek admittance must be authors of signed work, but need not be of

---

79 Margaret O'Leary was a playwright with the Abbey Theatre. Peig Sayers's autobiography was a record of her life on the Blasket Islands, and it was adopted for the Irish school curriculum. Stewart, "Ricorso".
80 Minutes of the Academy of Letters.
81 Minutes of the Academy of Letters.
82 Elizabeth E. Cullingford, *Gender and History in Yeats's Love Poetry* (New York: Syracuse University Press (1996), p.268. Hereafter Cullingford, *Gender and History*.
83 Cullingford, *Gender and History*, p.9.

Irish origin."[84] Within one year, they hosted an Annual Banquet and launched their Book of the Year literary prize.

The legacy of the Academy of Letters can be measured in its longevity as it lasted until 1981. It survived post-war travel restrictions and shortages, although participation at meetings fell considerably in the 1950s and there are no records of meetings for the years 1958 to 1960 or 1962 to 1968. The Academy continued to remain autonomous, despite a suggestion by Peadar O'Donnell that they merge with the Irish PEN on political issues. The motion, which was seconded by Sean O'Faolain at the seventh AGM in 1939, was rejected.[85] Instead, they set up a subcommittee known as "Friends of the Academy", to help raise funds, and promote the Club through banquets and lectures by visiting writers, including the modernist poet T. S. Eliot. In 1981, its successor, the government-funded organization Aosdána was established, and Yeats's desire for a type of "civil list" was finally realized. Over the period 1932 to 1981, the Academy fulfilled many of its objectives as an anti-censorship body, a forum for writers and a platform for Irish cultural expression.

O'Faolain described the Academy of Letters as Yeats's "plasma, nobody else's",[86] and indeed, Yeats's authority and the will to mold it led to the creation of a new activist writer: one who stood against unfair censorship practices and lobbied for recognition of the role of artists in the new state.

While Yeats's sustained struggle against censorship and advocacy for the creative freedoms of writers were in keeping with the aims and objectives of other intellectuals of the period, the exclusion policies and idiosyncratic qualification criteria of the Academy left a gap for a more egalitarian writing club. Inevitably then, when Edward Pakenham (Lord Longford) revived the Irish PEN Club in November 1934, an extensive cohort of male and female writers, playwrights, poets and publishers signed up. In a somewhat ironic gesture, the first public event organized by the Irish PEN in June 1935, honored the seventieth birthday of W. B. Yeats.

---

84 *The Irish Times*, September, p.933.
85 Minutes of the Academy of Letters.
86 O'Faolain, *Vive Moi!*, p.279.

The Irish PEN (1935–1960)

Three years following its launch on September 28, 1938, the Executive Committee of the Irish PEN received a letter from W. B. Yeats asking that his name be removed from the list of members. They duly issued a reply stating "the writer is not and never was a member of Irish PEN".[87] The directive from the Poet Laureate must have raised a few eyebrows around the coffee table at Robert's Café, which was attended by six executive committee members including the Irish Chief Justice and President of the Club, Kenneth Reddin, the critic and writer Andrew E. Malone, the journalist David Sears and the artist Lilian Davidson.[88] This instruction must have seemed even more astonishing, particularly in light of the extravagant dinner hosted three years previously in honor of Yeats's seventieth birthday. At this event, held in June 1935, the manifesto was announced by the young writer Sean O'Faolain. who praised Yeats's contribution to literature and introduced the PEN Club as a forum for ideas and intellectual debate:

> We have founded PEN partly in that spirit of fraternity – to create an atmosphere in which writers will feel that they are writers – feel the rivalry, the emulation, the excitement of ideas, of criticism, of everything that belongs to the world of imagination and ideas. And in a time when our politics are conservative and avid, and are given too much attention, it is proper to create the anti-dote.[89]

O'Faolain's opinion that Irish politics lacked vision and was based on economic materialist concerns with little regard for the arts was also apparent: "The only kind of culture our native governments seem to be interested in is beetroots. It should be the national vegetable – the colour of a blush."[90] Highly conscious of his audience of over

---

87 "Minutes Irish PEN", September 28, 1938.
88 "Minutes Irish PEN", June 27, 1935.
89 "Homage to Dr. Yeats: PEN's Club Dinner, Tribute by John Masefield, The Praise of his Heart's Desire", *The Irish Times*, June 28, 1935. This speech by Sean O'Faolain was given at a dinner held in the Dolphin Hotel, with tributes from John Masefield. It was arranged to coincide with Francis Hackett's festschrift on Yeats, known as "The Irish P.E.N. Book on Yeats". Despite contributions from such writers as John Eglinton, L. A. G. Strong and Sean O'Faolain, the Yeats festschrift was never published. The collection of letters, typescripts and news cuttings of this collection is held in the UCD Library Special Collections, E/UCD/SC/YEA.
90 The world economic situation in the 1930s had serious repercussions on the

140 guests representing the establishment including senators, district justice, commandants, professors, artists, critics, writers, poets and Irish aristocracy, he pressed for an end to censorship, and exhorted Irish writers to "fight to the last ditch" for the liberty of the press.[91] This was the first public declaration of the Irish PEN's intention to defend writers both nationally and internationally: a philosophical stance they continue to espouse to this day.

To begin with a brief history: the PEN Club was, and is, a part of an international organization whose first concern is "the promotion of literature and the defence of free expression".[92] As PEN stands for poets, playwrights, editors, essayists and novelists, it aims to promote friendship, freedom of expression, international goodwill and intellectual cooperation among writers across a wide variety of media. To date, little has been written of the history of the International PEN, with the exception of R. A. Wilford's 1979 account of the London PEN Club 1930–1950 and Rachel Potter's more recent history of International PEN, 1921–1936.[93] Both studies document the cultural politics of International PEN and examine the complex relationship between literature and human rights during the first half of the twentieth century. Drawing on the rich archival material available in PEN committee reports and newspaper reports of the period, the history of the Irish PEN situates the Irish center as a progressive and egalitarian writers' group within an international network of literary centers.[94]

From the outset, PEN evinced a clear didactic function: on one level, to promote the awareness of the role of the writer in an international context

---

economy of Ireland. A policy of self-sufficiency was implemented by the de Valera Government, spurred on by an economic war between Britain and Ireland. The analogy made by Sean O'Faolain at the PEN dinner most likely refers to the establishment of the Irish Sugar Industry (*Comhlucht Siúicre Éireann*) in the early 1930s. These factories produced sugar from beetroot.

91 *The Irish Times*, June 28, 1935.
92 Irish PEN, *Irish PEN: Defending the Freedom of Writers and Readers*, available at www.irishpen.com/the-irish-pen-committee/.
93 For an account of the international aims of PEN, see R. A. Wilford's account of the London PEN from 1930 to 1950. R. A. Wilford, "The PEN Club, 1930–50", *Journal of Contemporary History*, 14.1 (1979) (Hereafter Wilford, "The PEN Club, 1930–50") and Rachel Potter, "Modernist Rights: International PEN 1921–1936", *Critical Quarterly*, 55.2 (2013).
94 For further discussion of Irish PEN, see Deirdre F. Brady, "Writers and the International Spirit: Irish PEN in the Post-war Years", *New Hibernia Review*, 21.3 (2017). Hereafter Brady, "Writers".

through a worldwide network of PEN offices; and on another, to promote the works of its members. Inspired by International PEN's founder, Amy Dawson Scott, in response to the unprecedented carnage of the First World War, the Irish PEN was set up by Lady Augusta Gregory in 1921 and formalized as a club when a group of artists and writers met at the Mansion House on November 29, 1934.[95] This first meeting was presided over by Edward Pakenham (Lord Longford), with Andrew E. Malone as Honorary Secretary. The Club drew its membership from a broad range of writers including Sean O'Faolain, Andrew E. Malone, Seamus McCall, Dorothy Day (Dora McAuliffe), Bulmer Hobson, Edward Pakenham (Lord Longford), Desmond McCarthy, Blanaid Salkeld, Maurice Walsh, Dorothy Macardle, Hanna Sheehy Skeffington, Sheila Pim, Lilian Davidson, Gertrude Gaffney, Norah Hoult, Benedict Kiely, Flann O'Brien, Rutherford Mayne, Annie P. Smithson, Cecil Salkeld, Kate O'Brien, Seumas O'Sullivan, Francis Hackett, Maura Laverty and Temple Lane. Former Irish President Douglas Hyde was an honorary member. The PEN committee met on average ten times per year, usually breaking during the summer months of July and August, and also held an annual dinner and regular "at homes" and garden parties. As part of a vibrant network of international clubs, Irish writers within PEN were connected to forty-six key centers worldwide. Formal global networks extended to Brazil, USA, France, Netherlands, Sweden, New Zealand and England, where the offices of the International PEN were based.[96] The Belfast PEN, whose membership boasted the writers Alice Milligan, Forest Reid, Denis Ireland and Owen Meredith, frequently met with their Dublin counterparts, and harmonious inter-club relations were frequently noted in the minute books.

The grounding of PEN rests on belief in a world of letters unimpeded by geographical boundaries or interference from the state. The PEN's commitment to separating culture from national party politics was inspired by principles formalized at the 1933 International PEN Congress, which convened in Dubrovnik and was presided over by the then President, H. G. Wells. These principles were drafted in response to escalating pre-Second World War tensions and the rise of Nazism in

---

95 These writers are mentioned in the minute books of Irish PEN. Initially named Dublin PEN, the name was changed to Irish PEN in April 1937 and included Belfast PEN under the one club. This continued until 1953. See "Minutes Irish PEN", April 28, 1937 and October 1953.
96 The Irish PEN had a membership of 130 in 1940. *The Irish Times*, 14 October, 1940.

Germany.[97] Named for the Nobel Laureate, John Galsworthy, the first President of International PEN (1921–1933), the "Galsworthy Resolutions" clearly outlined the need to separate political ideology from art: "In all circumstances, and particularly in time of war, works of art, the patrimony of humanity at large, should be left untouched by national or political passions."[98] For the first few years, the Irish PEN built up its network of writers, invited visiting speakers to "at homes", and regularly corresponded with international centers. They also hosted a number of dinners, garden parties and performances. One such performance in 1938 included a "mock trial", which was "based on a trial either for libel or infringement of a supposed prohibition order under the censorship publications act in relation to *Alice in Wonderland*".[99] The PEN social events were an essential way of consolidating friendships and affiliations, and registering discontent with topical issues.

Major writers visiting Dublin were invited to speak to its members. Luminaries such as John Masefield, Desmond McCarthy, Elizabeth Bowen, Helen Waddell and Cecil Day-Lewis were included in the impressive lists of speakers during this period. The high-profile delegations dispatched to the PEN International Congress were reported in the national media. Throughout the 1930s, the Irish PEN kept faith with the basic spirit of an international club unbound by nationalist politics, and continued to fight for human rights leading up to and during the Second World War. Courageously, in 1938, when the rights of the Jewish community in Germany were threatened, they joined with International PEN in their condemnation. In a resolution signed by President Maurice Walsh, they issued the formidable statement: "The *Irish PEN* (Dublin) protests against the persecution of helpless people in Totalitarian States and pledges itself to do everything possible to assist them."[100] This was one of many forays into international affairs that continued throughout

---

97 International PEN Congress is an annual event held in various PEN centers. The Irish PEN hosted two International Congress events in 1953 and 1971.
98 Wilford, "The PEN Club, 1930–50", p.99.
99 "Minutes Irish PEN", January 12, 1938.
100 This statement was issued at an AGM of the Irish PEN in Jury's Hotel. The Irish PEN, November 26, 1938. It is worth noting that the International PEN continued to actively defend its apolitical stance. At the New York World Congress of Writers in 1939, a resolution was passed urging writers to actively defend peace and support civilization. This was viewed as support for the Allies, although the intellectual was left to "decide for himself where his duty lies". Wilford, "The PEN Club, 1930–50", p.105.

the decades. When the International Congress came to Dublin in 1953, the reputation of the Club was such that it was perceived as a conciliator between various dissenting PEN centers, and was invited to join UNESCO as a peace-broker.

In the context of post-revolutionary Ireland, this separation of nationalist politics from literary issues may have chimed with many Club members. The principle was further complicated by issues of wartime censorship and the contentious issue of Irish neutrality. From the onset of the Second World War, the Irish authorities, under the steady diplomacy of Eamon de Valera, maintained a policy of neutrality that gained wide acceptance in Ireland but attracted considerable censure from the Allies, particularly Britain and America.[101] With the threat of a German invasion of Britain at its greatest between 1940 and 1941, Ireland faced increasing pressure to enter the war and was accused of betrayal and moral irresponsibility.[102] By this time, the International PEN's endeavor to bridge the divide between nations through literature was rapidly unraveling as tensions between pro- and anti-Fascist intellectuals escalated. In July 1941, the Irish PEN received a letter inviting delegates to the International Congress hosted by the London chapter. The theme of which was "The *PEN* of the Future". A program of "post-war visions" was to be discussed and an International Book Exhibition formally opened by Desmond McCarthy. These, along with a poetry reading by Edith Evans, formed part of the overall program during this Congress, which was reported in Irish national newspapers.[103] Proposed topics discussed included nationalism, internationalism, refugee authorship and the position of the writer after the war.[104] In Dublin, there were differing views as to whether delegates should attend, since in light of Ireland's controversial neutrality "it was not clear [whether] writers in certain countries might now be precluded from attending owing to Great Britain being a belligerent in the present war".[105] Ultimately, in July 1941, it was "unanimously" agreed that a delegation would attend with a representative from the Belfast PEN as a "single delegation".[106] Denis Ireland and May Morton of the Belfast

---

101 This point is put forward by Terence Brown, see Brown, *Ireland*, p.160.
102 Diarmaid Ferriter, *Judging Dev* (Dublin: Royal Irish Academy 2007), p.253. Hereafter Ferriter, *Judging Dev*; Brown, *Ireland*, p.160.
103 *The Irish Times*, September 8, 1941.
104 *The Irish Times*, September 8, 1941.
105 "Minutes Irish PEN", July 21, 1941.
106 "Minutes Irish PEN", August 28, 1941.

PEN, and Peadar O'Donnell of the Dublin PEN were duly nominated as the PEN representatives for the island of Ireland.

For the Irish contingent, the Congress passed without any notable controversy. However, in January 1942, *PEN News* reported on a speech given at a memorial for the writer and former PEN President, Henry Nevinson, in which the speaker explicitly attacked Irish neutrality.[107] Members of the committee perceived the article as political provocation, as it forced the issue back onto the PEN agenda. Kenneth Reddin derided the speech as "propaganda, attacking the neutrality of Éire" and emphasizing that "all we wanted was to be left alone".[108] As a result, a subcommittee was formed from which Edward Pakenham (Lord Longford) issued a letter of objection to the General Secretary of PEN,[109] only to receive a swift and scathing response inquiring whether the Irish PEN "would have preferred the report of the speech to be suppressed".[110] Over time, the Irish PEN turned its focus away from this issue and concentrated on matters of professional justice.

Terence Brown makes the point that Irish life during "the Emergency" continued as normal for the majority of Irish men and women, with visitors to Ireland at that time describing a "prewar life in the midst of a sea of international change".[111] The Dublin literati's response to wartime was played out in the public sphere of annual balls, "at homes", ballad nights and garden parties, masking the strain of rationing and strict censorship. Intellectual life was complemented by an upsurge of amateur dramatics in rural villages, an influx of British touring companies to Irish towns, military spectacles and *tableaux*, and the "whiff of espionage" that permeated certain social atmospheres.[112] Thus, for those who could afford it, social life continued as usual and records of garden parties, annual dinners and "at homes" are regularly mentioned in the PEN minute books of the period. Denis Ireland's recollection of a PEN meeting in a luxurious mansion during the 1940s, with its "gilt

---

107 I have been unable to locate a copy of this article, although it is clear from committee reports that the contentious issue concerns Irish neutrality.
108 "Minutes Irish PEN", February 20, 1942.
109 "Minutes Irish PEN", March 27, 1942.
110 "Minutes Irish PEN", March 27, 1942.
111 Brown, *Ireland*, p.165.
112 Brown, *Ireland*, p.165. Clair Wills, "Neutrality and Popular Culture", *The Art of Popular Culture: From "The Meeting of the Waters" to Riverdance*, Series 1 [podcast] (2008), www.ucd.ie/scholarcast/scholarcast5.html.

chandeliers, whiskey, and opulent melancholy", hints at a literary set who remained isolated and out of touch with the international turmoil:

> Somebody switches on the gilt chandelier, making a subdued golden glitter in the dining-room, banishing the literary twilight. The glitter is reflected in rows of whiskey bottles on the mahogany sideboard, Irish aristocrats in front, backed by equally aristocratic cousins from remote Highland glens, a clear, amber-coloured gathering of the clans, flanked by black files of Guinness. No expense has been spared; it remains for the lions, if any, to start roaring.[113]

Here Denis Ireland captures the detached aristocracy and impartial literary set, happy to "abandon agenda and literary resolutions" and crowd into the "grey-panelled drawing room and literary conversation is thrown overboard"[114] and the casual indifference of singing songs of the Irish revolutionaries "Emmet, Tone and Dwyer ... to the crystal notes of the piano", while war raged around the world:

> Nobody in the party hears, except by newspaper headline, the sound of flying bombs over London, the chatter of machine-guns in the forests of Russia, the screaming of dive-bombers over the golden sands of Africa.[115]

Denis Ireland was not the only critic. The questioning of neutrality was a feature of Irish writing in both wartime and post-war Irish texts. According to Clair Wills, authors Elizabeth Bowen, Denis Johnston and Francis Stuart voiced increasing unease with the status quo.[116] It is common knowledge that Bowen worked for the British Ministry of Information during the war, while Francis Stuart's exile to Berlin at the time has remained a controversial move; particularly in light of his family connection to the nationalist Maud Gonne MacBride, as the estranged

---

113 Denis Ireland recounts his memory of life during the Second World War in the *Dubliner Magazine*. Denis Ireland, "Scenes from Irish Life: 1941–46", *Dubliner Magazine*, 5 (September–October) (1962), pp.30–31. Hereafter Ireland, "Scenes from Irish Life". Denis Ireland (1894–1974) was born in Belfast. He joined the Royal Irish Fusiliers and fought and was wounded in World War One. From 1930 onwards, he became a freelance writer, broadcaster, and Senator in the Irish Free State. Denis Ireland was a member of the Irish PEN. Dictionary of Ulster Biography, "Denis Ireland (1894–1974): Writer and broadcaster", available at www.newulsterbiography.co.uk/index.php/home/viewPerson/734.
114 Ireland, "Scenes from Irish Life", p.31.
115 Ireland, "Scenes from Irish Life", p.31.
116 Clair Wills has written extensively on the complexity of this issue. See Clair Wills, "The Aesthetics of Irish Neutrality during the Second World War", *Boundary*, 2. 31.1 (2004), p.120. Hereafter Wills, "The Aesthetics of Irish Neutrality".

husband of her daughter, Iseult. The debates about neutrality are palpable in the literature of the period. Although the authorial intention is unclear, Northern poet Louis MacNeice's complex view of the Irish position explored in his poem "Neutrality" is often read as a hostile and bitter anti-neutrality argument: a stance that Clair Wills suggests is problematized by the poet's acknowledgment of the uniqueness of the Irish situation.[117] Nevertheless, as the following excerpt illustrates, the final stanza is deeply critical of Ireland's non-participation in the war:

> But then look eastward from your heart, there bulks
> A continent, close, dark, as archetypal sin,
> While to the west off your own shores the mackerel
> Are fat – on the flesh of your kin.

According to the poet Derek Mahon, MacNeice was referring to the British seamen, and in particular, his friend Graham Shepard, who drowned off the Atlantic Coast of Ireland after being torpedoed by German submarines. MacNeice himself did not participate in combat, spending some of the war years teaching poetry at Cornell University in America, from January to June 1940, and moving to London in December 1940, where he worked as a feature writer and producer for the BBC during the war.[118]

Denis Ireland's critique should also be read in the context in which he wrote. As a former captain (retired through injury) of the British Army it is hardly surprising that his allegiance was with the Allies.

Memoranda from the PEN archives largely refute an Irish isolationist mindset. In reality, most Irish citizens sympathized with the Allies and were far from indifferent to the conflict. Behind the scenes, writers reached out to the broader international audience and continued to communicate with other PEN centers. One such correspondence includes a request from the Polish PEN to visit the Dublin center.[119] Accordingly, the visit was set for May 2, 1942 and the Polish Consul invited to attend. Bertie Smyllie, editor of *The Irish Times*, was also invited due to his experience as a foreign correspondent, his knowledge of Germany and his fluency in the German language. Four bottles of wine and one

---

117 Wills, "The Aesthetics of Irish Neutrality", p.120.
118 For details of MacNeice's life and works, see Derek Mahon, "MacNeice, the War and the BBC", *Studies on Louis MacNeice*, in J. Genet and W. Hellegouarc'h (eds), *Studies on Louis MacNeice* (Caen: centre de publications de L'Université de Caen, 1988).
119 Irish PEN, September 28, 1938 and Irish PEN, March 27, 1942.

of sherry, with the Chairman to have "discretionary power to order further refreshment if expedient", were commandeered; an impressive order during a period of severe shortages and rationing.[120] However, the meeting fell through with no explanation given. Another attempt to visit Dublin in September 1942 was made by Polish PEN (most likely, the Exiled Polish PEN) through the London office. The decision was postponed, though it was agreed to send a letter of goodwill to the London PEN. In essence, the debate about neutrality was both then and now hugely complex. For many Irish citizens, the Second World War was ultimately an imperial war, and Ireland's neutral stance was a form of self-legitimacy following British decolonization. In a report to the British government in 1940, Elizabeth Bowen observed that the "assertion of her neutrality is Éire's first free self-assertion: as such alone, it would mean a great deal to her. Éire (and I think rightly) sees her neutrality as positive, not merely negative."[121] As Bowen claims, many Irish people welcomed neutrality as the first real moment of autonomy since the War of Independence and considered a distinct foreign policy the logical outcome of the struggle for independence. Notwithstanding, over sixty thousand Irish citizens joined the Allied forces.

The primary issue dominating intellectual discussion revolved around the theme of censorship. Wartime censorship meant that writers and activists were identified and actively surveilled for any signs of dissident behavior. Strict censorship ensured that all forms of information coming into the public domain, including newsreel, film and fiction, was suppressed. As Rosamond Jacob revealed in her diary of January 1942, this had direct implications for the ease of association and the distribution of individual books:

> Went to 24 Beechwood Av [sic] in the evening to the sub-committee [WCA], very interesting. Le Brocquy [Sybil]made impassioned plea not to form official organisation, sure to be spied on & crushed in all sorts of ways, & so many thngs [sic] police have to spy on, they wd hate us anyway for giving them another. Suppression of free-thinking books wd follow etc. Very true, & they all saw it.[122]

Censorship turned out to be an effective means of silencing any subversion. The state had power over all forms of communication,

---

120 Irish PEN, April 24, 1941.
121 Ferriter, *Judging Dev*, p.255.
122 Papers of Rosamond Jacob, MS 32,582/9.

including private correspondence, and official organizations were closely watched. These measures extended to the censorship of books and booksellers:

> He [Peadar O'Donnell] sent me a grand open letter from the Bell [*Bell Journal*] to the Minister for Justice re censorship, telling lists of classics unofficially banned in Dublin & Cork public libraries – []Anna Karenina, Count of Monte Cristo, Deirdre, [] etc – & Halliday Sutherland's book Laws of Life, with bishop's imprimatur, banned because it treats of method of birth control allowed by Church.[123]

Sexual conservatism and the control of women's bodies through the banning of contraception and knowledge about birth control were consistent with Catholic social values and those of the Censorship Board. Movie censorship was pervasive, with popular films such as *Gone with the Wind* ruthlessly cut to prevent Irish audiences from viewing scenes suggestive of both sexual behavior and the reproductive body.[124] Books were more freely available. A list of "What Dublin is Reading", submitted to *The Irish Times* by Eason & Son, Ltd, reported *Gone with the Wind* by Margaret Mitchell to be the most popular book purchased in March 1937.[125] Browne & Nolan listed T. C. Murray's *Spring Horizon* as their most popular book of fiction. It was often the case that books were released onto the marketplace before they were banned by the Censorship Board, during which time they were accessible to a select reading audience.[126] For example. Signe Toksvig's novel *Eves Doctor* (1937) is on this list, though banned from March 27 that year. Those with connections continued to receive banned books, either by post from the North of Ireland or when traveling abroad. Nonetheless, by 1942, most of the world's leading writers had been banned in Ireland. Examples include writers such as Graham Greene, Ernest Hemingway, John Steinbeck, Ethel Mannin, Marcel Proust and Somerset Maugham, in addition to the prominent Irish writers, Frank O'Connor, Kate O'Brien, Norah Hoult, Sean O'Casey, Sean O'Faolain, George Bernard Shaw and Liam O'Flaherty.[127] Kate O'Brien's *The Land of Spices* and Eric Cross's *Tailor*

---

123 Brackets [] denote a word that is either missing or cannot be deciphered. Papers of Rosamond Jacob, 32,582/9.
124 Meaney *et al.*, *Reading the Irish Woman*, pp.183–185.
125 Anon, "What Dublin is Reading", *The Irish Times*, March 6 (1937).
126 See Chapter Four for the list of banned books read by Rosamond Jacob.
127 For further details on the effect of censorship on creative literature, see Donal Ó Drisceoil, "'The best banned in the land': Censorship and Irish Writing since

and Ansty initiated four days of Senate debate on the role of literature in Irish society, but ultimately remained on the banned list. The response of the Irish literati was to collectively form a Council of Action to agitate for the repeal the 1929 Act.

Some months before the Council of Action was established, several groups lobbied separately to persuade the government to reform legislation. Various means were adopted: petitioning ministers; appealing to other societies to debate the issue; inviting politicians to meetings; and sending delegations to the Minister of Justice. Notwithstanding, state censorship prevailed, prompting those in the book trade to forge ahead with vigorous anti-censorship campaigns. The Council of Action established by PEN led to a public debate in Jury's Hotel in late May 1942, to "deal with cases of injustice and misinterpretation of the Act".[128] It comprised fourteen literary and civil liberties organizations, including the Irish PEN. These are listed in committee reports as: the Irish Academy of Letters, the National University of Ireland, the Booksellers Association, the National Union of Journalists, the Dublin Literary Society, the Irish Association for Intellectual Freedom, the Women Writer's Club, the Librarians Association, the Institute of Journalists, WAAMA (the Writers Guild), the Books Fair Committee, the Royal Irish Academy and the Women's Social and Political Union.[129] While contemporary reports in *The Irish Times* firmly locate the "Council" "within a male-centred sphere of 'well-known writers, journalists, and university men'",[130] memoranda in the PEN archives reveal a different story and one that underlines the significant contribution of women writers to the establishment of the "Council".

According to PEN committee reports, in January 1942 the Club received a letter from the Irish Society for Intellectual Freedom (SIF) inviting them to send "delegates to a proposed meeting of representatives of literary and other societies to formulate an authoritative demand for the removal of the censorship of books".[131]

This triggered a series of exchanges that would, in time, culminate in legislative reform. The action was taken in April 1942 after a delegation

---

1950", *Yearbook of English Studies*, 35 (2005); Caleb Richardson, "'They are not worthy of themselves': The Tailor and Ansty Debates of 1942", *Éire-Ireland*, 42.3/4 (2007).

128 *The Irish Times*, June 1, 1942.
129 "Minutes Irish PEN", June 11, 1942.
130 *The Irish Times*, June 1, 1942.
131 "Minutes Irish PEN", January 16, 1942.

from the SIF, led by the feminist Hanna Sheehy Skeffington, was received by PEN.[132] After that, it was agreed that a special "symposium on the censorship of books (not including the censorship of publications under the emergency powers act 1939) would be held".[133] A third approach in the form of a letter from their secretary, "Miss [Rosamond] Jacob", confirmed arrangements for a special meeting on censorship in May.[134] This meeting is recorded in Jacob's diaries:

> Put on good clothes and went to Jury's to the PEN meeting. A good few there. Sat at table with M. Mickey and the 2 Emersons. Austin Clarke presiding, he said the Act is there for keeps but we can ask that it be carried out according to law, as its not new, & told of the 1670 Spanish play about St. Patrick's purgatory, which the Inquisition censors passed, but when a complaint was made of one scene in which a man did something shocking (I forget what, if he told) they left it in but ordered that the man be changed from a women's husband into her lover, because husbands must not be ridiculed. They had invited the Minister – Boland – & censors, but Boland "does not wish to take part in this discussion", Coffey & Williams wer [sic] "unable to accept" and Fr. Camac said Saturday was his busy night.[135]

The implication was that enforcement of the full Act would result in fewer Irish books being banned and would provide writers with a basis for compromise with the Censorship Board. The procedure for banning a novel requires some elucidation. Books were often banned based on a selection of passages in the book and not on the entire text. Moreover, when properly applied, the law stipulated that writers had the option to delete the offending passages, thereby avoiding censorship. Over the coming years, various appeals to government were made by those in the book trade. Within four years, legislation was revised, with new rights of appeal by authors or publishers, strengthening cultural ties between artists and government.

The relaxation of censorship was, in some ways, more symbolic than substantive, considering that many of the "unbanned" books were by then either out of print or unavailable. Although it took almost fifteen years for the power of the Catholic actionists to be broken, writers such as Sean O'Faolain, Liam O'Flaherty, Kate O'Brien, Maura Laverty, Austin Clarke and Sean O'Casey finally saw the release of their books.

132 "Minutes Irish PEN", April 24, 1942.
133 "Minutes Irish PEN", April 24, 1942.
134 "Minutes Irish PEN", May 15, 1942.
135 Papers of Rosamond Jacob, MS 32,582/98.

O'Faolain's impression of "the Emergency" and the issue of censorship was revealed in his influential journal *The Bell*:

> We emerge, a little dulled, bewildered, deflated. There is a great leeway to make up, many lessons to be learnt, problems to be solved which, in those six years of silence we did not even allow ourselves to state.[136]

His assertion reflects the prevailing mainstream notion of a cultural wasteland during the war. However, it ignores the dynamic cultural life that continued, despite the social realities of widespread poverty, rationing and emigration. Indeed, in some ways, it was a period of heightened creativity. Whenever possible, visiting authors to Dublin were invited to the "at homes" usually held in exclusive hotels or at the garden parties of certain members. Such luminaries as the poet Cecil Day-Lewis, the editor and journalist Kingsley Martin and the American press attaché Richard Watts were among those invited to speak at events.[137] Guest speakers regaled the audience with talks on "Poetry in the Theatre", "Critics the Parasites", "Can the Writer be Neutral?", "Irish Literary Magazines" and "Critics and the Artist".[138] Following the Armistice, the topics under discussion shifted to a more outward focus and included "Icelandic and Irish Folklore" and "Trends in Contemporary Spanish Literature", and to new technologies that opened up opportunities such as "Writing for the Radio", "Literature in Broadcasting" and "Writing for the Films".[139] In 1941, the PEN launched Ireland's first-ever Book Fair in the Mansion House,[140] and the founding of cultural associations such as the 1943 Irish Exhibition of Living Art by Sybil le Brocquy, Louis le Brocquy, Mainie Jellett and Evie Hone, represented a crucial point in modernist art. Likewise, avant-garde movements such as the White

---

136 Ferriter, *Judging Dev*, p.255.
137 Richard Watts was invited in September 1941 to speak at a PEN meeting in November, possibly as a public relations gesture following the bad publicity generated by the Congress in London. Cecil Day-Lewis was invited to speak to PEN in 1944, though it is unclear whether he attended. So, too, was Kingsley Martin invited with regular correspondence. See "Minutes Irish PEN", September 25, 1941; "Minutes Irish PEN", January 21, 1944; "Minutes Irish PEN", February 17, March 11, and June 13, 1943 respectively.
138 Respectively: "Minutes Irish PEN", November 3, 1937; "Minutes Irish PEN", December 7, 1939; "Minutes Irish PEN", September 15, 1939; "Minutes Irish PEN", October 4, 1940; "Minutes Irish PEN", March 16, 1945.
139 Respectively: "Minutes Irish PEN", February 1, 1946; February 7, 1947; January 23, 1948; December 4, 1948; January 28, 1949.
140 See Chapter Four for further details of this event.

Stag Group attracted the attention of artists seeking connections with international modernist movements.

As the country reached outward to the international community, relations between the artistic community and the government improved. The involvement of the state in cultural affairs, however small, signaled a new direction.[141] The Cultural Relations Committee was set up in June 1946, and within five years, the first Irish Arts Council was established. When the opportunity arose to host the International Congress in Ireland in 1953, the Irish government rowed in behind the Irish PEN in welcoming writers from around the world to promote Irish literature and tourism on an international stage.

International Congress 1953

The first item on the Irish PEN agenda for the organisation of the International Congress 1953 was the publication of an anthology of Irish poetry. Members had first proposed an anthology of their work in October 1946 as a means to raise funds for the Club (see Figure 2).[142] The publishing contract went to the Talbot Press, then one of the leading publishing houses in Ireland, which enjoyed links to the PEN. Ronald Lyons, son of the press's founder, W. G. Lyons, was an active member of the PEN and one of two delegates assigned to attend the Amsterdam Congress of 1954.[143] It was an ambitious publication, enthusiastically vaunted on the book jacket as a "glimpse of Irish poetic achievement in the present century".[144] No less than forty-one "past or present member[s]" from both the Dublin and Belfast PEN were invited to submit a poem. Aware of the opportunity to present their work to a worldwide audience, poets who accepted the invitation included

---

141 It is notable, too, that members of the Cultural Relations Committee included representatives from the Irish Tourist Association, Aer Lingus, Bord Fáilte, Irish Rail, and Córas Iompair Éireann, or CIÉ, all of which had vested interests in the development of tourism and were active patrons of the PEN Congress in 1953. See Eric G. E. Zuelow, *Making Ireland Irish: Tourism and National Identity Since the Irish Civil War* (Syracuse: Syracuse University Press, 2008), pp.57–58, and Brian P. Kennedy, *Dreams and Responsibilities: The State and the Arts in Independent Ireland* (Dublin: Criterion Press, 1998).
142 "Minutes PEN Papers", October 22, 1946.
143 "Minutes PEN Papers", February 24, 1954.
144 N. A., *Concord of Harp: An Irish PEN Anthology of Poetry* (Dublin: Talbot Press, 1952).

Austin Clarke, Blanaid Salkeld, Padraic Colum, Winifred M. Letts (Mrs Verschoyle), Seumas O'Sullivan, Mary Davenport O'Neill, Joseph Campbell, Rhoda Coghill and Stephen Gwynn. In April 1952, an octavo-sized book was produced with a light brown dust jacket set between cloth boards. Three quills on the circular frontispiece were individually marked with a letter to spell out "PEN" over a rising sun. The book was launched and advertised in the national newspapers for seven shillings and sixpence. The emphasis was on the music of Ireland, with a quotation from Moore's Irish Melodies setting the tone: "In every house was one or two harps, free to all travellers." At least four poems had the word "song" in the title.

The second item on the agenda was finance. After an initially shaky start, sponsorship to fund the event was sought and forthcoming from the Cultural Advisory Board.[145] Commercial enterprises soon followed, including the Irish Hospital Sweepstakes, Ireland's leading industrialists Messrs Jamesons, Powers and Jacobs,[146] and Aer Lingus, the national state-owned airline.[147] This alliance with commercial interests marked a radical shift in the relationship between culture and enterprise and exemplified a trend that was to characterize the book trade in the latter part of the twentieth century.

Third, the thorny issue of censorship was discussed, and the decision made to shelve any action or criticism of the government for the duration of the event. While the committee deemed it "unsuitable in the circumstances", provision was made to discuss it if the matter were raised by other PEN centers.[148] This extraordinary U-turn may be attributable to recognition of the importance of the Congress, not only to the PEN Club, but also to the general promotion of Irish books and what Peadar O'Donnell denoted the "economic circulation" of writers' work.[149] In an editorial in *The Bell* earlier that year, O'Donnell lamented the departure of Irish writers forced to turn to the "foreign market to make his living" and of their fear of speaking their minds "lest they suffer in their jobs or before their neighbours".[150] The implications for writers, then, in terms

---

145 For more on this, see Brady, "Writers".
146 "Minutes Irish PEN", November 9, 1951.
147 "Minutes Irish PEN", February 15, 1952.
148 "Minutes PEN Papers", April 24, 1953.
149 This term was used by Peadar O'Donnell, the editor of *The Bell* and a member of PEN. See Peadar O'Donnell, "And, Again, Publishing in Ireland", *The Bell*, 18.10 (1953). Hereafter O'Donnell, "And, Again".
150 O'Donnell, "And, Again", p.581.

of reputation, book sales and even employment, were severe enough to suspend criticism of the government to a world audience. Instead, PEN chose to accentuate the benefits of building bridges between rival factions within the international writing community by joining UNESCO to facilitate post-war relationships through cultural projects.[151] In November 1952, a PEN subcommittee adopted the theme "The literature of Peoples whose Language Restricts its Wider Recognition" with the expressed view of promoting the literature of smaller nations.[152] As the world media converged in the capital in June, the Dublin center joined forces with the newly autonomous Belfast PEN group for a five-day festival of literary debates, political resolutions and social entertainment.

Four hundred and thirty-nine PEN members from thirty-seven centers and twenty-seven countries across Europe, the United States, New Zealand, India, Indonesia and Japan took part in the Dublin International Congress. The event, which was co-organized with the Belfast PEN, hosted events throughout the two cities, with four-day sessions in Dublin and a one-day session in Belfast. For those five days, Ireland was the epicenter of the literary and intellectual world with celebrities including Storm Jameson, Joyce Cary, Shizue Masugi, Andre Maurois, Compton Mackenzie, Peter Ustinov, Stevie Smith, Neil Gunn and Arthur Koestler forming part of the impressive line-up of Congress delegates. The event was opened by French novelist Andre Chamson, with contributions in Welsh, Yiddish, Japanese and Irish. However, the ostensibly congenial gatherings belied much residual post-war hostility. The Irish PEN leaders had to tread a delicate diplomatic tightrope as they navigated the internal rifts that had emerged in the organization, and therefore concentrated on practical literary matters and the worldwide suppression of writers.

Opposition to censorship took the form of a resolution to send a telegram to the then Argentine President, Juan Peron, to protest at the arrest and imprisonment of cultural leader, Vittorio Ocampo.[153] A second resolution recognizing both Eastern and Western writers who had given their lives in the name of free expression was also passed and a minute's silence observed to commemorate their sacrifice.[154] The presence of both French and German delegates exacerbated post-combat tensions and was

---

151 After 1949, International PEN had a special "consultative" status with UNESCO.
152 "Minutes PEN Papers", November 14, 1952.
153 Ocampo was released before this telegram was sent. *The Irish Times*, June 13, 1953.
154 *The Irish Times*, June 13, 1953.

only resolved by the compromise of segregated receptions; one held in the French Embassy for the French delegation, and another in the Shelbourne Hotel for the German delegation. As one newspaper observed:[155]

> There is a delicate situation in the presence of delegates from both Eastern and Western Germany. Herr Eric Kastner, President of the PEN centre in Western Germany, is here with Mr. Bertolt Brecht, from the East German centre, but neither delegate recognizes the other, and relations are somewhat strained between the two delegations.[156]

Despite the tense atmosphere, social events continued unabated. Trinity College laid on a sherry reception for two hundred delegates and the Book Association hosted a luncheon for one hundred.[157]

The Irish government, keen to play a crucial role in cultural relations, extended four hundred invitations to visit Áras an Uachtaráin, the official residence of the President of Ireland. Accommodating one of the largest events ever held at Áras, reports described queues of one hundred yards to greet President Sean T. O'Kelly and his wife Phyllis, the then *Taoiseach* Eamon de Valera, opposition ministers and members of the diplomatic corps.[158] Guests were entertained in specially erected marquees to the music of the Army Number One Band.[159] The last day of Congress concluded with a literary session in the Mansion House where the UNESCO delegation and the Irish PEN put forward proposals for the formation of a committee to advise on the translation of little-known languages into world languages. The ensuing perception of the Irish PEN as a peace broker generated wide publicity in countries such as Holland, Austria and Belgium, and agreement on the "outstanding success" of the event. The minutes record that "numerous congratulations had been received, including some from official circles

---

155 The German reception was hosted by the German minister for delegates from the East and West German Centre, German writers aboard, and the Minister for Arts and Telegraphs. P. J. Little, "German reception for PEN", *Irish Independent*, June 13, 1953.
156 Andrea Orzoff notes, the German centers, East and West, were reconstituted in 1947, only to dissolve into two separate centers after 1951. During the Cold War, all German centers (four centers – East, West, Austrian and German Writers in Exile) remained involved with each other. See Andrea Orzoff, "Writing Across the Wall: The German PEN Clubs and East–West Dialogue, 1964–1968", *German History*, 33.2 (2015).
157 "Minutes Irish PEN", February 20, 1953.
158 *The Irish Times*, June 11, 1953.
159 *The Irish Times*, June 11, 1953.

here. Letter of thanks from the ministers to the President and Hon Secretary are still coming in".[160]

The Irish PEN's participation in the cultural life in Ireland from 1934 until 1960 was dominated by issues of censorship, the material welfare of Irish writers, and a humanitarian credo to defend those whose fundamental rights were threatened. Their commitment to human rights and courage in protesting against the persecution of fellow PEN members positions the Club at the forefront of international relations. Their egalitarian philosophy, indicative of a forward-thinking ethos, succeeded in attracting the main cohort of women writers involved in the Women Writers' Club. In 1953 the author and humanitarian Dorothy Macardle became the PEN President, followed by Temple Lane in 1954. What emerged from this period was a more politicized community of writers; each with individual aims and objectives, yet united in their shared goals to maintain a critical space for the arts in the new nation.

The mid-twentieth century was a time of new ideas and new associations. It was during this period that a myriad of writers' clubs, including the Women Writers' Club, the Academy of Letters and Irish PEN, were founded. Issues of art, censorship, politics and gender dominated debates within these circles and were often played out in the public sphere. As the next chapter will reveal, the contribution of the Women Writers' Club was critical to the advancement of women's writing and to their increased visibility in the cultural marketplace. Following the setback of exclusion from the Academy of Letters, membership of the Women Writers' Club offered the support and solidarity to overcome professional barriers, and the necessary networks to ensure that women writers were front and center of the literary life of this period.

---

160 "Minutes Irish PEN", June 26, 1953.

CHAPTER TWO

Coterie Culture and the Women Writers' Club, 1933–1958

> Recoil from life is not sufficient equipment for a novelist: it may – why not? – be a movement in every novelist's soul, but it must be offset by the outgoing wave; that balance and sanity and beauty our best novelists still possess.[1]

Beginnings

When thirty women signed up for membership of the Women Writers' Club at the Dublin home of poet Blanaid Salkeld at Morehampton Road on September 7, 1933, they heralded the establishment of a distinctive social and intellectual milieu with an overt feminist agenda to construct a role for professional women writers in the public arena. Many perceived the printed word as a powerful tool to serve their political agendas, and their engagement with the public through the medium of literature represented a constant reminder of a different order of things. Several of the older members of the club (at this time the average age was forty-nine) had already been part of powerful movements of the late nineteenth and early twentieth centuries advocating the ideals of socialism, pacifism, feminism and nationalism. It followed that they now expected full citizenship in a post-independent Ireland, a right they were determined to exercise and not relinquish lightly. Following in the tradition of writers as the conscience of the world and guardians of free expression as discussed in Chapter

---

1 Reynolds, "Thirty Years of Irish Letters", p.467.

One, the issues of human rights and gender equality originating in the Enlightenment were increasingly fermented, distilled and disseminated through coteries. Often regarded as forerunners to contemporary feminism, this multifarious professional women's writing club disseminated their ideas in small but influential artistic circles in local bohemian clubs, makeshift theatres and modernist "little" magazines, and internationally through the diverse channels available to worldwide network of cultural producers. Indeed, the intermingling of literary circles was a key characteristic of the period as is attested in the exchange of cultural, political and intellectual ideas evidenced throughout their works and events.

From the beginning, the Women Writers' Club was an active forum of intellectual discussion. A core group of women met in the informal and convivial public spaces of tearooms and hotels in the city center, and their influence was such that their events were routinely reported in the national newspapers. First mooted by the poet and *salonnière* Blanaid Salkeld, the idea was met with some skepticism. In a letter to Hanna Sheehy Skeffington following the inaugural meeting on September 7, 1933, the journalist Anna Kelly (then Women's Page editor of *The Irish Press*) described it as a "dining club" social gathering for professional women writers:

> I turned up at that Women Writers Club last Thursday. By the way, I notice in the Press that I am on the Committee, which, of course is wrong ... I liked the Club, or all I saw of it that night. Most people are still away on holidays, but have promised to join on return. I cannot remember (all the) people who were there: A Mrs Le Brocquy, W.M. Letts, Mrs Chevasse, Mrs whose name I cannot remember, Irene Haugh (I like her poetry), Mrs Clarke and Dorothy, whom I know. I told Mrs Salkeld that I had heard from you and that you would join. She was delighted ... It seems principally to be a dining club. I suggested that they should read each other's books.[2]

Kelly's first impression was misguided. This was no frivolous social club. On the contrary, the Club was a united, politicized female group of writers connected through cultural and social networks, who were fully intent on using the power of the pen to express their art in a form that was determinedly female, oppositional and in many cases radical.

In September 1933, the inaugural Annual Banquet of the Club was held in the Savoy Restaurant, one of the many exclusive venues in Dublin.[3]

---

2 Letter from Anna Kelly to Hanna Sheehy Skeffington. MS 82, Sheehy Skeffington Papers, MS 41,178/80, National Library of Ireland, September 9, circa 1933.
3 *The Irish Times*, September 28, 1933.

Twenty women writers were present including the honorary secretary Blanaid Salkeld, and committee members Dorothy Macardle, Irene Haugh, Winifred M. Letts (Mrs Verschoyle) and Sybil le Brocquy, and others including the actress Ria Mooney, the children's writer Patricia Lynch and the Sheehy sisters, Hanna Sheehy Skeffington and Kathleen Sheehy Cruise O'Brien. By November of that year, the constitution of the Club was adopted in the presence of Mrs James (Josephine) McNeill and Mrs Maeve Cavanagh-MacDowell, prominent members of the reading committee.[4] By 1934, the committee elected Dorothy Macardle as Chairman along with committee members "Mrs Salkeld, Miss Cynthia Franks, Mrs Kettle, Mrs le Brocquy, Mrs Verschoyle, Mrs Reddin, Mrs Sheehy Skeffington, Mrs Davidson and Mrs Lia Clark".[5] Their manifesto was announced by the President, Ethel G. Davidson, during the Annual Banquet of 1937.[6] In a nod to the famous Irish writer and wit Jonathan Swift, she formalized the Club's commitment to the "sharpening the wits, and improving the standard of criticism, as well as encouraging the writers".[7] This set the tone for the cultivation of a sophisticated coterie of like-minded intellectuals, encouraged a spirit of collegiality and also served to deflect any negative connotations of the club as a mere talking shop.

The Club actively ringfenced a separatist coterie culture, singling out women's literature for prizes and participating in public intellectual debates about art, literature and censorship as it pertained to women. Over time, they expanded the parameters of membership to include a broader network of writers, visual artists, playwrights and journalists, while carefully cultivating political and literary connections with transnational networks. They broadened eligibility criteria to include "authors of signed work [who] need not be of Irish origin", thus granting access to a wider diversity of members.[8] The inclusion of journalists

---

4 *The Irish Times*, November 3, 1933.
5 *The Irish Press*, October 26, 1934.
6 Ethel G. Davidson is generally referred to as "Mrs Davidson" or "Mrs Craig Davidson" in the newspaper reports of the period. Her role as President of the Women Writers' Club is noted in *The Irish Times* following her death in 1947. See J. P., 'Mrs Ethel Craig Davidson: An Appreciation', *The Irish Times*, March 18, 1947. For a list of Davidson's works, see Women in Modern Irish Culture database at https://warwick.ac.uk/fac/arts/history/irishwomenwriters/database/#!/people/-340794009, AHRC/University College Dublin/University of Warwick.
7 *The Irish Independent*, March 12, 1937.
8 *The Irish Times*, September 8, 1933.

meant a number of influential activists could form part of a cultural circle with a vast array of contacts in international feminist groups.[9] A perfect storm of events occurred that firmly politicized this group. To reiterate: the establishment of the male-dominated Academy of Letters prompted an immediate response from literary women. Socially, too, as female emancipatory or egalitarian ideas emerged, they were immediately countermanded by the reactionary Irish state's efforts to relegate women to the domestic sphere. This effectively enabled the regulation of Irish women's life to be articulated through a patriarchal church and state, a feature not uncommon in the aftermath of colonialism, as Gerardine Meaney points out:

> The psychodynamic of colonial and postcolonial identity often produces in the formerly colonized a desire to assert a rigid and confined masculine identity, against the colonizers stereotype of their subjects as feminine, wild, ungovernable. This masculine identity then emerges at state level as a regulation of "our" women, an imposition of a very definite feminine identity as guarantor to the precarious masculinity of the new state.[10]

The gender identity ascriptions that permeated Irish society were particularly evident in the Catholic Church's efforts to curb female sexuality. This manifested in attempts to control the publication/reading of certain books, visits to the cinema, dancing at the crossroads, traveling in motorcars (seen as literal vehicles of deviant behavior) and so-called "company keeping".[11] As Helena Moloney, an affiliate of Sheehy Skeffington and Jacob, and organizing secretary of the Irish Women Workers' Union, succinctly observed: "Disquieting signs were present that women were again to be segregated as a sex, and to have their lives ordered and restricted by the male portion of the population."[12] Female economic and unemployment concerns further exacerbated the dilemma as the social columnist Kitty Clive summarized in a 1935 edition of *The Irish Times*:

> It is very difficult for those responsible for the problem of unemployment at the present time not to feel it is a serious thing to have thousands of boys

---

9 For more on women journalists of the early twentieth century, see Karen Steele, *Women, Press, and Politics during the Irish Revival* (Syracuse: Syracuse University Press, 2007).
10 Gerardine Meaney, *Gender, Ireland, and Cultural Change: Race, Sex and Nation* (London: Routledge, 2010), p.5.
11 Regan cited in Lionel Pilkington, *Theatre and the State in Twentieth Century Ireland: Cultivating the People* (London: Routledge, 2001), p.98.
12 *The Irish Independent*, July 3, 1935.

and young men walking idly around while young women occupy posts in the country. But it is the danger which is evident of creating an inferior status for women than the traditional idea in Ireland.[13]

Clive's appraisal of the situation showed remarkably acuity and prescience in light of the ensuing concerted efforts to diminish the role of women in the public sphere and establish a second-tier female citizenry. This drove a raft of regressive legislation, including constraints to jury service, the criminalization of abortion and contraception, and employment restrictions in areas of traditional female occupations.[14] Mass emigration was a notable feature of women's experiences across the 1930s.[15] The Women Writers' Club was actively embroiled in these debates, challenging conservative modes and actively participating in issues concerning women's social status and a woman's right to "earn a living".

Women Writers and Political Campaigns

The American literary scholar Elizabeth Ammons makes much of "the crucial connection between political agitation and empowerment and art" demonstrated by female literary figures of the early twentieth century.[16] So too, during the interwar years, and in many cases in Britain and Ireland, women joined other reform groups and cooperated on an array of socio-political issues.[17] Their shared sense of themselves as fully fledged citizens and their commitment to improving the lives of women

13 Kitty Clive was a columnist with *The Irish Times* in the 1930s with a column entitled *Echoes of the Time*, a gossip-style column of social life in Dublin city. *The Irish Times*, July 19, 1935.

14 Maryann G. Valiulis states that this ideology dominated Irish life from 1922 until the 1950s. See Maryann Valiulis, "The Politics of Gender in the Irish Free State, 1922–1937", *Women's History Review*, 20.4 (2011).

15 For a fuller discussion of women, work and emigration during this period see Louise Ryan, "Leaving Home: Irish Press debates about female employment, domesticity and emigration to Britain in the 1930s", *Women's History Review*, 12.3 (2003), and Louise Ryan, *Gender, Identity and The Irish Press 1922–1937: Embodying the Nation* (New York: Edwin Mellen Press, 2002).

16 This is quoted in Elaine Showalter's influential book, *A Jury of her Peers*. See Elaine Showalter, *A Jury of Her Peers: American Women Writers from Anne Bradstreet to Annie Proulx* (London: Virago Press, 2009), p.330.

17 For more on this, see Caitriona Beaumont, "Women, Citizenship and Catholicism in the Irish Free State, 1922–1948", *Women's History Review*, 6.4 (1997). Hereafter Beaumont, "Women, Citizenship and Catholicism".

in public society encouraged them engage in the contentious gender and human rights debates of the period; not least, the Status of Women debates and the 1936 Geneva Convention.

Debate around the drafting of Irish Constitution was inherently tied to the battle for female financial independence. This issue was part of an overall push by international feminists to empower women to become fully participating citizens. The demand for single and married women's right to "earn a living'" was largely driven by the dire necessities of a depressed national economy, which directly impacted Irish families. For literary women, this was determined by their class in some instances, and by their family wealth. Some members, such as Dorothy Macardle, had access to private finance, while others, like Rosamond Jacob, hailed from monied families, but were obliged to earn their living independently.[18] Owing to a dearth of information on the book sales of this period, it is difficult to assess the financial situation accurately. However, clues abound in the biographies of these women writers and throughout their private correspondence. Jacob's biographer, Leeane Lane, maintains the author was unable to support herself through her writing alone and published her novels at her own expense. By 1959, less than four hundred copies of her most popular novel *The Rebel's Wife* had been sold, for which Jacob was paid the princely sum of £30 by her publishers.[19] Fellow members Dorothy Macardle, Maura Laverty and Patricia Lynch were more successful and forged well-paid careers from their writing. The financial statements of Patricia Lynch's publisher, Dent & Sons, Ltd, held in the depositories of the National Library of Ireland, reveal the author received a lucrative income from royalty payments.[20] At the other end of the scale, economic imperatives obliged Hanna Sheehy to draw on her wide social network to secure teaching or journalism jobs to support her writing career.[21] Crucially then, any efforts to stymie the ability of literary women to engage in the public sphere had significant implications in terms of both their

---

18 Dorothy Macardle inherited vast sums of money and was financially independent. One of her family business interests included the famous Macardle brewery in Dundalk. Leeann Lane, *Dorothy Macardle* (Dublin: University College Dublin, 2019), p.13.
19 Lane, *Rosamond Jacob*, pp.303–304.
20 Papers of Patricia Lynch and R. M. Fox, MS 40,314/1.
21 In the 1930s, Hanna Sheehy Skeffington regularly corresponded with the British newspaper *Time and Tide* asking for work. See letters dated May 15 and July 7, MS 82, Sheehy Skeffington Papers, MSS 41,181/8.

earning capacity, and perhaps more importantly, their reputation as professional writers.

The appeal of professional status rested on the premise that individuals be judged not on matters of gender, but on their merits and attainments. However, as patriarchal societies had proven less likely to advance women in traditionally occupations, women realized they needed to adopt new strategies for advancement. Thus, increased female entry into the professions became a key demand of feminists, especially in the more "learned" areas of law, medicine and academia. They saw this as a means of shifting power within society in the belief that "organized knowledge *is* power".[22] These developments must be considered in the broader context of international feminism, where, aided by achievement of suffrage and new forms of traveling and commuting, the notion of professionalism was seeping into all aspects of life. Thus, the "hallmarks of the professions were training and service, open to idealization by aspiring women – all you needed was brains and commitment".[23] British women responded by setting up professional groups for women whom they could join according to trade or industry. The Federation of British Professional and Business Women, the Advertising Club and the Venture Club, were among the many bodies established to develop professional women-centered networks.[24] The perception was, and is, that supportive networks advance equality in work. Mirroring their counterparts, the Soroptimists, a sister club of the Venture Club, was founded in Ireland by Women Writers' Club member Professor Agnes O'Farrelly.[25] Within the Club, a more professional image was promoted, from the development of the social activities outlined above to material culture, including the printing of banquet leaflets, formal printed invitations and headed paper with a logo for 1958 specially designed by the artist Lilian Davidson.[26]

22 Nancy Cott, *The Grounding of Modern Feminism* (New Haven: Yale University Press, 1987), p.216. Hereafter Cott, *The Grounding of Modern Feminism*.
23 Cott, *The Grounding of Modern Feminism*, p.217.
24 For more on the rise of professional women's group during the interwar years, see Linda Perriton, "Forgotten Feminists: The Federation of British Professional and Business Women, 1933–1969", *Women's History Review*, 16.1 (2007); and Linda Perriton, "The Education of Women for Citizenship: The National Federation of Women's Institutes and the British Federation of Business and Professional Women 1930–1959", *Gender and Education*, 21.1 (2009).
25 The Venture Club which was a club for professional women where they could meet and exchange ideas and business methods. It was run on the lines of the Rotary club.
26 *The Irish Independent*, November 28, 1958.

Debates about the status of women and the visionary role of women writers in promoting an equal rights agenda contextualize the Club within other women's movements of the period. Indeed, many members of the Club operated within transnational feminist and reform groups of the period; particularly the feminist groups at the League of Nations. Their hope, along with that of other international interwar feminists participating in the Geneva Conference (1936), was to elevate the status of women worldwide, and in particular the treaties affecting citizenship in South America.[27] Arrangements began at a public meeting in July 1935, when delegates from the Irish Women Workers' Union, the National Council of Women, the Women Citizen's Association, the Federation of University Women, the Irish Matrons' Association and Save the Children Society agreed to prepare a memorandum on the status of women in the Free State for submission to the Women's Consultative Committee at Geneva and to the head of the government, Eamon de Valera.[28] A deputation was nominated to meet with de Valera to discuss this and the government's attitude and policy regarding issues of legalized discrimination based on sex throughout Irish legislation, including issues of jury service, criminal law amendment and the Conditions of Employment Bill.[29] De Valera's positive response was a promise to give "sympathetic consideration to the views expressed by the deputation".[30]

At this juncture, the activist Hanna Sheehy Skeffington was a leading member of the National Council of Women in Ireland whose stated objective was "to encourage sympathy of thought and purpose among the women of Ireland and to promote joint action for the welfare of the community".[31] The Council maintained strong relationships with the International Council of Women and the International Alliance of Women for Suffrage and Equal Citizenship in promoting

---

27 Carol Miller makes the point that Latin American feminists were supported by American women from the National Women's Party who encouraged them to act of their behalf within the League of Nations in order to advance gender equality. See Carol Miller, "'Geneva – the key to equality': Inter-war Feminists and the League of Nations", *Women's History Review*, 3.2 (1994). Hereafter Miller, "Geneva".
28 *The Irish Press*, July 1, 1935.
29 *The Irish Times*, September 3, 1935. Individual deputies included a "Mrs" M. Cosgrave, Lucy Kingston, Louie Bennett and Dorothy Macardle.
30 *The Irish Times*, September 3, 1935.
31 Sheehy Skeffington Papers, MS 24,166.

equality.[32] Carol Miller asserts that the Geneva Convention formed part of a continuum of events leading eventually to the creation of the United Nations Commission on the Status of Women in 1946.[33] Certainly, Geneva was seen as the epicenter of the international women's movement of the period, and a fertile ground for feminist networking.[34] During the interwar years, major international feminist groups set up their headquarters in Geneva, having turned to the League of Nations to support their legal and social reform agendas. Their progressive agenda for an equality treaty, proposed under the heading Women's Organizations for World Order, called for equal rights for women in the professions and a leading role for women in all political and economic bodies that "have an influence in moulding the political and economic life ... as half the population, [women] claim the half of the representations".[35] Their precepts around family and intimate life were scandalous by Irish standards and included the rights of a wife to initiate divorce proceedings, reproductive autonomy and equal parental duties for mothers and fathers "regardless of sex, race, creed, tongue, or position". Unsurprisingly, such ideas, regarded as antithetical to prevailing Irish social norms and Catholic dogma, became a hotbed of debate during Ireland's campaign against the draft Constitution in 1937.

Much has been written about the role of women in the campaign against the draft Constitution.[36] According to Maria Luddy, the short-lived campaign, which lasted all of two months, was the "last major battle of the suffrage feminists" who deemed the Constitution a "charter of rights and liberties of the citizen within the framework of

---

32 Sheehy Skeffington Papers, MS 24,166.
33 Miller, "Geneva", p.219.
34 Miller, "Geneva".
35 Sheehy Skeffington Papers, MS 24,166.
36 Maria Luddy, "A 'Sinister and Retrogressive Proposal': Irish Women's Opposition to the 1937 Draft Constitution", *Transactions of the Royal Historical Society*, 15 (2005), pp.177 and 185. Hereafter Luddy, "A 'Sinister and Retrogressive' Proposal". See also Caitriona Beaumont, "Gender, Citizenship and the State in Ireland, 1922–1990", in S. Brewster et al. (eds), *Ireland in Proximity: History, Gender, Space* (London: Routledge, 1999); Margaret Ward, *Hanna Sheehy Skeffington: A Life* (Dublin: Attic Press, 1997); Senia Paseta, "Women and Civil Society: Feminist Responses to the Irish Constitution of 1937", in J. Harris (ed.), *Civil Society in British History: Ideas, Identities, Institutions* (Oxford: Oxford University Press (2003), p.213.

the State".[37] In accordance with Catholic social teachings of the period, the exacting language of the draft Constitution fixed women immutably within the domestic sphere of wives and mothers: a move that feminists construed as a diminution of their status as equal citizens. Their fears lay in the premise that the wording of the proposed article was occasionally vague and indeterminate, and thus liable to (mis)interpretation. The most contentious clauses for many feminists in the draft Constitution were based on Articles 40, 41.2.1, 41.2.2 and 45.4.2 and the omission of the phrase "without distinction of sex" stated in Article 16 of the 1922 Constitution.

Since this section specifically delineated the right of women to vote, feminists were swift to intervene. They organized public meetings, and wrote numerous letters to the media, to government ministers and to de Valera himself. Political heavyweights such as Hanna Sheehy Skeffington, Mary Kettle and their associates in the Women Graduates Association, Professors Mary Hayden and Agnes O'Farrelly, united in the Joint Committee of Women's Societies, which was a lobby group made up of representatives of different women's organizations to monitor social legislation.[38] The Women Writers' Club, the International Alliance of Women for Suffrage and Equal Citizenship, the National Council of Women and the Irish Women Workers' Union also exhorted de Valera to revise certain sections of the draft.[39] In May 1937, a "group of writers" petitioned de Valera listing their grievances.[40] Twenty-nine women writers, including prominent Club members Blanaid Salkeld, Dorothy Macardle, Mainie Jellett, Rosamond Jacob, Patricia Lynch, Helen Staunton (Sybil le Brocquy), Lilian Davidson and Christine Longford, were among the signatories to the petition, which reads:

---

37 This latter statement was made by Professor Mary Macken, a member of the WGA.
38 The first committee meeting of this organization was held in March 1935 at Ely Place in central Dublin. Notable attendees at the initial meeting were Mary Kettle, Hanna Sheehy Skeffington, Louie Bennett, Jennie Wise-Power and Madeleine ffrench-Mullen. The Joint Committee was made up of representatives from a number of women's organizations, and met initially to discuss a response to the rejection of proposed amendments to the Criminal Law Amendment Act, which outlawed contraception. National Archives of Ireland (NAI) 9814.
39 Ferriter, *Judging Dev*, p.239.
40 Letter from a "group of writers" to Eamon de Valera, May 25, 1937: NAI, Department of the Taoiseach Files (1922–1979), S9880. Hereafter NAI, S9880.

> We regard with utmost dismay the clauses in Articles 40, 41 and 45 of the Draft Constitution which provide for legislation to discriminate among certain classes of citizens and especially against women. They endorse the arguments put forward by Miss Louie Bennett in her letter to the President which appeared in the "Irish Press", 12 May 1937. "We urgently beg that you will favourably consider the deletions and the amendments suggested in the letter". Twenty nine women are listed: Constance Powell-Anderson, Nina Barrett, Ethne Byrne, Nancy Campbell, Eibhlin bean Mic Cearbaill, Mairead bean Ni Ciosain, Ethel G Davidson, L Davidson, Dorothy Day, Peggy Doyle, Edna C Fitz Henry, Kathleen Garrett, Mary Hayden, Rosamund Jacob, Mainie Jellett, Lucy O Kingston, Dorothy M Large, Christine Longford, Patricia Lynch, Dorothy Macardle, Hester Sigerson Piatt, Blanaid Salkeld, Fay Sargent, Helen Staunton, Marion E Tennant, Edith D Twiss, Edith L Twiss, AC Wheeler and Florence M Wilson.[41]

Two days later, the letter was re-sent with signatures including those of Teresa Deevy, Kathleen Sheehy Cruise O'Brien, Winifred M. Letts (Mrs Verschoyle) and Nora Connolly O'Brien:

> We urgently beg that you will favourably consider the deletions and the amendments suggested in the "letter". Eleven women are listed: Truda Barling, Maedbh Caomhanach, Teresa Deevy, C Maire Ni Dubhgaill, Alice M Finny, Eibhlin bean Mac Ceisdhealbha, Isa M Macnie, Nora Connolly O'Brien, Katharine S Cruise O'Brien [Kathleen Sheehy Cruise O'Brien], M Roswell and Winifred M Verschoyle.[42]

This "group of writers" is representative of the artistic milieu that constituted memberships of the Women Writers' Club and other cultural groups throughout Dublin whose influential networks and connections assured unrivaled access to the upper echelons of government. Dorothy Macardle, a close friend of de Valera and signatory of the above letter, wrote to him privately: "I do not see how anyone holding advanced views on the rights of women can support it, and that is a tragic dilemma for those who have been loyal and ardent workers in the national cause."[43] This argument was often deployed by Republican women to remind the government of their pivotal role in the nationalist struggle and their longstanding support and loyalty to de Valera.

---

41 NAI, S9880.
42 NAI, S9880.
43 Nadia Smith, *Dorothy Macardle: A Life* (Dublin: Woodfield Press, 2007), p.84. Hereafter Smith, *Dorothy Macardle*.

The campaign against the draft Constitution is integral to any discussion of women writers of the period. The solidarity demonstrated within the Club and wider collective unity of literary women serves to highlight the issue of equal rights within the cultural sphere; bringing on board British feminist organizations who regarded such these issues as universal to all women. These included the British Six Point Group, led by Betty Archdale, Chairman and associate of Hanna Sheehy Skeffington. In a letter sent to de Valera, Archdale unequivocally denigrated the offending clauses as "based on a fascist and slave conception of woman being a non-adult person who is weak and whose place is in the home".[44] Somewhat ironically underscoring the role of women in the fight for freedom from Britain, she added: "Ireland's fight for freedom would not have been so successful if Irish women had obeyed these clauses."[45] Similarly, the succinct text of a May 1937 telegram to de Valera from Miss Winifred Lesueur, Secretary of the Open Door Council, read: "Women's organisations are deeply distressed at section forty one sub section two of the new draft Constitution and urge substitute of excellent status for women laid down in 1916 Proclamation and 1923 Constitution."[46] The internationalization of this issue stemmed from the concerns of women in the broader international field of any efforts to curtail newly found freedoms, and the increasing apprehensions following the rise of fascism in Europe. These fears were reiterated in a letter from trade unionist Louie Bennett to de Valera that was republished in *The Irish Press* in May 1937.[47]

Bennet's argument foregrounds the ambiguity of the wording of the draft Constitution and possible interpretations of the law, and were "inspired by a real anxiety to safeguard the position of women irrespective of class or party prejudices".[48] The letter focused on clauses that feminists perceived as barriers to entry into the workplace: according to Bennett, the "highly dangerous" wording could be misconstrued and used to restrict civilian rights.[49] She claimed that such "undefined and subtle" qualifications meant the law could be deployed in ways that did

---

44 Ferriter, *Judging Dev*, p.247. Betty Archdale's father was an Irish professional soldier in the British army. Her godmother was the famous suffragette Emmeline Pankhurst.
45 Ferriter, *Judging Dev*, p.247.
46 NAI, S9880.
47 *The Irish Press*, May 12, 1937.
48 *The Irish Press*, May 12, 1937.
49 Bennett mentions the word "danger" three times.

not promote equality and liberty and she drew an analogy between the draft and "Fascist ideology".[50] At the time, any attempt to diminish citizen rights, and its knock-on consequences for women, was seen as dangerously veering toward the right wing.

In her letter, Bennett reminded de Valera of women's success in the public sphere and their role in nation building; in particular, "the part played by women for the common good outside the home, in education, in social service, in culture, in workshop and on the farm has now become indispensable to a civilized state".[51] The implication was that efforts to dilute their status would suggest a regressive state, which was anathema to the international image that de Valera was determined to portray.[52] Bennett's letter emphasized clause 45.4(2), which concerned the right of women to choose their own vocation and stated it was "most indefensible" to deny women this freedom, adding: "It would hardly be more possible to make a more deadly encroachment upon the liberty of the individual than to deprive him or her of this right."[53] In clear alignment with both working-class and intellectual women, Bennett warned, "women who think and women who work all view this clause with indignation and apprehension".[54] She therefore proposed recognition for women within the professions by suggesting a change to the wording in Article 41.2.1 to read "by her work *for* the home' rather than "*within* the home", insisting that women be given due regard for their contribution to society, particularly for those with "specialized knowledge for legislation affecting home and family".[55] Here, Bennett was staking a claim, not only for working-class women, but also for professional women in politics, law and academia.

Growing unease with the patriarchal tone of the Constitution was also mirrored in a letter to *The Irish Times* from the President of the Women Writers' Club, Ethel G. Davidson,[56] in which she referred to the "fatherly government" and voiced concerns that it would affect professional women even more than working-class women:

---

50 The word "Fascist" is mentioned twice within the letter.
51 *The Irish Press*, May 12, 1937.
52 For more on de Valera's international ambitions, see Ferriter, *Judging Dev.* pp.121–146.
53 *The Irish Press*, May 12, 1937.
54 *The Irish Press*, May 12, 1937.
55 *The Irish Press*, May 12, 1937.
56 Letter to *The Irish Times*, May 11, 1937.

> We may believe that it will not result in a depreciable decrease in the army of charwomen but will operate in other directions. This predicates a return to the position against which women fought so long, and ultimately successfully, which opened to them the doors of honourable independence.[57]

This resonates with the view of the Joint Committee of Women's Societies and Social Workers, who also put this argument in a letter to de Valera, and enquired whether:

> The hard-worked charwoman, running her own home, as well as doing the hard and uninteresting work of other households, or the nurse, with her long hours of day and night duty, be considered or would it only be used to prevent women entering occupations in which they would be in competition with men.[58]

The interrogatory tone of these letters reveals women's suspicions of intent and widespread distrust of male politicians following the erosion of women's legislative status in the emerging nation.

As a result of feminist objections, the term "without distinction of sex" was added to Article 16, and the phrase "inadequate strength of women" was removed following Joint Committee deputations to de Valera.[59] By engaging with contentious political debates such as the draft Constitution, the collective efforts of women writers drew specific attention to the rise of the professional woman writer, which forced the government to accept their presence as a social and political force. This political campaign was their first united public political stance, but it was not their last. Indeed, Gerardine Meaney refers to "a certain revolutionary force", which continued to make itself felt through cultural activities and literary means.[60] These challenges to authority characterize the various energies of this cohort. Nonetheless, the glamour of cultural politics required cultivation through social networks and connections.

---

57 Letter to *The Irish Times*, May 11, 1937.
58 Beaumont, "Women, Citizenship and Catholicism", p.577.
59 Beaumont, "Women, Citizenship and Catholicism", p.577.
60 Meaney, "Fiction, 1922–1960", p.187.

Relationships and Networks

At the core of this Club were its leaders. Following the adoption of the constitution of the Club in November 1933, members elected Blanaid Salkeld as Honorary Secretary, and "Mrs Pope" as Honorary Treasurer.[61] While details are somewhat sparse and fragmentary, the following women are credited with the role of President: Dorothy Macardle (1934–1936 and 1958);[62] Ethel G. Davidson (1937 and 1938);[63] Winifred M. Letts (Mrs Verschoyle) (1940);[64] Sybil le Brocquy (1942 and 1944);[65] Maura Laverty (1946);[66] Temple Lane (1945);[67] Lorna Reynolds (1948);[68] Kate O'Brien (1950); Madeline Ross (1957); and founding member Blanaid Salkeld (1939, 1941 and 1942).[69] While the Club's policy of rotating the role of President ensured that no one person could dominate, the consistent presence of key members reveals how the different personalities shaped its ethos over the twenty-five years of its existence. Blanaid Salkeld, credited with founding the club in 1933, remained an influential figure throughout its lifespan. Her public stance against the draft Constitution in 1937, prominent role as owner of the Gayfield Press, and unflinching commitment to art and literature, encapsulate the energies of this cohort of women.[70] Ethel G. Davidson was a particularly vocal President, publicly protesting against the draft Constitution as discussed, while Dorothy Macardle's influence was also immense. As one of the Club's

---

61 *The Irish Times*, November 3, 1933. Dorothy Macardle is not listed as President for 1935 but is likely to have been elected.
62 *The Irish Times*, December 11, 1934, March 20, 1936, and December 2, 1958, respectively.
63 *The Irish Times*, March 12, 1937 and February 4, 1938.
64 *The Irish Press*, December 18, 1940.
65 *The Irish Times*, November 2, 1942, and May 4, 1944.
66 *The Irish Times*, April 4, 1946.
67 *The Irish Times*, June 27, 1945.
68 *The Irish Independent*, December 17, 1948.
69 *The Irish Times*, June 8, 1939, December 19, 1941, April 10, 1942, November 17, 1950, and December 4, 1957. There appear to be two Presidents in 1942. Sybil le Brocquy was elected President after the AGM in November 2, 1942.
70 Salkeld made a public appeal to women writers to resist sections of the draft constitution of 1937, joining with Edna Fitzhenry in issuing a circular to members. This was reported in the Irish Press. *The Irish Press*, May 25, 1937. During her reign as President in 1942, she appealed to fellow members to "do their best to keep art and literature flourishing". *The Irish Times*, April 10, 1942. Her involvement with the Gayfield Press is outlined in Chapter Five.

more successful writers, she was highly appreciated as a historian of note, and as a dramatist and critic. Moreover, as a powerful figure in politics, with connections to the higher ranks of national and international governments, her presence held great sway. It was during her period of office that texts of a more political nature dominated nominations for the Book of the Year awards.[71]

Other notable members include Sybil le Brocquy, an authority on Jonathan Swift whose political networks extended to powerful international organizations, including the Women's International League of Peace and Freedom (WILPF) and the League of Nations.[72] Her association with modernist artists also forged positive links between artists and writers in the Club. Assuming the role of President in 1942, she followed this with the successful launch of the Living Art Exhibition in 1943 co-founded with her son, the artist Louis le Brocquy, and committee member Mainie Jellet.[73] Le Brocquy remained a prominent member of the Club throughout its lifespan, lending support to other writers and working on several books with fellow members. One such collaboration included a "diet section" contribution to the first cookery book written by fellow member, Maura Laverty.[74] Interestingly, Laverty's tenure was marked by controversy since by the time she first assumed office two of her books had been banned, including the winning text of the 1944 Book of the Year award, *Alone We Embark*.[75] Her 1946 novel, *Lift up our Gates*, was also banned. While the ensuing presidencies of Letts, Lane and Reynolds may have been less stormy, their steadying guidance and leadership ensured the longevity of the Club despite turbulent international conditions.

As part of their aim to promote women in the professions, the Women Writers' Club accentuated the academic nature of the group by inviting female graduates such as Mary Hayden, Agnes O'Farrelly and Lorna Reynolds to join. The Club's association with the National University Women Graduates Association reinforced this image of an intellectual milieu, and their prominence, admittedly a rarity, attracted media attention and "a great deal of interest" in political circles. This was heightened after the intention of founding the Women's Social and

---

71 See Lane, *Dorothy Macardle*.
72 Stewart, "Ricorso".
73 For more on this exhibition, see Riann Coulter, "Hibernian Salon des Refusés", *Irish Arts Review*, 20.3 (2003).
74 For more on this, see Chapters Three and Four.
75 Caitriona Clear, "'The Red Ink of Emotion': Maura Laverty, women's work and Irish society in the 1940s", *Saothar*, 28 (2003).

Political League (WSPL) was announced in the wake of the controversies surrounding the draft Constitution in 1937.[76]

The stated aim of this new party was to "organise women voters through the country in an effort to secure the principle of equal opportunity for men and women, with equal pay for equal work".[77] As part of the international WSPL, they were afforded useful connections with political affiliates both in Britain and farther afield.

As with any organization, tensions occasionally arose within the Club committee. One minor quarrel between Macardle and Salkeld stands out. At the first Annual Banquet of the Women Writers' Club, Macardle awarded Salkeld the Book of the Year, extolling her as "the greatest woman writer of the year".[78] Again in 1948, Macardle made a presentation to Salkeld at the home of Sybil le Brocquy to honor her role in founding the Club. However, by 1955, their relationship was showing strains regarding the nature of the founding of the Club; an issue that Salkeld outlined in a letter to her friend Sybil le Brocquy following the Annual Banquet:

> Several people had been asking me who started the Club – acting on a blind impulse, I thought out a speech of how it all happened – for the occasion. You cannot imagine how <u>amazed</u> and <u>shocked</u> I was ... when our <u>Guest</u> in most sarcastic tones ... apologised for the great wrong she had done me in allowing some Press interviewers to get away with the idea that she had started the Club. I had never seen it in the papers. If I had – I wouldn't have chosen just the occasion of a dinner in her honour – w. get my own back ... I was horrified at what I had done – really and all who didn't know that I didn't know – must have thought I was a horrible person.[79]

The quarrel was never resolved but was most likely forgotten. This is evident in another letter from Salkeld to le Brocquy in which she

---

76 Some of the most prominent members were academics. For example, Mary Hayden was the first professor of modern Irish history at UCD, which appointment she was awarded in 1911. She also founded the Irish Association of Women Graduates (WGA) in 1902 and was later a leading member of the National University Women Graduate's Association who were actively involved in the campaign against the wording of some of the aspects of the draft Constitution in 1937. For a full account of this, see Luddy, "A 'Sinister and Retrogressive' Proposal". See also *The Irish Times*, November 29, 1937.
77 *The Irish Times*, November 29, 1937.
78 *The Irish Times*, December 11, 1934.
79 Underlined text in the original. Blanaid Salkeld to Sybil le Brocquy, July 20, 1955. Le Brocquy Papers, MS 24,232/1.

expresses her pleasure at receiving a bouquet of flowers from the Club on her seventy-fifth birthday: "Such a beautiful arrang [*sic*]– and the perfume wonderful, I feel very important at the moment."[80] Such kind gestures reveal the commitment to support their founding member and the friendships that developed within the Club.

From a social perspective, activities in the public sphere drew the attention of the national papers of the period. Photographs from that time feature a consciously cosmopolitan group of artists arriving at the Annual Banquet in exclusive hotels, including the aforementioned Royal Hibernian, Jury's, the Russell, the Dolphin, the Savoy and the Gresham, while write-ups give detailed accounts of the proceedings and a list of attendees (see Figure 4). These venues provided the context from which the status of authors emerged, which in turn, conferred recognition and prestige.

Newspapers of the period portray evenings of celebration and merriment where lists of published books and poems were read out, "songs and recitations were given to members", and guests feasted on six-course dinners. Rosamond Jacob recollections of the Silver Jubilee festivities – which included a "Big birthday cake with twenty five candles" and a menu of grapefruit followed by mushroom soup, fish (which she declined), sprouts, a baked potato, and an ice-cream "bomb" with chocolate sauce for dessert – situates such events within a privileged environment, and highlights the extravagance of the occasion and Jacob's lifelong vegetarianism.[81] However, the annual ritual of dining with "60 or more" guests and attendant media presence also afforded rich opportunities for political activism. During her acceptance speech for the Book of the Year, for instance, Jacob reflected on the merits of her novel *The Rebel's Wife*, offering two excerpts; including a quotation on "the bad effects of giving power to 1 man – then the want of a monument with quote from Lucien Buonaparte".[82] This reference to the need to immortalize the revolutionary Theobald Wolfe Tone and his free-minded intellectual milieu underscores Irish sensitivity to French views of democracy and European liberal views. As a social visionary, advocating for change, Jacob *et al.* are framed by an influential public and intellectual sphere that represented changing paradigms of thought.

The Annual Banquet also served a more radical agenda. At the 1939 banquet, when Elizabeth Bowen was guest speaker, Blanaid Salkeld

---

80 Blanaid Salkeld to Sybil le Brocquy, July 20, 1955. Le Brocquy Papers, MS 24,232/1.
81 Papers of Rosamond Jacob, MS 32,582/164.
82 Papers of Rosamond Jacob, MS 32,582/164.

seized the opportunity to lobby for more books in the Irish language, and to promote Maud Gonne MacBride's autobiography, *A Servant of the Queen* (1938). Describing it as "a glorious book full of sincerity, by the most beautiful woman of our age", Salkeld sought to remind the educated readership of *The Irish Times* of Gonne's cultural clout and her prestigious connections in the literary world.[83] Likewise, in 1942, a blanket resolution was passed expressing the Club's regret about the application of the Censorship of Publication Act 1929, while in 1944, Sybil le Brocquy used the occasion to defend the reputation of Maura Laverty following the banning of her novel *Alone We Embark*.[84] Both politically and culturally then, the Annual Banquet garnered symbolic capital to the members of the Club, and disrupted embedded cultural ascriptions of the author as male.

In many ways, the sense of belonging and *esprit de corps* nurtured at the event was unique. The novelist Elizabeth Bowen remarked on this on accepting the Book of the Year award on the occasion of her birthday in 1939; referring to it as "one of the happiest birthday parties she had ever had".[85] Bowen particularly noted the friendly ambience, and the "kindness, friendliness, sympathy and imagination" that she had enjoyed at the Club.[86] On another occasion, Jacob's diary records the joy of receiving the Book of the Year prize and her delight at the glowing panegyric offered by Owen Sheehy Skeffington "prising [sic] me beyond everything, my work in good cases & charity to old women, making me a real angel. I was amazed and much impressed."[87] Lorna Reynolds also recalled the importance of the Annual Banquet in forging new relationships, in particular, her first meeting with Kate O'Brien:

> In November 1946 Kate O'Brien was invited as guest of honour to the Annual Dinner of the Women Writers' Club in Dublin. The intention was to celebrate *That Lady* which had had an immense success and become a best-seller. Micheál MacLiammóir was asked to propose the toast to our

---

83 Maud Gonne MacBride is widely recognized as the friend and muse of W. B. Yeats. See also *The Irish Times*, June 8, 1939.
84 *The Irish Times*, May 4, 1944.
85 *The Irish Press*, June 8, 1939.
86 *The Irish Press*, June 8, 1939.
87 Papers of Rosamond Jacob, MS 32,582/164. In addition, Sheehy Skeffington's wife Andrée wrote a memoir of her husband's life where she records the Silver Jubilee of the Women Writers' Club and Skeffington's speech. See Andrée Sheehy Skeffington, *Skeff: A Life of Owen Sheehy Skeffington 1909–1970* (Dublin: Lilliput Press, 1991).

guest and I to second it. With her usual graciousness she came up to me afterwards and congratulated me on my speech ... A few days later she invited me to lunch, and so began a memorable and stormy friendship.[88]

This account of their first meeting, and subsequent relationship, reveals the reciprocity of Dublin's literary community and hints at the possible homoerotic bonds between certain writers. Certainly, the emergence of a more sexually liberated intellectual community was evident at the time. Aintzane Legarreta Mentxaka claims that Reynolds was the inspiration for the lesbian relationship in O'Brien's novel, *As Music and Splendour* (1956).[89] Gerardine Meaney also suggests that analysis of the writings and readings of the period reveals "different sexualities and lives at odds with the dominant ideology of their day, often invisible to the dominant histories since".[90]

In general, the multifarious and potentially conflicting affiliations within the Club, both internally and externally, were held together by a shared sense of purpose. The importance of friendship and the sense of camaraderie for members was clearly visible to those who attended the Annual Banquet, prompting Edward Pakenham (Lord Longford) to remark that "it was unusual to find an artistic body lasting for longer than a year or a club where everyone was friends" and applauded Club members for their "harmony and enterprise".[91]

An estimated nineteen Annual Banquets were held over twenty-five years; with the five held between Second World War period 1939 and 1945/6 boasting the largest attendance numbers in spite of the obvious difficulties with transport and rationing. One columnist in *The Irish*

---

88 Micheál MacLiammóir, Edward Pakenham (Lord Longford), Hilton Edwards, Denis Johnston, Mary Manning and Sheila Richards feature among the list of actors, producers and patrons of the Gate Theatre during the 1930s. See Lorna Reynolds, *Kate O'Brien: A Literary Portrait* (Buckinghamshire: Colin Smythe, Ltd, 1987), p.83. Hereafter Reynolds, *Kate O'Brien*.

89 Aintzane L. Mentxaka, "Orpheo, Eurydice, and Co.", *SQS Journal of Queer Studies in Finland*, 2 (2006).

90 Meaney et al., *Reading the Irish Woman*, p.194. For details on the discussion of lesbian relationships in the works of Rosamond Jacob and Blanaid Salkeld, respectively, see Meaney, "Regendering Modernism", and Moynagh Sullivan, "'The Woman Gardener': Transnationalism, Gender, Sexuality, and the Poetry of Blanaid Salkeld", *Irish University Review*, 42.1 (2012). Hereafter Sullivan, "'The Woman Gardener'".

91 The first of these was held in the Dolphin Hotel in Dublin on December 10, 1934, and was attended by fifty-five guests from Dublin's artistic community. *The Irish Times*, December 11, 1934.

Times wryly summed up the prevailing mood of the time: "In such circumstances – when half the world is at war, and the shadow hangs heavy over the other half – it seems unwise to plan for anything more than ten days ahead."[92] Yet remarkably, it was at this juncture that a more united front developed between writers' groups in an effort to promote their books.[93] As the then President Blanaid Salkeld somewhat idealistically declaimed, the Club "must do our best to keep art and literature flourishing".[94]

Privately, the Club held "at homes" in their city residences. For centuries, coterie and salon culture had formed an important part of female literary life in Ireland as a way of facilitating writing and discussing literature. Salkeld hosted gatherings in her home at 43 Morehampton Road where writers such as Patrick Kavanagh and Flann O'Brien were regular visitors. Indeed, a contemporary article in *The Irish Times* confirmed the practice of meeting in one's home was "very popular and brings the writers together closely during the season".[95] Such "at homes", suggestive of hospitality and conviviality, were also sites of serious literary lectures, inspirational talks and advice for members. Moreover, they served to admit or exclude members, since private parties require an invite from the host. Notable absentee women writers and poets of the period include Mary Lavin, Sheila Wingfield and Annie P. Smithson. While the reasons for their absence remain speculative and require further investigation, some affiliations were known to exist with specific members. For instance, and as further elucidated in Chapter Five, Wingfield and Salkeld developed a professional relationship through the Gayfield Press, and both Lavin and Smithson were active members of the Irish PEN, which was often the writing group of choice for younger writers.[96]

Coterie culture provided support and assistance for writing and publishing matters as well as a site for intellectual discussion. Ethel G. Davidson, as President of the Club in 1937, reiterated this aim at the Annual Banquet, where she "described the objects of the Club, and pointed out the great assistance derived by members from their fellow-writers through discussing their works and comparing their views of

---

92 *The Irish Times*, December 18, 1940.
93 This will be discussed in more detail in Chapter Four.
94 *The Irish Times*, April 10, 1942.
95 *The Irish Times*, March 24, 1939.
96 Both Lavin and Smithson were members of PEN. Wingfield was not a member but was a contributor to the Gayfield Press, a publishing venture of Salkeld's. See Chapter Five for further details.

literature".[97] Examples include Rosamond Jacob, who received considerable support from fellow members such as Patricia Lynch when searching for a publisher for her children's book *The Raven's Glen*. Similarly, Sybil le Brocquy advised Jacob on practical publishing matters when she presented extracts of her novel *The Rebel's Wife* at a work-in-progress meeting of the Women Writers' Club.[98] These novels were ultimately published in 1957 and 1960 respectively.

Yet these women were no "parlor radicals".[99] They were active, professional women writers engaged in promulgating a specific type of female writing: one that was radical, liberal and contemporary. As such, their discussions largely centered on literature, human rights and women writers. Rosamond Jacob recalls attending one such talk at the "shop" (Country Store) in 1934 and following a heated debate between "Dorothy & Hanna" on the issue of "anti-vivisection": "Dorothy, all for vivisection, partly because she had heard doctors speak of trying new form of operation on poor patients in hospital, & thought it wd be better try it on animals."[100] Another "interesting and animated" discussion held in the home of Dorothy McAuliffe concerned the French novelist George Sand (1804–1876): "an extraordinary woman, who was at the center of the French world of letters in the eighteenth century".[101] Sand's reputed affairs with Chopin and "particularly de Mussett" were considered "almost as exciting as the Dreyfus case".[102]

Dissident women and unorthodox sexuality were themes that ran through the fiction of many members, despite the potential repercussions of having their books banned. In light of this, Maura Laverty held a discussion on seventeenth-century women writers that focused on the risqué writings of the playwright and prose writer Aphra Behn (1640–1689). Often cited as one of the first professional female authors,[103] the resilience of their earliest foremothers in thwarting criticism held special appeal for a Club that was still grappling with patriarchal and conservative constraints in the twentieth century.

---

97 *The Irish Times*, March 12, 1937.
98 Lane, *Rosamond Jacob*, pp.281–301.
99 Elizabeth Harding quoted in Elaine Showalter, *A Jury of Her Peers: American Women Writers from Anne Bradstreet to Annie Proulx* (London: Virago Press, 2009), p.338.
100 Papers of Rosamond Jacob, MS 32,582.
101 *The Irish Times*, March 24, 1939.
102 *The Irish Times*, March 24, 1939.
103 Lane, *Rosamond Jacob*, pp.264–265.

The ensuing alliances and affiliations formed over the twenty-five years reinforced solidarity among members. At times, friendship and professional pairings intersected and overlapped. Examples include Blanaid Salkeld's friendships with Maud Gonne MacBride and Sybil le Brocquy, while Dorothy Day (Dora McAuliffe) and le Brocquy were also close personal friends. Ethel Mannin and Hanna Sheehy Skeffington shared socialist beliefs and regularly corresponded in the 1940s, while Rosamond Jacob's wide circle of friends included Sheehy Skeffington, Patricia Lynch and Teresa Deevy, for whom she worked as secretary. Jacob also lived with Dorothy Macardle for a time. Although their personal relationship was often tempestuous, their friendship nonetheless provided "mutual intellectual support" for their respective writing endeavors throughout the 1920s and 1930s.[104] Sheehy Skeffington's relations spanned multiple interrelated networks of familial and political ties. These included committee member "Mrs" Cavanagh McDowell, the satirical poet and sister of cartoonist Ernest Cavanagh, and Mary Kettle, ardent feminist and sister of Hanna Sheehy Skeffington.[105] Many writers formed temporary affiliations with the Club but were not involved in its day-to-day activities. The writers Norah Hoult, Madeleine French-Mullen (member of the Joint Committee of Women's Societies and Social Workers and friend of Rosamond Jacob) and Róisín Walsh, the first female Chief Librarian for the City of Dublin,[106] were among this cohort of influential women.

Male colleagues were also welcomed. Despite the Club's decision to remain a "female-only" entity, men were regularly invited to events over the years. Playwright, novelist and Chief Justice Kenneth Reddin, PEN member and journalist Seamus McCall, playwright Denis Johnston, artist Jack B. Yeats, politician James McNeill, scholar and editor of the short-lived *The Klaxon* Con Leventhal (A. J. Leventhal), director

---

104 According to Nadia Smith, tension arose in their living arrangements when Jacob began a relationship with a prominent IRA member Frank Ryan who visited the apartment many times during 1925–1926. Smith, *Dorothy Macardle*, pp.53–56.
105 *The Irish Times*, December 11, 1934.
106 Róisín Walsh was a regular attendant at the annual banquet although she is not listed as present on this date. Walsh, political activist as well as Chief Librarian of County Dublin, was the only woman on the first editorial board of the journal *The Bell*. Her circle included female activists Maud Gonne MacBride, Hanna Sheehy Skeffington and Mary Kettle. Niall Carson and Paddy Hoey, "The Bell and the Blanket: Journals of Republican Dissent", *New Hibernia Review*, 16.1 (2012).

of broadcasting for national radio (Radio Éireann) C. E. Kelly[107] and poet Austin Clarke, number among the prominent male guests invited to attend the various Annual Banquets. Men were occasionally invited to attend monthly meetings, but their presence was sporadic. For example, an invitation was extended to Austin Clarke, a friend of Blanaid Salkeld, to attend a monthly meeting in April 1938.[108] Yet, when the writer and critic Andrew E. Malone suggested they "give up a little of their independent existence to become an autonomous section of the PEN Club", Club President Ethel G. Davidson explained that "they belonged to other literary clubs, but this was a sort of side-show".[109] Their determination to choose their own canvas and remain independent was seen as a source of female empowerment and freedom from patriarchal control. In short, Malone's suggestion was politely but firmly ignored.

These important networks encapsulate the compelling world of the coterie and club culture of the mid-twentieth century. No doubt, further research will capture and elucidate further elements of this story, as yet undiscovered. For now, what *is* clear is that the supportive network of the Women Writers' Club enabled their members to push for the right to participate as equal citizens, promote their literary works and encourage women into the professions. As the following chapter reveals, this was achieved in part through the prestigious Club's literary prize, which they titled the Book of the Year.

---

107 *The Irish Press*, December 13, 1949. Dorothy Day (Dora McAuliffe) worked as a broadcaster on Radio Éireann (RE), the national broadcaster.
108 Madeleine Ross to Austin Clarke, MS 83, Austin Clarke Papers, MS 38,674, National Library of Ireland, April 28, 1938.
109 *The Irish Times*, February 4, 1938.

Figure 2: Advertisement for the PEN Anthology of Poetry: *Concord of Harp: An Irish PEN Anthology of Poetry* (Dublin: Talbot Press Ltd, 1953). *Irish Independent*, June 10, 1953.

Figure 3. Detail from photograph of Women Writers' Club Dinner. February, 1938. Press Photographs of Eamon de Valera (1882–1975). P150/PH/3664/4.

Figure 4. Newspaper cutting of Ena Dargan (left) and Kate O'Brien (middle) at the Women Writers' Club Dinner in the Hibernian Hotel in 1950. *Irish Press*, December 19, 1950.

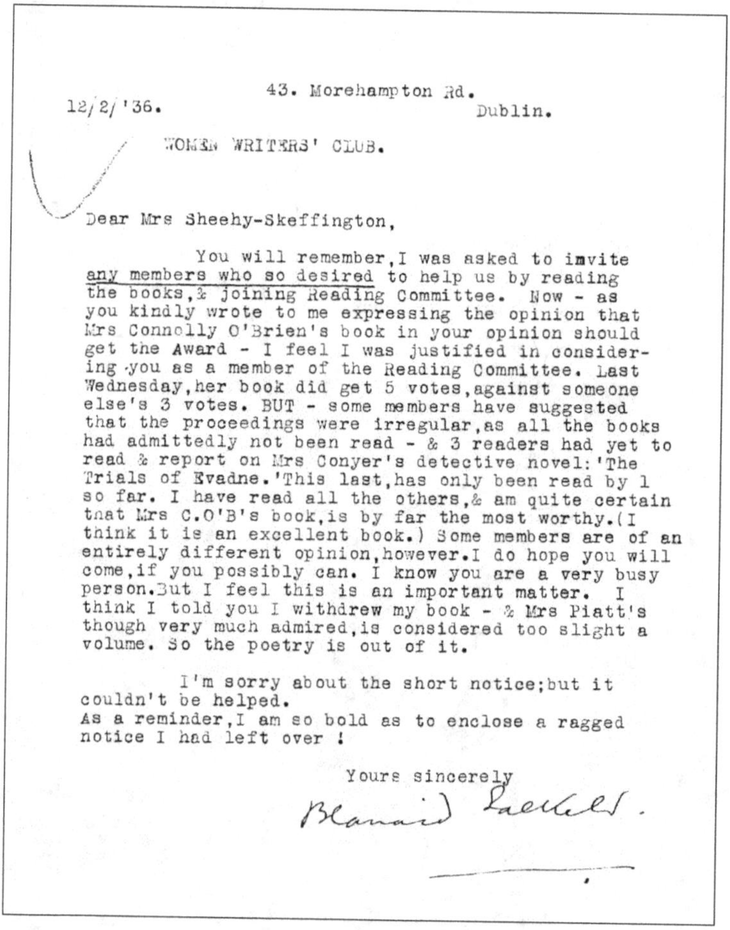

```
                        43. Morehampton Rd.
    12/2/'36.                           Dublin.

         WOMEN WRITERS' CLUB.

    Dear Mrs Sheehy-Skeffington,

             You will remember, I was asked to invite
    any members who so desired to help us by reading
    the books, & joining Reading Committee. Now - as
    you kindly wrote to me expressing the opinion that
    Mrs Connolly O'Brien's book in your opinion should
    get the Award - I feel I was justified in consider-
    ing you as a member of the Reading Committee. Last
    Wednesday, her book did get 5 votes, against someone
    else's 3 votes. BUT - some members have suggested
    that the proceedings were irregular, as all the books
    had admittedly not been read - & 3 readers had yet to
    read & report on Mrs Conyer's detective novel: 'The
    Trials of Evadne.'This last, has only been read by 1
    so far. I have read all the others, & am quite certain
    that Mrs C.O'B's book, is by far the most worthy.(I
    think it is an excellent book.) Some members are of an
    entirely different opinion, however. I do hope you will
    come, if you possibly can. I know you are a very busy
    person. But I feel this is an important matter.  I
    think I told you I withdrew my book - & Mrs Piatt's
    though very much admired, is considered too slight a
    volume. So the poetry is out of it.

             I'm sorry about the short notice; but it
    couldn't be helped.
    As a reminder, I am so bold as to enclose a ragged
    notice I had left over !
                            Yours sincerely
                            Blanaid Salkeld.
```

Figure 5: Letter from Blanaid Salkeld to Hanna Sheehy Skeffington, February 12, 1936. MS 47, Sheehy Skeffington Papers, MS 33,607/13, February 12, 1936. Thanks to the Sheehy Skeffington family for permission to use this material.

Figure 6: *Fisherman's Wake* (Dublin: Talbot Press, 1940), collection of poetry by Temple Lane.

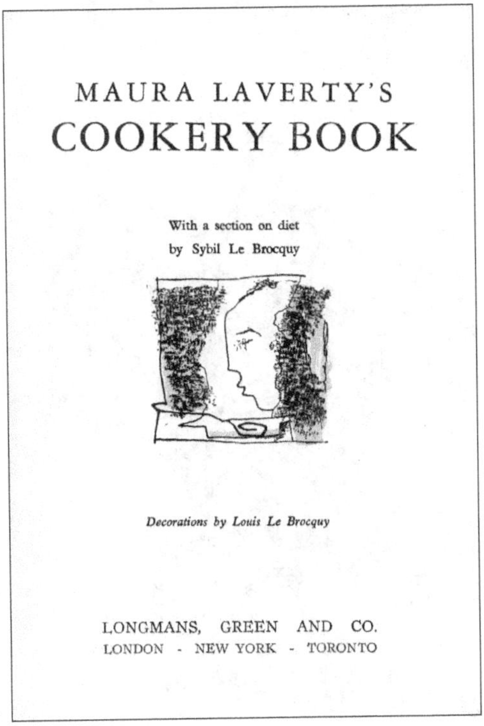

Figure 7: Frontispiece of Maura Laverty's *Cookery Book* (1946), with a section on diet by Sybil le Brocquy and decorations by Louis le Broquy.

Figure 8: Newspaper cutting of Ethel Mannin (middle) with Lorna Reynolds (right) at the Women Writers' Club Dinner, circa 1948.

Figure 9: Leaflet announcing Extraordinary General Meeting of the Women Writers' Club, 1958.

Figure 10: Photograph of "The Inca King: Folk-play at Oruro Carnival". Photographer: Ena Dargan. From: Ena Dargan, *The Road To Cuzco: A Journey from Argentina to Peru* (London: Andrew Melrose, 1950).

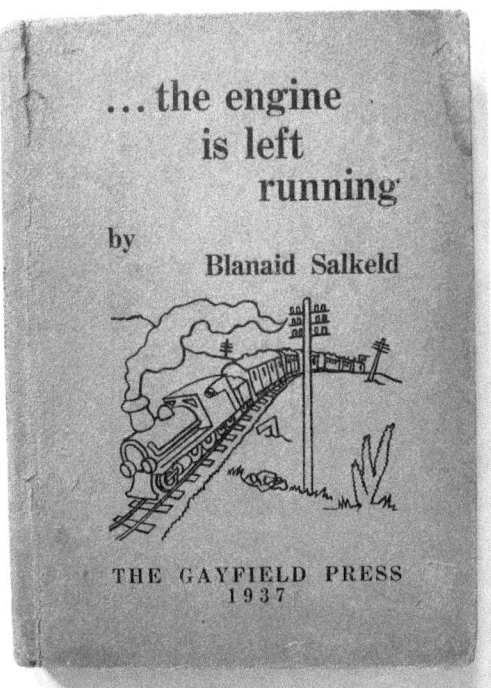

Figure 11: Cover of ... *the engine is left running* (1937), first publication of the Gayfield Press.

Figure 12: Illustration by Cecil ffrench Salkeld for children's book *Once Upon a Time ... Being Stories about a fierce Ogre and a small Boy, and a little Princess and a tiny Bird* (circa 1938), published by the Gayfield Press.

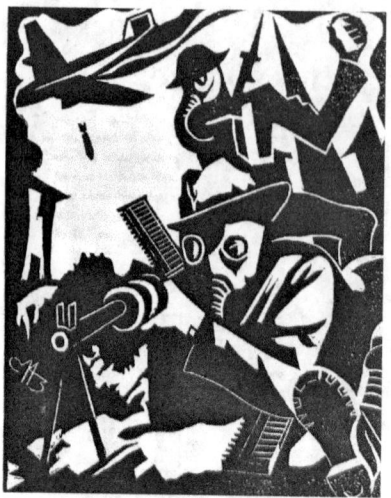

Figure 13: Illustration by Cecil ffrench Salkeld for Ewart Milne's poem "Oboe for Yeats" in the Gayfield publication *Forty North Fifty West* (1938).

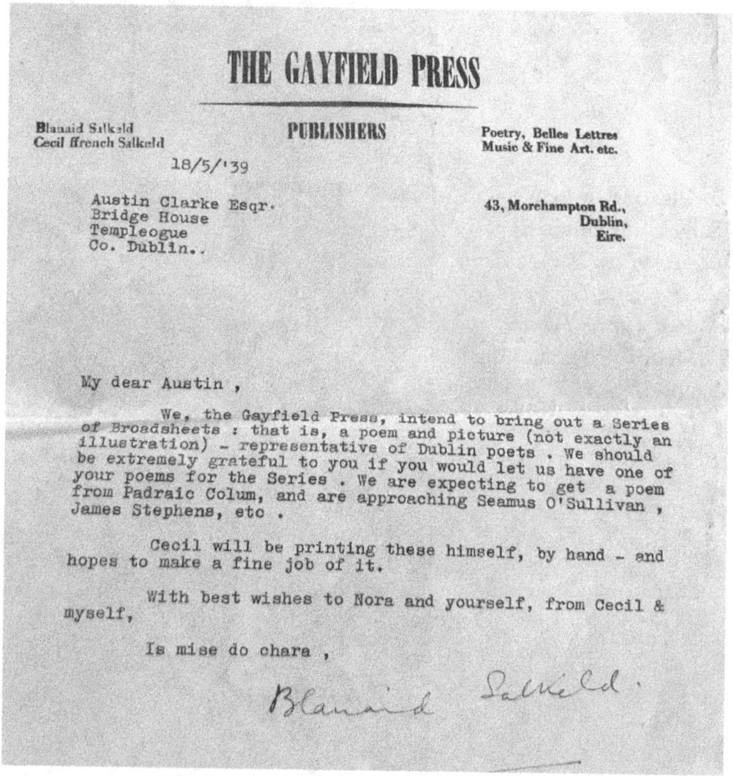

THE GAYFIELD PRESS

PUBLISHERS

Blanaid Salkeld
Cecil ffrench Salkeld

Poetry, Belles Lettres
Music & Fine Art. etc.

18/5/'39

Austin Clarke Esqr.
Bridge House
Templeogue
Co. Dublin..

43, Morehampton Rd.,
Dublin,
Eire.

My dear Austin ,

We, the Gayfield Press, intend to bring out a Series of Broadsheets : that is, a poem and picture (not exactly an illustration) - representative of Dublin poets . We should be extremely grateful to you if you would let us have one of your poems for the Series . We are expecting to get a poem from Padraic Colum, and are approaching Seamus O'Sullivan , James Stephens, etc .

Cecil will be printing these himself, by hand - and hopes to make a fine job of it.

With best wishes to Nora and yourself, from Cecil & myself,

Is mise do chara ,

Blanaid Salkeld.

Figure 14: Letter from Blanaid Salkeld to Austin Clarke regarding the Gayfield Press's series of broadsheets, May 18, 1939. Thanks to Aoife Clarke, granddaughter of Austin Clarke, for permission to use this material.

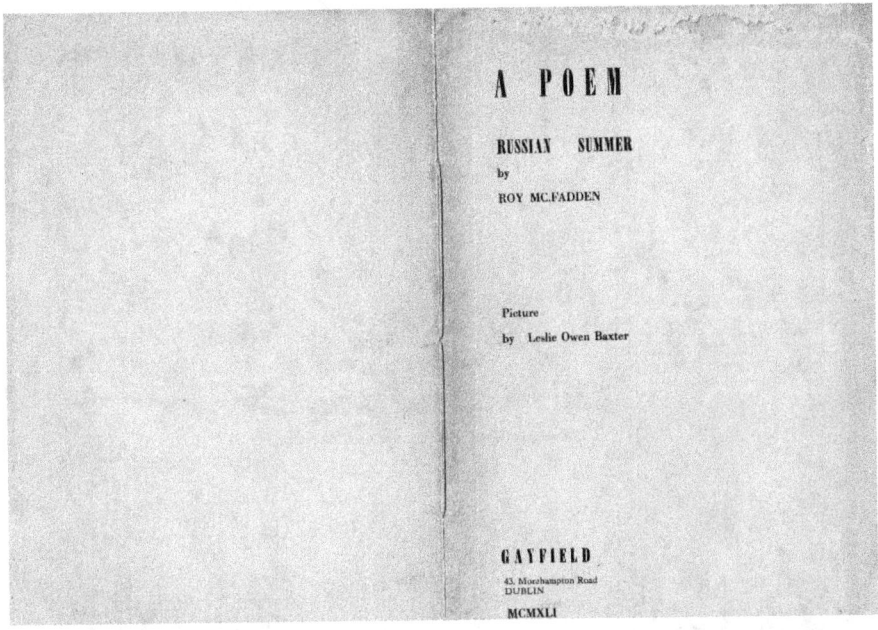

Figure 15: Roy McFadden's poem "Russian Summer", published in 1941 by the Gayfield Press for their series of broadsheets, with illustrations by Leslie Owen Baxter.

Figure 16: Photograph of the interior of the restaurant Jammet with waiters in attendance. Postcard (2012). *Restaurant Jammet*. 9. https://arrow.tudublin.ie/jamres/9.

Figure 17: Frontispiece from Helen Waddell's book, *The Desert Fathers* (London: Constable, 1936).

CHAPTER THREE

"A Wild Field to a Later Generation"

The Book of the Year Award

Writing in the influential periodical *Irish Studies* in 1951, Lorna Reynolds, academic, writer and one-time President of the Women Writers' Club, described her generation of writers' wish to bequeath an heroic tradition of their own. Particularly singling out Elizabeth Bowen's novel *Death of the Heart* and Kate O'Brien's novel *That Lady*, which won the Book of the Year awards in 1939 and 1946 respectively,[1] she listed what she saw as a "wild field to a later generation" of thirty noteworthy poets, including Blanaid Salkeld and Temple Lane, to highlight "the chiming voices that rise from the pages" of Irish literature of the mid-twentieth century. In naming these women writers, Reynolds ringfenced a space for her female contemporaries in the print culture of the period and proposed a particular canon of post-revival writing, which was promoted through the annual Book of the Year literary award of the Women Writers' Club.

As previously mentioned, over a period of twenty-three years, the fifteen books that won the Book of the Year and the runners-up were celebrated at an award ceremony held at the Annual Banquet. The two-fold aim of the prize was to reinforce the collegial ethos of the club and market its members' books. The title of the award speaks for itself. The cultural artifact, a specially bound edition of the "the writers' own book, beautifully and artistically bound", replete with gold lettering, was promoted as a symbol of material value and literary worth.[2] It operated as a means of negotiating access to the public sphere and fostered the collective identity of a professional and creative club. The award was a

1 Reynolds, "Thirty Years of Irish Letters".
2 *The Irish Times*, February 4, 1938.

metaphor for the complex and diverse nature of contemporary feminist thinking and the socio-political contexts of book production. As such, it reflected not only the radical ideologies of its members, but also what Adams and Barker refer to as the effect of "that society on the book". In an increasingly conservative and patriarchal Irish state, many of their works contested established notions of womanhood and societal norms, pushing back against restrictive legislation.[3] As a corpus of female writing, they represented a dissident voice in the Irish literary field between the years 1933 and 1958, contesting nationalist narratives and religion and positing a uniquely feminist value system.

The Reading Committee

The intricacies of bringing a book to the marketplace involves a communicative process that harnesses intellectual influences and readers groups.[4] To facilitate this, the Club convened a reading committee to function as an arbiter of personal taste and judgment. Drawing on members from academic, political and artistic backgrounds, the committee served to construct an alternative canon of reading reflecting the ethos of Club members and the diverse ideas within their writings.

The reading committee underscores both the private and public responses of the Club to the dissemination and marketing of books. Privately, it consisted a group of readers with specific political and cultural agendas. It functioned as a mediator of talent; a filter through which texts were read, discussed and disseminated that celebrated the wide range of female influences in the book cycle process. Publicly, its prime objective was the targeting of readers and those in the book trade through reviews and newspaper reports, while commending the collective identity of a "woman-centred network of readers and writers".[5] The interchange of cultural, political and intellectual ideas evinced through the various nominations intermingled with this intellectual grouping exerted significant influence on the outcome of the books chosen. As social visionaries advocating for change, the reading committee was

---

3 Adams and Barker, "A New Model for the Study of the Book", p.49.
4 For a useful discussion of what constitutes reading committees, see Janice Radway, "A Feeling for Books: The Book-of-the-Month-Club, Literary Taste and Middle-class Desire", in D. Finklestein and A. McCleery (eds), *The Book History Reader*, 2nd edn (London: Routledge 2006).
5 Travis, "The Women in Print Movement", p.276.

intrinsic to an influential public sphere that supported radical changes in attitude and behavior. While precise knowledge of this committee is limited by the lack of information available, correspondence between the various literary participants goes some way to advancing a better understanding of the reading committee's politics, the make-up of its members and its overarching impact. In particular, letters between Salkeld and Hanna Sheehy Skeffington in 1936 and 1937 provide unique insights into the machinations of the process, the composition of the reading committee, and the interplay between members.

The driving force behind the committee was Blanaid Salkeld, with Dorothy Macardle also playing an active role. Members of the Club "who desired to join" were encouraged to submit reviews and/or critiques based on any of numerous novels, radio plays, translations and poetry collections published by its members.[6]

Those who expressed an opinion on the award were also invited, as a letter from Salkeld to Sheehy Skeffington in 1936 attests: "You kindly wrote to me expressing the opinion that Mrs Connolly O'Brien's book in your opinion should get the Award [sic] – I feel I was justified in considering you as a member of the Reading Committee" (see Figure 5).[7] Up to this point, Sheehy Skeffington had remained on the fringes of the reading committee, despite previous pleas from Dorothy Macardle to join properly: "We are a dud lot from the point of view of efficiency and your name got a large vote. It's good too to have the Committee Republican [sic]."[8] Skeffington acquiesced, joining the reading committee alongside others including the "Irish" readers "Dr. Byrne, Mrs McNeill, Mrs C MacDowell and myself (I don't think [sic] other members of Reading Committee have Irish)".[9] While gaps remain in its composition, the heart of this reading committee comprised a virtual powerhouse of influential women who were deeply imbedded in the wider community of Irish political and literary life. "Mrs [Josephine] McNeill['s]" networks extended to the political associates of her husband, James McNeill, Governor General of the Irish Free State (1929–1932), who regularly

---

6 Blanaid Salkeld to Hanna Sheehy Skeffington, MS 47, Sheehy Skeffington Papers MS 33,607/13, February 12, 1936.

7 Blanaid Salkeld to Hanna Sheehy Skeffington, MS 47, Sheehy Skeffington Papers, MS 33,607/13, February 12, 1936.

8 Dorothy Macardle to Hanna Sheehy Skeffington, MS 82, Sheehy Skeffington Papers, MS 41,178/81, circa 1933.

9 Blanaid Salkeld to Hanna Sheehy Skeffington, MS 47, Sheehy Skeffington Papers, MS 33,607/13, February 12, 1936.

attended the Annual Banquet.[10] Her commitment to Irish affairs included acting as Chairman of the Irish Countrywomen's Association in 1950 and being the first female to represent Ireland in a ministerial capacity at the Hague in 1949.[11] Artistic connections included Christine Longford, Elizabeth Bowen, Lennox Robinson and Micheál MacLiammóir. Eithne Byrne's role as advocate for the Irish language and her wide international connections are exemplified in a 1936 *Irish Times* report that focused on her Women Writers' Club lecture discussing her recent tour with Irish and British architects to Czechoslovakia, in which she emphasized the difficult nature and longevity of the revival project. Similarly, Maeve Cavanagh McDowell formed part of this network of women, all of whom were former Cumann na mBan members. Lucy Collins lists her as an important poet of 1916 along with fellow club member Winifred M. Letts (Mrs Verschoyle), while the revolutionary James Connolly once referred to her as "the fair poetess of the revolution".[12] While judgments on their taste and influence on the decision-making process is complicated by lack of material evidence, there is a distinct sense that their personal and political allegiances were close to that expressed by Sheehy Skeffington below and reflected in the nature of books that won the award during this period. Initially, the decision-making process seemed rather haphazard. Each member of the reading committee was given a vote and reviewed the nominated books. The prize went to the book that got the most votes, while the runners-up received second prize and "honorable mention" at the Annual Banquet. Initial proceedings were also similarly disorganized and Club correspondence noted several complaints about "irregular proceedings":[13]

> Last Wednesday, her book [Connolly O'Brien's] did get 5 votes, against someone else's 3 votes. BUT – some members have suggested that the proceedings were irregular, as all the books had admittedly not been read – & 3 readers had yet to read & report on Mrs Conyer's detective novel: "The Trials of Evadne". This last, has only been read by 1 so far. I have read all the others, and am quite certain that Mrs C. O'B's books, is by far the most

---

10 See for example, the list of attendance at the Annual Banquet in 1937 and 1938. *The Irish Times*, March 12, 1937, and February 4, 1938 respectively.
11 Papers of Josephine McNeill, P234, Descriptive Catalogue, UCD Archives (Dublin: University College Dublin, 2009). Hereafter Papers of Josephine McNeill.
12 Stewart, "Ricorso".
13 Blanaid Salkeld to Hanna Sheehy Skeffington, MS 47, Sheehy Skeffington Papers, MS 33,607/13, February 12, 1936.

worthy. (I think it is an excellent book.) Some members are of an entirely different opinion, however. I do hope you will come, if you possibly can.[14]

By 1937, a more formalized and structured process had evolved. Readers were asked to review, evaluate and determine the scoring and criteria for their judgments. In a 1937 note entitled, "Memo on books for W.W. Club", Sheehy Skeffington outlined her assessments of the nominated books as follows: Winifred M. Letts's schoolgirl novel *Pomomos Island* was described as "a good school girl yarn", and her radio script *The Dean's Tree* as "a charming little radio play & Swift-Stella theme but too short & sketchy to be [] as equalling a book".[15] Christine Longford's light-hearted "biography" of Dublin was described as "superficial & slight ... A gossipy sort of guide book – readable but easily forgotten". Caitriona McCleod's biography of Robert Emmet was deemed "good for a first book & shows a certain amount of research tho no very deep study", and Helen Waddell's book was described as "mainly translation under thread of narrative & [], I do not class it with [] work & do not place is as high as some of the authors [*sic*] other works".

Privileging historical research over other forms of literary output, Sheehy Skeffington ultimately nominated *Henry Joy McCracken* for the Book of the Year award:

> Henry Joy McCracken by Edna Fitz. Henry an excellent historical biography of [] M C written with sympathy and understanding & showing painstaking research of original documents & close study of various documents. Account of Ulster background & Belfast conditions add greatly to value of book. Many French lights thrown on important figure & events. Style clear & vivid. Consider this the best of the series/great Irishmen, by Talbot Press & the best of book of W.W. submitted for year 1936. Recommended for 1st Prize.[16]

Fitzhenry's book was one of a series of politically educative books celebrated by the Women Writers' Club. As outlined later in the chapter, these texts call into question contemporary historical narratives

---

14 Blanaid Salkeld to Hanna Sheehy Skeffington, MS 47, Sheehy Skeffington Paper MS 33,607/13, February 12, 1936. "Dorothy Conyers" refers to Dorothea Conyers (1871–1949), a Limerick writer who wrote over fifty novels, specializing in humorous tales of the Irish sporting set.

15 Brackets [] denote a word that is either missing or cannot be deciphered. See "Memo on Books for W.W. Club", MS 47, Sheehy Skeffington Papers, MS 33,619/14.

16 MS 47, Sheehy Skeffington Papers, MS 33,619/14.

of nationalism and prioritize the role of women in historical events. In second place was Rosamond Jacob's fictional novel *The House Divided* (1937) – later renamed and published as *The Troubled House* (1938),[17] which was based on actual events during the War of Independence. Sheehy Skeffington's review notes:

> Black & Tan phase of Anglo-Irish war in which members of an Irish household have divided allegiance which rears – in one case in tragedy. Characters well drawn [] espec mother & sons, character of Nix []the woman artist very interesting and "live" … Essentially a feminine & feminist picture: the sons very well set off the mother and her frame of story[] opportunity for contrast & climax. Would [] this no. 2 on list.[18]

While Jacob's novel chillingly predicts the type of tensions that divided Irish families for decades following the Civil War of 1922–1923, it also reads as a feminist novel that questions societal mores and incorporates progressive views on sexuality and art. Sheehy Skeffington gave third prize to Waddell's "translation" of *The Desert Fathers*. The final marks were handwritten in the right-hand margin. They ranged from "3" votes for *Robert Emmet*, "4" for *Dublin*, "8" for *House Divided* and a surprising joint first of "8½" votes each for *Henry Joy McCracken* and *The Desert Fathers*. All three books were celebrated at the Annual Banquet in 1937 with a toast proposed by Josephine McNeill to all members "whose works have been published during the past year".[19]

It is likely that Waddell's book was the choice of Salkeld. In a letter to the poet Austin Clarke the following year, she praised Waddell while bolstering the Club's reputation: "we have some very distinguished members – notably Helen Waddell – and – are we not as strong as our strongest link? (I think we are)".[20] But if private responses reflected the various likes and dislikes of the reading committee, they were nonetheless given in the spirit of solidarity and harmony. Sheehy made reference to this in the aforementioned letter, suggesting that "all members who produced books and on this list should be included as our guests & in affiliation, two prizes for English & one for Irish". Despite this intention, no prize was awarded to Irish language books.

17 Rosamond Jacob, *The Troubled House: A Novel of Dublin in the Twenties* (Dublin: Browne & Nolan, 1938).
18 MS 47, Sheehy Skeffington Papers, MS 33,619/14.
19 *The Irish Times*, March 12, 1937.
20 Blanaid Salkeld to Austin Clarke, MS 83, Austin Clarke Papers, MS 38,670/2, March 11, 1938.

"A WILD FIELD TO A LATER GENERATION"

The cultural and commercial impact of the Book of the Year award was keenly observed, and every opportunity was taken to exploit it. At the Annual Banquet of 1936, Macardle toasted the winning authors while at the same time she "presented women writers with some amusing ideas of how best to further the sale of their books".[21] Her speech was followed by the modernist artist Mainie Jellett, who "gave a list of books and poems published during the past year by members of the club". The singularity of the prize to individual writers had positive implications for other writers, as publicity was extended to all. Leveraging their networks in the media also enabled them to promote their works ahead of publication. Examples include the "Women in the News" section in *The Irish Press* in 1936, which featured book discussions at the Annual Banquet including "several suggestions for increasing book sales", and listing the winning books and all-woman shortlist:

> There are two books for children, "The Turf-cutter's Donkey Goes Visiting" by Patricia Lynch, and a charming western book by Winifred Letts. Mrs Piatt has each contributed a volume of poetry, Dorothy Conyers has a novel, "The Trials of Evadne["] and of Irish interest there are Catriona McLeod's "Life of Emmet" and Edna FitzHenry's "Anthology of 1916," the first edition of which was sold out in a few days last Christmas … .We are all waiting for Miss MacArdle's great work, which is now in the hands of the printers.[22]

Also in 1937, following the announcement of the winners, Josephine McNeill proposed a toast to all the nominees: "Miss Rosamond Jacob, Lady Christine Longford, Winifred Letts, Mairead Ni Grada, and Miss McCloud".[23] The event was lauded in *The Irish Press* for "again dividing their yearly award for the best book written by a member".[24]

These public responses expertly positioned the Club as professionals in the book trade while the notion of a reading committee marked their shortlist and winners as signifiers of taste and merit. As one report enthused: "The idea of a Reading Committee to whom the writers can send their books, and on whose recommendation the society awards prizes, is interesting."[25] However, any in-depth analysis

---

21 *The Irish Times*, March 20, 1936.
22 "Women in the News", *The Irish Press*, March 25, 1936. The reference here to McArdle's work (usually spelt Macardle), refers to Dorothy Macardle's history book *The Irish Republic* (1937).
23 *Irish Independent*, March 12, 1937.
24 *The Irish Press*, February 19, 1937.
25 *The Irish Times*, March 28, 1936.

of their decision-making process is hampered by the lack of relevant committee reports and notes. Furthermore, the impact of their choices on book sales is difficult to assess accurately without statistical records. Yet the images of these dynamic women bestowing their members with awards, and pointedly marketing their books in the public sphere, serves to document their formidable cultural presence in literary life of the period. In what follows, I will explore the body of works that won the Book of the Year award, examining their texts thematically to reveal what Donald McKenzie describes as a "a more authentic reconstruction of cultural history".[26] The winning texts are considered under three headings: namely, "An Experimental Form of Literature", "A Broader Republican Identity" and "Censorship and Women Writers: Ethel Mannin, Maura Laverty and Teresa Deevy". The first section interrogates the works of Blanaid Salkeld, Temple Lane, Helen Waddell, Kate O'Brien, Patricia Lynch, Christine Longford and Ena Dargan; critically examining common themes through the social, political and religious debates of the period. The next section considers the historical writing of its members, and the political and educative nature of these books. The third and final section explores the societal impact on the book, examining the nature of censorship and its impact on the writings of Ethel Mannin, Maura Laverty and Teresa Deevy. As a strategic weapon against literary censorship, or harsh reviews, the award came to represent unity and solidarity within the club and afforded its members a form of protection from the effects of literary censorship.

An Experimental Form of Literature[27]

The first book to win the Book of the Year prize was Blanaid Salkeld's poetry collection *Hello Eternity!* (1933). Published by the London house Elkin Mathews & Marrot, its light blue cardboard cover, stamped with a modern black typeface, boldly brought to light a corpus of literary texts that was radical and ahead of their time.

---

26 McKenzie, "History of the Book", p.296.
27 This sub-title is taken from Clair Wills, "Women Writers and the Death of Rural Ireland". In this essay, Wills argues that alongside the realist novel and short story, other experimental forms, "mixed forms in the novel and short story" are important to the study of literary culture in the mid-twentieth century. Clair Wills, "Women Writers and the Death of Rural Ireland: Realism and Nostalgia in the 1940s", *Éire-Ireland*, 41.1&2 (2006), p.197. Hereafter Wills, "Women Writers and the Death of Rural Ireland".

Blanaid Salkeld (1880–1959) was born in India and brought up in Fitzwilliam Street, Dublin. Her early influences included the English poet John Keats and the Bengali poet Rabindranath Tagore, a friend of her father, whom she met as a young girl in India.[28] She married an Englishman in the Bombay Civil Service in 1902 but was widowed and returned to Ireland in 1906 with her son Cecil, who later became a well-known artist. She joined the Abbey Theatre, appearing under the stage name Nell Byrne, and took the lead role in George Fitzmaurice's *Country Dressmaker* in 1907. One of the early members of the Gaelic League, she attended George Russell's (Æ) Sunday evening gatherings. Salkeld's bohemian lifestyle left her free to hold regular "at homes" for those involved in the creative arts and subsequently to host her own Dublin *salon* at her home in Morehampton Road.[29] Close proximity to the inner city afforded easy access to centers of creativity and left her ideally placed to host meetings for the Women Writers' Club. In the late 1930s, her home became the site of her private printing operation, the Gayfield Press. Her publishing record represents the shifting tensions and influences in her poetry. Moynagh Sullivan writes that Salkeld's work was influenced by the literary revival, although her later work became more formally experimental with influences from the aforementioned poet Tagore, W. B. Yeats, Ezra Pound and Marianne Moore.[30] One of her last published poems, "The Woman Gardener", based on her memories of her childhood in Chittagong, mirrors that of Tagore's work "Gardener", and has a preface that draws on Yeats's "The Fiddler of Dooney".[31] Justin Quinn considers the style of her first collection, *Hello Eternity!*, an "archaic sub-Yeatsian mode which appealed to American audiences", although he states that her later feminist poetry in *The Fox's Covert* (1935) embraced a kind of "hectic futurism".[32] While Quinn clearly regards Salkeld's poetry as an unsuccessful anomaly, her publishing record suggests otherwise.

During her lifetime, she published four collections of poetry: *Hello Eternity* (1933), *The Fox's Covert* (1935), *... the engine is left running* (1937) and *Experiment in Error* (1955). Other publications included poetry pamphlets

---

28 *The Irish Times*, December 19, 1958.
29 Patrick Kavanagh, Flann O'Brien, Ernie O'Malley were amongst the attendees. Stewart, "Ricorso".
30 Sullivan, "'The Woman Gardener'".
31 Sullivan, "'The Woman Gardener'", p.55.
32 Justin Quinn, *The Cambridge Introduction to Modern Irish Poetry: 1800–2000* (Cambridge: Cambridge University Press, 2008), p.80.

produced by her own publishing house, the Gayfield Press. In 1935 her poem "One in Dublin" was published in the prestigious modernist journal *Poetry* under the editorial direction of T. S. Eliot.[33] Salkeld's poetry was also published in the *Spectator*, the *London Mercury* and T. S. Eliot's edited journal, *Criterion*.[34] A gifted translator, she also translated and reviewed the works of Alexandra Blok, Ezra Pound and Anna Akhmatova for the Irish periodicals *The Dublin Magazine, Ireland Today, Motley* and *The Bell*.[35] In addition, her poetry collections received two awards from the Women Writers' Club for the aforementioned *Hello Eternity* (1933) and *... the engine is left running* (1938); the latter winning second prize. Her verse play, *Scarecrow over the Corn*, was produced at the Gate Theatre and she also wrote pieces for the ballet and radio.[36] As with other members, she played an active role in the Irish PEN, and was awarded "life membership" in 1954. She was elected to the Council of the Irish Academy of Letters in 1956.[37] Temple Lane paid particular tribute to *... the engine is left running* at the 1938 Annual Banquet. According to Lane, Salkeld's work spanned "the gulf between thought and the machine and evolving something intelligent. This was the product of a fine, sensitive mind."[38] The machine aesthetic to which Lane refers, the material *things* or artifacts (machines, radios, hammers, trains) that drive this collection, was a popular theme in the avant-garde literature of America and Europe in the 1920s.

Salkeld's oeuvre also addresses issues of female sexuality, desire and the restrictions of institutional religion; ideas that link her poetry with that of other female poets such as Sheila Wingfield, Lorna Reynolds and Temple Lane. Susan Schreibman describes the "modernist sensibilities" of their poetry forms as "overwhelmingly female".[39] Their work engaged with the often taboo issues affecting women's lives such as sexuality, domestic violence and lesbianism.

---

33 *Poetry* refers to a Chicago-based journal set up in 1912 by Harriet Munroe. The editor, T. S. Eliot, published a series of Irish poems for a special edition in January 1935, which featured Salkeld's poem "One in Dublin". See also *The Irish Press*, February 19, 1937, which features an article on Blanaid Salkeld and her poetry.
34 *The Irish Press*, October 25, 1937.
35 For more details on Salkeld's publishing history, see Chapter Four.
36 *The Irish Times*, December 19, 1958.
37 *The Irish Times*, December 19, 1958. Her "life membership" was proposed by her friend Temple Lane at a PEN meeting in 1954 after Salkeld resigned (presumably for health reasons). See "Minutes Irish Pen", December 17, 1954.
38 *The Irish Times*, February 4, 1935.
39 Susan Schreibman, "Irish Women Poets 1929–1959: Some Foremothers", *Colby Quarterly*, 37.4 (2001), p.314.

A characteristic of women's poetry of the period was its tendency toward self-reflection, as exemplified in Blanaid Salkeld's poem "Terenure", from her *Hello Eternity* collection:[40]

> Across the dark road, the cottages gleaming with light
> Seemed more like dolls' houses than men's, as I passed
> At night –
> Dreaming that I had power to reveal spouse to spouse,
> To give children and the love of children to every house.
> Broken and sad and helpless, on my lonely road –
> I wished passionately, seriously, that I was God.[41]

This poem tackles the subject of marriage within urban middle-class families and critiques the restrictions on women within the institution and the lack of experiential autonomy in women's role as wives. The reference to Henrik Ibsen's controversial play *A Doll's House* echoes with the theatrical world in which Salkeld circulated and international plays that were popular in the Gate Theatre in the early 1930s. The theme of feminine self-discovery within Ibsen's play also resonates with Salkeld's life journey "on my lonely road", a subject to which she regularly returns within her poetry.

The topic of religion and the harshness of the implacable Church informs her third volume of poetry, *... the engine is left running*, which was runner-up in the Book of the Year award in 1938.[42] Salkeld's poem "Leave us Religion" registers her discontent with Catholic moral values and rejects institutional religion, instead appealing for an autonomous voice for women: "we have all been given Saints names / Whether you call Bernadette, Philomena, or Margaret", and are tainted with original sin and "our follies legion".[43] She exhorts women to "refute Authority and bite the Mother's hands", a radical notion during a period marked by repressive Catholic sensibilities. Margaret MacCurtain praises this as a "robust" poem, which "speaks of the reality of many women's desire to

---

40 Terenure was considered a middle-class area in Dublin city during the mid-twentieth century.
41 This poem, entitled "Templeogue", is the fifth in Blanaid Salkeld's collection of poems *Hello Eternity* (1933).
42 See Chapter Five for further details about this collection.
43 Margaret MacCurtain, "Poetry of the Spirit, 1900–95, Blanaid Salkeld (1880–1959)", in A. Bourke, S. Kilfeather, M. Luddy, M. MacCurtain, G. Meaney, M. Ni Dhonnchadha, M. O'Dowd and C. Wills (eds), *The Field Day Anthology of Irish Writing: Irish Women's Writing and Traditions, Volume IV* (New York: New York University Press, 2002).

give a human face to a harsh church" at a time when the Church was increasingly policing women's lives.

The conditions of women's lives are further explored in the works of fellow member, Temple Lane. Temple Lane (1899–1978), pseudonym for Mary Isabel Leslie, became the second poet to win the Book of the Year award for her 1940 collection of poetry entitled *Fisherman's Wake* (see Figure 6). Born in Dublin and raised in County Tipperary, she was educated at Trinity College Dublin, where she received her doctorate. Lane wrote over fifteen novels including *The Trains go South* (1939), and two collections of poetry, including *Fisherman's Wake* (1940) and *Curlews* (1945). Like Salkeld, Lane was a regular contributor to periodicals such as *The Dublin Magazine*, *Poetry Ireland* and *Irish Writing*. Under the alternative pen-name Jean Herberts, Lane wrote some light-hearted novels, and her successful novel, *Friday's Well* (1943), was adapted as a three-act comedy for the stage by Frank Carney in 1950. Lane's poetry explores the complexity of sexuality in the mid-twentieth century and the strict influence of the Irish Church on gender relations. Anne Fogarty describes her poetry as close in style to the early writing of W. B. Yeats, but with a feminine perspective and a "subtle irony".[44] Schreibman purports Lane's poetry to be influenced by the poetry of the Celtic Revival; replete with a modernist "psychological" approach to issues of sexuality and gender roles.[45] Such poems were composed during an historical period when investigative committees were convened to deal with sexuality, particularly issues of sexual crime, deviancy, women's dress and the dangers of sociability.[46] Socially, Catholic teaching burdened women with upholding the nation's virtue, and pastoral sermons propounded the view that women's sexuality needed to be controlled. The Pope issued a statement condemning modern dress codes as "one of the great evils of the time – the immodest fashions in women's dress", a point that was seized upon and reiterated in the sermons of the Irish Catholic Clergy.[47] It was through the cultural space that women poets could voice their opposition and express their discontent with patriarchal religious authority without fear of reprisal or criticism.

---

44 Fogarty, "The Influence of Absences", p.266; Collins, *Poetry by Women in Ireland*, p.266.
45 Susan Schreibman, "Irish Women Poets 1929–1959: Some Foremothers", *Colby Quarterly*, 37.4 (2001), p.313.
46 Maria Luddy, "Sex and the Single Girl in 1920s and 1930s Ireland", *Irish Review*, 35 (2007). Hereafter Luddy, "Sex and the Single Girl".
47 Luddy, "Sex and the Single Girl", p.79.

The diversity of their literary awards was also their strength, encompassing a range of genres, styles and modes of writing. This included not only poetry and fiction, history and plays, but also travel narratives and translations. *The Desert Fathers* (1937), Helen Waddell's (1889–1965) translation of the Latin *Vitae Patrum* (Lives of the Desert Fathers), won joint first with Edna Fitzhenry's history of the republican Henry Joy McCracken in 1937. Waddell was born in Tokyo, the daughter of Hugh Waddell, a Presbyterian minister and orientalist. Her brother, Rutherford Mayne (Samuel John Waddell), was a playwright with the Ulster Literary Abbey Theatres, a committee member of the Irish PEN and a highly regarded *salonnière*. Sometimes called "Ulster's Darling", Helen Waddell was an accomplished scholar who attended Somerville College, Oxford, and was the recipient of a PhD in Medieval French.[48] During the 1930s and 1940s, when her international success was at its height, Waddell was "feted by Prime Ministers and society hostesses" alike.[49] She was an enthusiastic supporter of Patrick Kavanagh, encouraging him to write his novel *The Green Fool*. Although she lived abroad for much of her life, Waddell's Irish roots were important to her and she identified as Irish. Perhaps her most significant creative work is *Peter Abelard: A Novel* (1933), but her enduring fame rests on her ability as a translator of medieval texts, including the prizewinning book *The Desert Fathers*. Both texts are still in print.

The Desert Fathers deals with the theme of religion in the early Christian period of the fourth century. It narrates the lives and teachings of monastic fathers and mothers, and the development of intellectual thought before seventeenth-century humanism. Grant Lomis, a contemporary reviewer, noted her ability to fuse "dry learning with an understanding for the popular touch", and lauded the work of the author in "culling from many hundred pages of dull reading".[50] The text also served as a critique of the modern world, which Waddell felt had "fallen to ancient anarchs of cruelty and pride".[51] For Waddell, the notion of a self-conscious intellectual life, such as that lived by the desert fathers, was a heroic existence in which "The Desert has bred fanaticism and

---

48 Stewart, "Ricorso".
49 Olivia Neill, *The Lost Decade of "Ulster's Darling" Helen Waddell: A Biography* by D. Felicitas Corrigan, reviewed in *Fortnight*, 235, March 10–23 (1986).
50 Grant Lomis, *The Desert Fathers, Translations from the Latin with an introduction by Helen Waddell*, reviewed in *Speculum*, 12.2 (1937).
51 Helen Waddell, *The Desert Fathers* (London: Constable, 1936), p.viii. Hereafter Waddell, *The Desert Fathers*.

frenzy and fear: but it also bred heroic gentleness".[52] The call for a more introspective cerebral life was endorsed by many members of the Women Writers' Club, including Kate O'Brien, whose novel *That Lady* (1946) won the Book of the Year prize in 1946.

Kate O'Brien (1897–1974) was born in Limerick to a wealthy Catholic horse-dealer. Her mother died of cancer when she was five and she spent the next twelve years as a boarder at the Laurel Hill French Convent in Limerick. After the death of her father in 1916, she won a scholarship and entered University College Dublin, where she received a Bachelor of Arts in English and French. Throughout her distinguished international career as a writer, and reviewer for *The Guardian*, she wrote ten novels, including two that won the Book of the Year award. O'Brien moved with ease in artistic circles in London, including those of her close friend Marie Belloc Lowndes, a sister of Hilaire Belloc. She became President of the Women Writers' Club in 1950. Throughout her life, she won many prestigious literary accolades including the Prix Femina, the Book of the Year award and the British Hawthornden and James Tait Black prizes.

O'Brien set her most successful novel, *That Lady* (1946), in the sixteenth century. The novel broaches the topics of sexual freedom, autonomy and religion. *That Lady* tells the story of Ana de Mendoza, a widow of the Spanish prime minister and a member of a noble aristocratic family during the turbulent reign of King Philip II. The novel presents the heroic narrative of de Mendoza, her personal friendship with the despotic monarch, and her love affair with a married man, Antonio Perez, against the wishes of Philip. It deals with the issue of personal choice and integrity and questions fundamental values, including the right to a private life. As Ana points out to King Philip:

> *But* my private life *is* truly private. There have been, Philip, as long as I can remember, thoughts and even acts in that private life which, presented to the world, would seem to injure this or that. That is so, I should think, from everyone from cradle to grave. But I do not present my private life to the world. Which is not the same thing as saying that I sacrifice it to the world. I own it, Philip. If I do wrong in it, that wrong is between me and Heaven. But here below, so long as I don't try to change it into public life, I insist that *I* own it.[53]

In the above defense of her sexual relationship with Perez, Ana insists on the individual volition inherent in the private act. In the case of *That*

---

52 Waddell, *The Desert Fathers*, p.viii.
53 Kate O'Brien, *That Lady* (London: William Heinemann, 1946), p.236.

Lady, Ana ultimately chooses "sin", but it is a choice that she makes as a free individual.

O'Brien's oeuvre repeatedly asserts the right and the freedom of the individual to control her own moral behavior; an ethical stance that ran counter to the prevailing discourses of morality in Ireland during this period.[54]

Lifelong friend and academic Lorna Reynolds suggests that O'Brien was attempting something new by writing about the mother–daughter relationship in her novel *The Flower of May* (1953), which won the Book of the Year award that year.[55] It deals with the theme of education, and the ideals of sisterhood, as female characters support each other in their quest for autonomy and education. In the novel, the protagonist, Fanny, is given the resources to further her education, and by implication, her future profession as a writer by her Aunt Eleanor:

> The father has neither the means nor the desire to give her such freedom of education. He has sons, he is not rich, and he is selfish and sentimental about this daughter. I want, therefore, to put a weapon in her hand, at the right time. Education, to be vital, should flow onward from school. It would be an arid, staccato business, to start one's self-education when one had fought out into the twenties – having fussed round over Father in the intervening years![56]

Mirroring the ideals of the modernist writer, Virginia Woolf, O'Brien links financial autonomy with education and success as a professional writer; a theme also taken up by Bridget MacCarthy as outlined later in this chapter. Other links to Woolf include the symbol of the lighthouse, a central theme of Woolf's 1927 novel of that name and a recurring motif of maternal supremacy.[57] In O'Brien's novel, it is at Fanny's mother's home, Glasalla, that maternal supremacy reigns free from patriarchy. In *The Flower of May*, the lighthouse flashes its beam "every minute,

---

54 This was an issue that concerned intellectuals of the period; for example, Rosamond Jacob argued in *A Bagail Timpal* for the importance of individual liberty and the dangers of "lowering the value set upon individual liberty". See Michael Cronin, "Kate O'Brien and the Erotics of Liberal Catholic Dissent", *Field Day Review*, 6 (2010), p.31.
55 Kate O'Brien, *The Flower of May* (London: William Heinemann, 1953). Hereafter O'Brien, *Flower of May*. See also Reynolds, *Kate O'Brien*, p.87.
56 O'Brien, *Flower of May*, p.277.
57 For more on this, see Aintzane, L. Mentxaka, *Kate O'Brien and the Fiction of Identity: Sex, Art and Politics in "Mary Lavelle" and other Writings* (North Carolina: McFarland, 2011), p.105.

night after night" into the drawing room, like a heartbeat, calming her mother, Julia, and her Aunt Eleanor. Glasalla becomes a space for Fanny that even "the hard beat from a lighthouse could not trouble", while ownership of her own property allows her freedom to determine her own fate.[58]

O'Brien's fate as a writer in Ireland was marred early in her career by the banning of her novels *Mary Lavelle* in 1936 and *The Land of Spices* in 1942. Lorna Reynolds claimed that O'Brien suffered a "failure of nerve'" after the outcry caused by the proscription of her work.[59] The impact on her family troubled her, while the fear of having her book burned caused her to rethink her writing subjects.[60] Her membership of an influential network mitigated against the damage to her professional reputation while public endorsements by influential members provided much-needed support.[61] Critically, *That Lady* was a commercial success. The novel was dramatized for radio and television by the BBC (1954 and 1961), and made into a Hollywood film starring Olivia de Havilland in 1955. It was a Book Society choice in 1945 and adapted for Broadway in 1949, helping to rebuild O'Brien's reputation in Ireland as a writer of note.[62]

Another female writer of international note was Patricia Lynch. Lynch (1891–1972) was born in Cork city and received her education in Ireland, England and Belgium. As a young girl, she was left in the care of landladies, boarding schools, and an impoverished aunt in Cork while her mother and brother traveled the world on business. She married the historian R. M. Fox, a socialist writer whom she met while living in London, returning to Dublin with him in 1922, where they remained for the rest of their lives. A prolific writer, Lynch published over forty-eight novels and two hundred stories.[63] She was one of the most popular children's writers in Ireland, publishing in London and New York. She won several literary prizes including the Tailteann Silver

---

58 O'Brien, *Flower of May*, p.40.
59 Reynolds, *Kate O'Brien*, p.82.
60 Kate O'Brien's book *Land of Spices* was referred to as the "Sodomy Book" by one of the chairpersons of the Censorship Board, which resulted in an outcry by those involved in the arts.
61 As reiterated in Chapter Two, O'Brien was President of the Women Writers' Club in 1950.
62 Eibhear Walshe, *Kate O'Brien: A Writing Life* (Dublin: Irish Academic Press, 2006), pp.107–108.
63 Stewart, "Ricorso".

Medal for Literature (1932), as well as two Book of the Year prizes.[64] Her nomination for children's fiction, *The Turf-cutter's Children*, later renamed *The Turf-cutter's Donkey* (1934), underscores the progressive and inclusive nature of the reading committee. The novel featured illustrations by Jack B. Yeats and was the first in a series of children's books. It won second prize in 1934.

Lynch's oeuvre draws on oral folklore and legend, traditional rural family units and an Irish landscape, lovingly invoked. These scenes were tremendously popular with many artists of the time and aligned with the ideology of the newly established Irish state, and with the precepts of the Gaelic League and of many members of the Women Writers' Club. In a letter to the poet Austin Clarke some years later, Salkeld praised Lynch's artistry: "I do think Patricia Lynch is a great writer – not a mere story-writer for children. Her *Turf Cutter's Donkey* is a classic."[65] Dorothy Macardle also thought highly of Lynch, regaling her "Shanachie's traditional bag of tricks"[66] in her *Irish Press* column, while Amanda Piesse suggests that *The Turf-cutter's Donkey* typifies the theme of a family contained within the social landscape and engagement with past mythical worlds from which future children's writing could be framed.[67] Indeed, Piesse maintains that all subsequent Irish literature "loops back to Lynch" in its treatment of family, nation, history and landscape.[68]

---

64 The *Aonach Tailteann*, was a sporting and artistic festival that took place in Dublin in 1924, 1928 and 1932. The objective was to project the positive attributes of the Irish Free State and it was supported financially by the government. Other recipients of the literary awards included Oliver St John Gogarty (poetry) in 1924, David Sears (best novel) in 1928 and George Bernard Shaw (imaginative literature), and were presented by W. B. Yeats. It is likely that these prizes inspired Yeats (and the Women Writers' Club) to award prizes for literature for their members. For more information on this festival, see Michael Cronin, "Projecting the Nation through Sport and Culture: Ireland, *Aonach Tailteann* and the Irish Free State, 1924–32", *Journal of Contemporary History*, 38.3 (2003).
65 Blanaid Salkeld to Austin Clarke, Austin Clarke Papers, 83, MS 38,670/2. Letter dated May 25, 1957.
66 The Shanachie is an Irish storyteller of Gaelic tales or legends. *The Irish Press*, November 19, 1935, p.3.
67 Amanda Piesse writes of the influence of children's literature on society. Amanda, Piesse, "Fictionalizing Families", in V. Coughlan and K. O'Sullivan (eds), *Irish Children's Literature and Culture: New Perspectives on Contemporary Writing* (New York: Routledge 2011), p.87. Hereafter Piesse, "Fictionalizing Families".
68 Piesse, "Fictionalizing Families", p.92.

Lynch's next Book of the Year prize followed in 1942 for the immensely popular book *Fiddler's Quest* (1941). This took first prize. Like its predecessors, themes of family and motherhood reflect the values of the new nation state. However, Leeann Lane's reading suggests that the text both sanctions and destabilizes the patriarchal family through representations of strong women within the family unit: women who are independent of often ineffectual or absent men.[69] This paradox is evident in *Fiddler's Quest*, where the deserted "widow" Rafferty raises her children in an impoverished home, but one where "the kettle was singing and the table was laid for tea".[70] Lane also suggests a reflective nationalism within Lynch's texts, which she argues mirrors the ideals of Patrick Pearse, one of the leaders of the 1916 Irish Rising.[71] In *Fiddler's Quest*, the main protagonist, Ethne, searches for her grandfather who lives on the mystical Island of Inishcoppal. Raids by an occupying army feature regularly within the plot:

> Sometimes they pulled up outside a house. If the door did not open at once to their knocks, the soldiers burst it in. Then came shouts and cries, the smashing of pictures and furniture and often, when the soldiers came out again, they dragged with them a struggling prisoner.[72]

The soldiers are depicted as aggressive and violent, "thundering through streets, where the people watched with hostile or anxious looks",[73] and the dilemma of insurrection is openly discussed between Ethne and her friend Nono:

> Sometimes you must fight! declared Nono. If you love your country you want her to be free and the only way to get freedom is by fighting. That's what Eamon says. Twas Nial told him and he knows. You do love your country, don't you, Ethne?

Lynch's characterization of Nono echoes Pearse's conviction that love of one's country requires blood sacrifice. These views are hardly surprising. Her writings are littered with allusions to the nationalist struggle and

---

69 Leeann Lane, "'In my mind I build a house': The Quest for Family in the Children's Fiction of Patricia Lynch", *Éire-Ireland*, 44 (2009), p.177. Hereafter Lane, "'In my mind I build a house'".
70 Patricia Lynch, *Fiddler's Quest* (London: J. M. Dent & Sons, Ltd, 1941), p.118. Hereafter Lynch, *Fiddler's Quest*.
71 Lane, "'In my mind I build a house'", p.172.
72 Lynch, *Fiddler's Quest*, p.123.
73 Lynch, *Fiddler's Quest*, p.123.

her texts have meaningful links with the work of other writers in the Club. In fact, the name "Nono" is the childhood name of Nora Connolly O'Brien, daughter of the 1916 revolutionary James Connolly and prominent Club member. While the unflinching depictions of the violent raids of the British soldiers are highly evocative of Rosamond Jacob's *The House Divided/Troubled House*, the overtly political themes of Lynch's book had little impact on book sales. Indeed, such was its popularity in Britain that the first London edition numbered 4,500 copies, despite the paper shortages of the Second World War.[74]

During Lynch's acceptance speech at the Book of the Year award at the Annual Banquet in April 1942, she spoke of her yearning to write about "a lovelier and happier world" as a refuge from "life in its present state", which she described as "part of our heritage of human beings".[75] Commercially, too, Lynch's identity as an Irish writer was critically important, as correspondence in 1953 from her editor at the London-based publisher Dent & Sons, Ltd attests:

> I wonder if you could bring over with you a green scarf or handkerchief as Miss Lloyd has the idea of drawing you with slight colour in the picture, and thinks that possibly the handkerchief over your hand could give an attractive touch to it, and also a slightly Irish feeling![76]

Dent & Son's insistence on "greening" the author was motivated by their international ambitions. As a marketing strategy it was successful, and Lynch's work was ultimately translated into many languages.

Like Lynch, Irish identity and the connection between the peasantry and the oral tradition were themes explored in Ena Dargan's travel fiction *The Road to Cuzco: A Journey from Argentina to Peru* (1950). The book is set in the 1930s, when Dargan worked for the British Cultural Institute in Buenos Aires. It won the Book of the Year award in 1950. Little is known of Ena Dargan, although some traces remain of her short literary career. As a critic with *An Irish Quarterly Review*, she reviewed J. C. J. Metford's book *San Martin the Liberator* in 1951, based on her own experiences in Argentina.[77] In 1959, she published *The Holy Ghost*, a translation of the sermons of the popular John of Avila; a contemporary

---

74 *The Irish Times*, November 15, 1943.
75 *The Irish Times*, April 11, 1942.
76 Carey to Patricia Lynch, circa 1951. Papers of Patricia Lynch and R. M. Fox, MS 79, MSS 34,923–34,931; 40,248–40,419.
77 Ena Dargan, *San Martin the Liberator* by J. C. J. Metford, reviewed in *An Irish Quarterly Review*, 40.157 (1951).

of Teresa of Avila. Further links to French liberal writer Georges Cattaui can be traced through her collaboration with him on the translated work *Saint Bernard de Clairvaux* (1966). She was nominated to the Irish PEN by Sheila Pim in 1950 and represented them at the International PEN Congress of that year, traveling to Edinburgh with Pim and the writer Maurice Walsh.[78] One newspaper report of the period describes Dargan as an "intrepid traveller in the South Americas" and claims that the book *The Road to Cuzco* formed the background to another book, *Bright is the South*, "now with the publishers and should be out fairly soon".[79] To date, no record can be found of this title.

Nevertheless, Dargan's prodigious book places her within a continuum of other Irish women explorers and writers, anticipating travel writers such as Dervla Murphy, and building on the work of her predecessors. These include the Ulster writer May Crommelin, who wrote of the South Americas in *Over the Andes from Chile to Peru* (1896); Beatrice Grimshaw (1871–1953), the travel explorer whose first book, *Strange South Seas* (1907), concerned the Cook Islands archipelago in the South Pacific; and Pamela Hinkson (1900–1982), writer of *Indian Harvest* (1941) and daughter of the well-known novelist Kathryn Tynan.[80]

The Road to Cuzco explores themes of dislocation and displacement of the South American Inca following colonization by the Spaniards in the sixteenth century. Traveling unaccompanied along the old trade route used by the Incas and Spaniards from Buenos Aires in Argentina to the "heart of the Inca Empire" in Cuzco, Bolivia, Dargan excavates the forgotten folk-history of the Incas, long thought lost, which finds expression through performance cultures within the Indian community. Indeed, the rich cultural traditions and colorful pageantry of the native Indians are comprehensively presented throughout the text with in-depth descriptions of the performances and the costumes. The search for truth, or what the Spanish intellectual and historian Salvador de Madariaga's preface to *The Road to Cuzco* (1950), calls "the truth of the matter", was the inspiration for Dargan's work. The geographical complexities of traveling in this vast continent meant that many misconceptions and

---

78 This is recorded in the minute books of Irish PEN. See Irish PEN, 12 May 1950. Sheila Pim was a detective novelist and a member of the Women Writers' Club and Irish PEN She is also known as the author of *Bringing the Garden Indoors* (1949), a book on flower arranging.

79 *The Irish Times*, October 20, 1950.

80 For a useful discussion of Irish women travel writers, see A. A. Kelly, "Irish Women Travel Writers: An Overview", *Linen Hall Review*, 10.1 (1993).

dubious theories had developed about the history of South America. In pondering "who was going to get there and find out the truth of the matter",[81] it is clear that de Madariaga considered Dargan, as an Irish writer, to be "the ideal interpreter between English and Spanish culture", since she privileged the post-colonial perspective of the "outsider" subject in the pursuit of history.

The book reads as a fascinating homage to the life of the Indians; their organic agricultural methods, the adverse intrusions of modernity, and the colorful fusion of Pagan and Christian religious beliefs. It also registers the dissidences within the cultural field. Regarded by the natives as the "strange *Irlandesa*", Dargan begins her travels among a group of displaced foreigners:

> We were a motley company: A Spanish professor of law on his way to lecture in Bolivian universities; some university professors from Argentina, an Argentine architect and his wife, intending to write up Bolivian architecture; a young couple lately escaped from Hitler's Europe, he Bolivian and she Belgian, visiting her husband's country for the first time; an elderly pair of Argentine honeymooners; a few North Americans and refugee Jews on business; as always in Bolivia, a sprinkling of miners, Germans and Czecho-Slovakians; and lastly, my Irish self".[82]

Dargan's literary identity as a marginalized figure operates outside the bounds of prescribed cultural modes. This distinction is acknowledged as she travels unhindered through this patriarchal terrain. During her trip, she is afforded the freedoms withheld from native women: for instance: "no Bolivian female would ever be sitting round cafés by herself".[83]

As the book unfolds, it draws the reader away from the viceregal cities of the High Perus to isolated areas where authentic Indian ways and original language, beliefs and customs still prevail: an "ageless" region, where "neither time nor humanity will ever make any lasting impress".[84] It is here she first notices the unchanged traditions of Inca and Spanish ways of life (see Figure 10).

Dargan's exegesis of South American life ringfenced a theoretical space through which her own ideals of nationhood and culture could

---

81 Ena Dargan, *The Road to Cuzco: A Journey from Argentina to Peru* (London: Andrew Melrose Limited, 1950), p.7. Hereafter Dargan, *The Road to Cuzco*.
82 Dargan, *The Road to Cuzco*, p.19.
83 Dargan, *The Road to Cuzco*, p.50.
84 Dargan, *The Road to Cuzco*, p.28.

be addressed. In their study of travel writers, Faith Binckes and Kathryn Laing agree that "distance from 'home' could be liberating, giving leeway to criticize, but also creating a conceptual space through which ideas about nation and selfhood could be re-imagined".[85] Indeed, Dargan foregrounds the similarities between ordinary Indian villages and Irish rural communities that "most closely approximate[s] to our own conception of rural life".[86] In cultural terms, comparisons between the two communities are explored through the images and descriptions of oral traditions, superstitions, folk customs and pageantry, wherein crucial moments in history are re-enacted and re-imagined through cultural performances. Her nod to Irish theatre and particularly to Yeats's preoccupation with *Cuchulain*, the mythical hero of ancient Ulster, is evident in her account of the Oruro Carnival performances, where folk plays, with their rich display of costumes and masks, projected dissidence and disharmony.[87] One review of the time described Dargan in particularly glowing terms:

> Miss Dargan's brilliant description of the Oruro Carnival, has now fallen – a rich trophy – into the hands of this Irish girl armed with no other weapons than her research instinct, her linguistic skill, her enthusiasm, her native courtesy and her intrepidity in the face of dangers known, unknown or dimly sensed.[88]

The idea of a single woman questing alone through this vast hinterland had doubtless appeal for many within the Club. The concept of women as adventuring explorers, and the belief that women were the physical and intellectual equal of men, was a stated contention of the international woman's movement of the time.[89] *The Road to Cuzco*

---

85 Faith Binckes and Kathryn Laing, "A Vagabond's Scrutiny: Hannah Lynch in Europe", in E. D'hoker, R. Ingelbien and H. Schwall (eds), *Irish Women Writers: New Critical Perspectives* (Bern: Peter Lang, 2011), p.113.
86 Dargan, *The Road to Cuzco*, p.37.
87 For more on this performance play, see Deirdre F. Brady, "The Road to Cuzco: An Irish woman writer's journey to the 'navel of the world'", *Irish Migration Studies in Latin America*, 9.1 (2018).
88 M. M. Macken, *The Road to Cuzco* by Ena Dargan, reviewed in *An Irish Quarterly Review*, 39.154 (1950), p.233.
89 Nancy Cott outlines the ways in which women in the early to mid-twentieth century entered the male sphere of professional work, eased by their ability to travel, and encouraged by a general fascination with high-achieving women. Even in Hollywood, celebrity culture enabled Mary Pickford to rise to the top-earning ranks of cinema and earn a salary of one million dollars. In keeping with these

was published in London by Andrew Melrose Publishers, and marketed throughout English-speaking countries, including Ireland, Britain and the United States of America. The prestigious New York-based journal *Foreign Affairs* was unstinting in its praise. Writing for the magazine, Henry L. Roberts lists *The Road to Cuzco* among his "Recent Books on International Relations" describing it as "an account of a journey from Buenos Aires, across Bolivia to Cuzco in upper Peru, told with skill", an accolade rarely extended by the magazine.[90]

Admittedly, the choice of Dargan as a prizewinning author was considered an anomaly by some. As an article in *The Irish Times* put it: "To have written a book for the first time is an achievement in itself, but to receive an award for a first work is something that does not often happen to an author."[91] What this commentator clearly failed to recognize was the quality of Dargan's stylistic writing, and the themes of dislocation and isolation so sensitively portrayed in the book that clearly resonated with the work of other writers connected to the Women Writers' Club, not least Elizabeth Bowen's prizewinning text *The Death of the Heart*.[92]

Bowen (1899–1973) was born in Dublin and spent her youth between Ireland and Britain. In 1931, she inherited the family home at Bowen's Court, County Cork, and while living there, hosted numerous literary parties. Her Cork guests included Bloomsbury friend and writer Virginia Woolf, who visited Bowen at her home in Cork in 1934,[93] while Bowen's London circle in the 1930s included the prominent authors David Cecil, Isaiah Berlin, Cyril Connolly and John Buchan.[94] She was also a close friend of Josephine McNeill, a key member of the Women Writers' Club reading committee, mentioned earlier.[95] She wrote for the BBC and was awarded a CBE in 1948 and a Honorary Doctorate of Letters from Trinity College Dublin in 1949. Somewhat controversially from

---

times, she announced she was "proud to be one of ... the girls who earn their own living". Cott, *The Grounding of Modern Feminism*, p.217.
90 Henry L. Roberts, "Recent Books on International Relations", *Foreign Affairs: An American Quarterly Review*, 29.104 (1951).
91 *The Irish Times*, November 17, 1950.
92 Elizabeth Bowen, *The Death of the Heart* (London: Jonathan Cape, 1938).
93 Heather Ingman, *Irish Women's Fiction: From Edgeworth to Enright* (Dublin: Irish Academic Press, 2013), p.93. Hereafter Ingman, *Irish Women's Fiction*.
94 Ingman, *Irish Women's Fiction*.
95 Papers of Josephine McNeill.

the Irish standpoint, Bowen was an operative of the British Ministry of Information during the Second World War. Working under cover of her married name, "Mrs Cameron", she reported on the state of opinion in Ireland throughout "the Emergency".[96] Bowen is considered one of the most significant Irish writers of the twentieth century, producing eleven novels. *The Death of the Heart* (1938) was one of her most successful books, and, was according to Maud Ellmann her "most celebrated writing" alongside her novel *The Heat of the Day* (1948).[97]

Bowen's *The Death of the Heart* has been hailed as the "most intensive consideration of the private world" and "one of the most memorable novels of the last thirty years".[98] The central themes of displacement and dislocation are sympathetically represented through the character of the main protagonist, Portia; a troubled child whose attempts to understand the world around her render her disconcertingly vulnerable. The *mise-en-scène* is the urbane exclusivity of Regent's Park in the 1930s, into which Portia, an orphaned sixteen-year-old, arrives to live with her half-brother Thomas and his wife Anna following her parent's death. Portia's unconventional European upbringing and the fact that she is the lovechild of an extra-marital affair between her father and "scrap of a widow" mother introduce a challenging unconventionality to traditional family structures.[99] Themes of displacement and insecurity mirrors that of her life as an Anglo-Irish writer. Bowen never quite resolved this sense of insecurity, though when challenged, she resolutely asserted her identity as an Irish writer.[100] Consequently, when Bowen received her Book of the Year award in 1939, she underscored her identity as a Dublin-born Irish writer and praised the vitality and fluidity of the English language

---

96 Bowen married Alan Cameron in 1923. They lived for a period in Clarence Terrace opposite Regent's Park, London, the setting for the Quaynes' household in the novel *Death of the Heart*.

97 See Maud Ellmann, "Shadowing Elizabeth Bowen", *New England Review*, 24.1 (2003).

98 Reynolds, "Thirty Years of Irish Letters", p.466.

99 Bowen, *The Death of the Heart*, p.22.

100 Bowen's identity as an Irish writer was frequently questioned, then and now, by critics who read Bowen in terms of her ethnicity and affiliations as an Irish writer. Heather Laird's essay on "placing" Bowen considers contemporary critics and their analysis of Bowen under different classifications. These include the "Anglo-Irish Bowen", the "modernist Bowen", the "woman writer", and so on. See Heather Laird, "The 'Placing' and Politics of Bowen in Contemporary Irish Literary and Cultural Criticism", in Eibhear Walshe (ed.), *Irish Writers in their Time: Elizabeth Bowen* (Dublin: Irish Academic Press, 2009).

on "the Irish tongue", thereby firmly aligning her status as an Irish writer in English to the Anglo-Irish tradition.[101] The dislocation of the Ascendancy was also taken up in Christine Longford's wry novel *Printed Cotton* (1935), albeit in the witty bantering tone that was wholly characteristic of her style. The novel received honorable mention at the Book of the Year award ceremony of 1936.

Christine Longford (1900–1980), addressed formerly as Lady Longford or the Countess of Longford, was born in Somerset, England. As daughter of an upper-middle-class family, she completed her education at Oxford University. As a young woman, she moved in the brilliant social and intellectual Oxford circles and was a regular Sunday Afternoons visitor to Garsington Manor, the Elizabethan home of the *salonnière* Lady Ottoline Morell. There she rubbed shoulders with such literary luminaries such as Lytton Strachey, E. M. Forster, W. B. Yeats (whom she knew and admired) and Bertrand Russell.[102] She married Edward Pakenham (Lord Longford) in 1925, whereafter they lived between Pakenham Hall, County Westmeath and Dublin. Friends and visitors to Pakenham Hall included Yeats, Desmond and Mabel Fitzgerald (Desmond would later become Minister for External Affairs), the poet laureate John Betjeman, Evelyn Waugh and the painter Henry Lamb (husband of Edward Pakenham's [Lord Longford] sister, Pansy). Her first book, *Vespasian and Some of his Contemporaries* (1928), presages the witty, light-hearted style that characterized *Printed Cotton*. After it was published by the Dublin publishers Figgis, one reviewer recommended *Vespasian* for its "scintillating sketches of Vespasia, Agrippa I, and his daughter Bernice [mistress of the Emperor Titus]", and likened it to a Gilbert & Sullivan opera.[103] Her first novel, *Making Conversation* (1931), was published by Victor Gollancz and republished forty years later by Faber & Faber.[104] This was followed by two further novels, *Country*

---

101 *The Irish Independent*, June 8, 1939.
102 John Cowell writes that Christine Longford (née Trew) won a scholarship to Oxford, where she studied Latin, Greek, ancient history and philosophy. According to Cowell, her contemporaries included writers Graham Greene, Robert Greacen, Evelyn Waugh and John Betjeman. Betjeman would become the British attaché in Ireland during the Second World War. See John Cowell, *No Profit but the Name: The Longfords and the Gate Theatre* (Dublin: O'Brien Press, 1988), p.19. Hereafter Cowell, *No Profit but the Name*.
103 Donald McFayden, *Vespasian and Some of His Contemporaries* by Christine Longford, reviewed in *The Classical Journal*, 24.8 (1929), pp.617–618.
104 Cowell, *No Profit but the Name*, p.76.

Places (1932) and the award-winning *Printed Cotton* (1935), and the guide book *A Biography of Dublin* (1936).

Longford and her husband were actively involved in the management of the Gate Theatre and key figures in literary circles. One of their most valuable contributions to the history of theatre is their account of the early years of the Gate Theatre in *The Gate Theatre Book* (1934), edited by Bulmer Hobson. The book was a limited edition, bound in cloth boards, with black and red-gold lettering, and the now familiar frontispiece of the Gate Theatre, which had previously featured in *Motley* magazine. In its preface, Edward Pakenham (Lord Longford) outlines the theatre's "mission statement": "The Gate is an intellectual theatre in that it presents a selection of dramatic masterpieces of all nations and all periods chosen for their intellectual and technical significance."[105] And indeed, European plays produced by the Gate Theatre included the German Gothic play, Goethe's *Faust*, Shakespeare's *Hamlet*, a translation of the *Oresteia* and Chekhov's *The Cherry Orchard*, starring the Irish Hollywood sensation Sara Allgood. Irish works included the Denis Johnston's play *The Old Lady Says No*, gothic drama *Carmilla* by Joseph Sheridan Le Fanu, and Christine Longford's most popular play, *Mr Jiggins of Jigginstown*.

Longford's *Printed Cotton* is a witty social commentary on the artistic life of Dublin. John Cowell, a contemporary and friend of the Longfords, welcomed it as both an "accurate picture of the arty Dublin of the 1930's" and "a delightfully amusing read".[106] The protagonist, Eileen, is presented through the fictional autobiography of a young Protestant woman. Her character represents the disjuncture between the Anglo-Irish ascendancy of her nostalgic parents who long for the time when "there were balls at the Castle, and the British Army was there", and the new generation of emerging middle-class Dubliners and a city that Eileen's mother describes as "full of Catholics and Sinn Feiners and people 'of a different class' who spoke with Dublin accents".[107] The book is a thinly veiled gossip column that parodies the "club bore", the "eminent *littérateurs*" who boast "a Gaelic Christian name and a un-Gaelic surname" and the incessant talk of "mysticism".[108]

---

105 Bulmer Hobson (ed.), *The Gate Theatre Book* (Dublin: Gate Theatre 1934).
106 Cowell, *No Profit but the Name*, pp.104–105.
107 Christine Longford, *Printed Cotton* (London: Methuen, 1935), pp.114–115. Hereafter Longford, *Printed Cotton*.
108 Longford, *Printed Cotton*, pp.182–183.

Longford's depiction of a high-blown "Protestant intelligentsia" dinner party, featuring a self-conscious mix of traditional, modern and Celtic drawing-room furniture, is one particularly scathing rendering of the Anglo-Irish in the novel.[109] Nonetheless, the sense of isolation felt by the Protestant Anglo-Irish is driven home through candid social comedy in which the "[p]olitics were hopeless and Protestants were persecuted", and where they could still "afford modest holidays on the Continent, if it was only in the lesser known little hill-towns".[110]

While the novel reads as a straightforward parody of the Anglo-Irish, it is also a novel of possibilities. In it, Eileen, represents the possibility of a new identity within the Irish nation that operates between the old Ascendancy or "Big House" and an emerging Catholic middle class. In fact, Longford puts forward the case for the Anglo-Irish within Irish society and their legitimate Irish status. As Eileen reflects: "I heard rebel songs as early as orange songs; and though I do not think I have any accent, I am always recognized as being Irish."[111] Longford's concern with assimilating both traditions in the new nation resonates with the preoccupations of intellectuals of the 1920s and 1930s.[112] Eileen's two love interests, the English Tony and the Irish Sean, symbolize the dual traditions within the Irish state, and locate a space for more than one religious, political or national identity. As the title suggests, the novel is concerned with beginnings exemplified through the printed cotton bedspreads of Eileen's flat. One contemporary reviewer was unimpressed with this "esoteric" title, describing it as ambiguous and vague: "It might as well have been called *Double Knitting* or *Baked Beans*."[113] However, a closer reading of the title suggests a different view. For autonomous women like Eileen, the optimism of the new nation state was transposed into everyday experiences and things: "I think printed cotton is very characteristic of my life: bright and cheerful and varied, but definitely makeshift. One day I shall settle down to

---

109 Longford, *Printed Cotton*, p.169.
110 Longford, *Printed Cotton*, pp.169–170.
111 Longford, *Printed Cotton*, p.3.
112 By the 1920s, Catholic nationalist Ireland had the majority within the Irish Free State and Parliament and the Protestant Ascendancy was in the decline. Terence Brown suggests the struggle between the Anglo-Irish tradition and the Gaelic tradition was based not on cultural differences but on religious affiliations. See Brown, *Ireland*, pp.114–117.
113 M. L., *Printed Cotton* by C. Longford, reviewed in *The Irish Book Lover*, 23 (1935), pp.97–98, National Library of Ireland, IR 0154II1.

something better."[114] This optimism was sadly short-lived. The year of its publication coincided with introduction of legislation including the Conditions of Employment Act, 1935, which placed restrictions on women's participation in the workforce and had implications for the rights of the professional woman writer.

Rising to professional status as a writer was paved with obstacles for women, both socially and legislatively. One way to circumvent this was to raise public awareness of the extensive heritage of women's writing. In 1945, Bridget G. MacCarthy, a professor of English at the University of Cork, won the Book of the Year award for her treatise on *Women Writers 1621 to 1744*. This work charts the contribution of female writers to the development of the novel and the importance of education in fostering writing. Citing Virginia Woolf's polemical text, *A Room of One's Own* in the foreword, MacCarthy interrogates the factors that impede women's writing: "If Shakespeare had had a sister endowed with literary powers, could she have won to success in that earlier period? What factors would have impeded her development as a writer?"[115] This question sets the tone for the book, which features biographical notes and excerpts from writers such as the Countess of Pembroke, the Duchess of Newcastle, Aphra Behn, Sarah Fielding and a host of other writers from the fifteenth to the eighteenth centuries. However, it stops short at demarcating Irish women writers per se; a point noted earlier by Heather Ingman and Clíona Ó Gallchoir.[116] While the reasons for this remain speculative and require closer investigation, the overall erudition, transnational Club membership and the feminist ethos of the book appealed to the reading committee. At the 1945 award ceremony, Maura Laverty hailed it as a book of "vigorous scholarship" and "'treasure trove' of women's writing".[117] MacCarthy took the opportunity of her acceptance award to state: "Women writers of earlier times had established a tradition and an equality which was valued by the women writers of the present day."[118] This matrilineage of equality was particularly appealing to the committed republicans within the Club, as their shortlist for the Book of the Year award attest.

---

114 Longford, *Printed Cotton*, p.278.
115 Bridget MacCarthy, *Women Writers: Their Contribution to the English Novel 1621–1744* (Cork University Press, Cork 1944).
116 Ingman and Ó Gallchoir (eds), *A History of Modern Irish Women's Literature*, p.1.
117 *The Irish Times*, March 17, 1945.
118 *The Irish Times*, June 27, 1945.

A Broader Republican Identity

The impulse to keep the "real story of Ireland" alive was a dominant discourse of the mid-1930s and the period was characterized by the blaze of revolutionary histories.[119] Women writers made a significant contribution to this genre. Examples include Edna Fitzhenry's *Henry Joy McCracken* (1936), Catriona Macleod's *Robert Emmet* (1935), Rosamond Jacob's, *The Rise of the United Irishmen 1791–94* (1937), and her historical novel *The House Divided/The Troubled House* (1937/1938), Nora Connolly O'Brien's *Portrait of a Rebel Father* (1935), and Dorothy Macardle's *The Irish Republic* (1937).

The first history to win the Book of the Year award was *Portrait of a Rebel Father* (1935). The book is an account of the life of James Connolly, the socialist trade unionist and revolutionary martyr of the 1916 Rising, as seen through the eyes of his eldest daughter Nora, or Nona, as she is called in the novel. Nora Connolly O'Brien (1893–1981) was born in Scotland but moved to Belfast with her family in 1910. As a political activist, she organized the Belfast branch of Cumann na mBan, was involved in the 1918 elections, and served as a member of the Senate for fifteen years. *The Unbroken Tradition* (1918) and *Portrait of a Rebel Father* (1935) are among the chief works that she wrote under her maiden name of Nora Connolly.

The valorization of James Connolly as an "ideal parent" at the 1935 Annual Banquet simultaneously subverts entrenched ascriptions of motherhood and womanhood and privileges the socialist-republican mind as an ideal.[120] A contemporary review placed it as one of the most interesting novels published by the Talbot Press, though not without reservation: "The book is disappointing because a reader will look for and fail to find an insight into the philosophy of this leader of Irish Labour."[121] This viewpoint overlooks the authorial intention to privilege the insights of the female child Nora/Nono, and by implication, that

---

119 These include Ernie O'Malley's *On Another Man's Wound*, Edmund Curtis's *History of Ireland* (1936), Joan Heaslip's *Parnell* (1936), and a number of short lives published by the Talbot Press, on the subject of the revolutionary men such as Theobald Wolfe Tone, Robert Emmet, Patrick Sarsfield and Henry Joy McCracken. See also Edna Fitzhenry (comp.), *Nineteen-Sixteen: An Anthology* (Dublin: Browne & Nolan 1935), and *The Irish Times*, August 6, 1936.

120 *The Irish Times*, March 20, 1936.

121 B. O. C., *Portrait of a Rebel Father* by Nora Connolly O'Brien, reviewed in *The Irish Monthly*, 64.753 (1936).

of the whole family. In the book, Nono is influenced by her father but displays independence of mind, much to her father's approval:

> [*Nono*] "If ... we are really sincere in our belief in an Irish Republic, and that we must struggle, work, and fight for it, it is better to carry on the struggle, and work with the possibility of success in the forefront of our minds rather than the certainty of defeat." [*Daddy*] "You can justify yourself," said daddy, twinkling at her; "and now you don't need the approval of older people, not even mine."[122]

Despite her young age, the child is conscious of the family upheavals that stem from her father's work. For instance, she witnesses her mother Lilian's frustration at having to move: "It seems as soon as we get settled anywhere we have to break up and go somewhere else. What's the use of building up a home when you know that it's bound to be broken up again?"[123] Nonetheless, Lillian accepts her fate and the personal sacrifices the family must make for the cause: "'Oh, well', she said, smiling at him, 'Let's finish the packing. As long as we are together, James, I've no cause for complaint.'"[124] Despite these disruptions, Nono's childhood is depicted as exciting and the republican community as an inclusive space. Robert Lynd's preface lauded the novel as a "vivid and moving narrative" that confirms the personal sacrifices the Connolly family made for the nationalist struggle. Lynd noted the support and endurance of Connolly's "heroic wife and children", likening it to that of the family in *Little Women*, and praised the "affections of the home" and the family's devotion to the revolutionary leader.[125]

The heroic family is also reprised in Edna Fitzhenry's biography *Henry Joy McCracken* (1936), which was published by the Talbot Press as part of the Noted Irish Lives series and awarded the Book of the Year prize in 1937.[126] Fitzhenry's credentials as a historian of note had been firmly established following the publication of her critically acclaimed anthology *Nineteen Sixteen: An Anthology* (1935).[127] So successful was it

---

122 Nora Connolly O'Brien, *Portrait of a Rebel Father* (Dublin: Talbot Press, 1935), p.172. Hereafter Connolly O'Brien, *Portrait*.
123 Connolly O'Brien, *Portrait*, p.96.
124 Connolly O'Brien, *Portrait*, p.97.
125 Connolly O'Brien, *Portrait*, p.9.
126 Edna Fitzhenry, *Henry Joy McCracken* (Dublin: Talbot Press, 1936). Hereafter Fitzhenry, *Henry Joy McCracken*.
127 In 1936, *Journal of Modern History* printed a bibliography of history books published in 1935. Included in this list is Catriona MacLeod's *Robert Emmet*, part of the Noted Irish Lives series, issued by the Talbot Press in 1936. See

that it sold out in a matter of weeks and had to be reprinted to meet demand; a school edition was also produced a few months later, and a souvenir copy was published by Browne & Nolan on the fiftieth anniversary of the Irish Rising. In fact, *Henry Joy McCracken* was so ardently acclaimed that one reviewer urged readers to buy the book "even if you get no other for ten years".[128]

The book relates the involvement of Henry Joy McCracken, the founding member of the Society of the United Irishmen, and his family in the republican movement: a politico-familial theme that was not lost on a reviewer of the time: "As I read the foreword, I can say that the very thing that was most apparent in the book was this very attention to the family of the Joys and McCracken's and to their milieu."[129] The role of the family, and in particular that of his sister Mary-Ann, and the many sacrifices associated with the process of nation building, are evenly handled by the author. The text valorizes the self-reliance and industrious nature of women in the McCracken family who are represented as progressive, forward-thinking and non-conformist. Fitzhenry's depiction directly challenges the received notions of eighteenth-century womanhood as submissive, dependent and uneducated. On the contrary, McCracken's mother is depicted as a business woman who had "in her early twenties established herself in a millinery and fancy goods shop"; his Aunt Eleanor is revealed as the editor who "became her father's right-hand man in editing the paper [*The Belfast News-Letter*]"; while his sister Mary-Ann's intellect "astonished them all" by demonstrating expertise "in finance and mathematics" and an imagination that "far outstripped her practical ability".[130]

Women writers also feature in the book. When Mary-Ann visits her brother in jail, she brings a travel book written by the feminist Mary Wollstonecraft and suggests he read the *Memoirs of Emma Courtney*. This epistolary novel written by Mary Hays, a professional woman writer and friend of Wollstonecraft, evokes the tradition of women writing with republicanism, feminism and equality: ideas that were advanced by the

---

Anon, "Bibliography", *Journal of Modern History*, 8.2 (1936). *Robert Emmet* was nominated for the Book of the Year award in 1937.

128 *The Irish Press*, February 19, 1937.
129 Their milieu included Theobald Wolfe Tone and his wife Matilda. See, Riobárd Ó Faracháin, "Henry Joy McCracken" by Edna Fitzhenry, reviewed in *The Irish Monthly*, 64.761 (1936).
130 Fitzhenry, *Henry Joy McCracken*, pp.17–30.

Irish revolutionaries of the early twentieth century.[131] Furthermore, the book privileges the life of Henry's sister Mary-Ann on an equal footing with her revolutionary brother. At the end of the book, when Henry's "bones" are recovered, they are poignantly interred alongside his sister.[132] In this way, Fitzhenry suggested a space for family within the heroic tradition and reified women's role in the founding of the independent Irish state. These themes form striking parallels with other winning texts celebrated through the awarding of the Book of the Year prize; in particular, the writings of Jacob, Connolly O'Brien and Macardle. Fitzhenry explicitly acknowledges her influences in the preface to her book, whom she lists as "Rosamond Jacob, C [Constantia] Maxwell, Alice Milligan, Nora Connolly O'Brien, Professor Mary Hayden, D. Litt., and Róisin Walsh, Chief Librarian for County Dublin".[133] Her strategy of recognizing the influence of fellow members and pointedly marketing the works of her fellow members is echoed in the introduction to Macardle's history book, *The Irish Republic*, wherein Macardle acknowledges the contribution of Nora Connolly O'Brien and Mary Hayden.[134]

In the same year, Rosamond Jacob was nominated for her fictional account of the war of independence. Her book *The House Divided/The Troubled House* took second place and was mentioned at the Annual Banquet in 1937. As discussed earlier, this novel was primarily a historical fiction concerning the Irish War of Independence (1919–1921), the events surrounding "Bloody Friday" and the consequences for one Irish family. Couched in the realist mode, issues of violence, sexuality and art are explored against a backdrop of non-conformist characters who question the prevailing notions of nationalism. This may have caused some disquiet among a nationalist readership, who were inclined to purchase more heroic nationalist tales.[135] However, the following year she also

---

131 Fitzhenry, *Henry Joy McCracken*, p.104.
132 Henry Joy McCracken was buried in Belfast, but his grave was desecrated and built over. In 1902, bones and a coffin were uncovered, which were believed to be McCracken's, and his remains were placed beside Mary-Ann 1909.
133 Fitzhenry, *Henry Joy McCracken*, p.8.
134 Dorothy Macardle, *The Irish Republic* (London: Victor Gollancz, 1938), p.24. Hereafter Macardle, *The Irish Republic*.
135 This point is made by Danae O'Regan in her analysis of Jacob's writing. See Danae O'Regan, "Representations and Attitudes of Republican Women in the Novels of Annie M. P. Smithson (1873–1948) and Rosamond Jacob (1888–1960)", in L. Ryan and M. Ward (eds), *Irish Women and Nationalism, Soldiers, New Women and Wicked Hags* (Dublin: Irish Academic Press, 2003).

won the 1938 second prize for her history of Protestant republican Theobald Wolfe Tone in *The Rise of the United Irishmen 1791–94* (1937). This text, which traced the history of the revolutionary movement, was described by one reviewer in *The American Historical Review* as "a masterly work".[136] It was during her research for *The United Irishmen* that Jacob became aware of Matilda Tone's role in the nationalist struggle as the wife and confidant of the revolutionary leader. Over the next ten years she researched the biography of Matilda, and sourced her novel from the writings of "Tone, Matilda, and Mary-Ann McCracken, and Matilda's letter to the New York *Truthteller*".[137] Unable to find a willing publisher for this history, Jacob recast it as the historical novel that was eventually published in 1957 by *The Kerryman*.[138] Jacob was awarded the Book of the Year at the Silver Jubilee of the Women Writers' Club and was the last known recipient of the award.

Rosamund Jacob (1888–1960) was born to an upper-middle-class Waterford family. As a lifelong and prominent feminist republican, she was active in numerous organizations including Cumann na mBan, the Gaelic League, the Women's International League for Peace, the Irish Women's Social and Progressive League and the Women Writers' Club. Her moral compass aligned with the Quaker traditions of her family, and she remained a pacifist throughout her life. Living most of her adult life in Dublin, her political and literary milieu included the foremost feminists of the day: Hanna Sheehy Skeffington, Louise Bennet, Lucy Kingston, Helena Moloney and Dorothy Macardle. A prolific writer and diarist, she published five books, wrote political articles for the suffrage newspaper *The Irish Citizen*, and produced an array of plays, poetry, children's fiction and a number of unpublished novels. Her novels particularly speak to the period in which they were written, questioning the sexual mores of Irish society and engaging with various contemporaneous socio-political debates.

The novel *The Rebel's Wife* carves out a place for the wife of Theobald Wolfe Tone in the struggle for Irish independence. In her private papers Jacob writes of Matilda:

---

136 J. Pomfret, *The Rise of the United Irishmen, 1791–94* by Rosamond Jacob, reviewed in *The American Historical Review*, 44.1 (1938), p.109.

137 Rosamond Jacob, *The Rebel's Wife* (Tralee: The Kerryman 1957). Hereafter Jacob, *The Rebel's Wife*.

138 The original manuscript *Matilda* is held in the repositories of the National Library of Ireland (MS 33,167/11–12). See also Lane, *Rosamond Jacob*, pp.299–304.

> From the materials, tantalizingly incomplete as they are, we know her, and we see her as a human being surpassed in quality by scarcely any character in our history, although in that history, technically speaking, she has no place.[139]

Jacob's unstinting admiration for Matilda is evident throughout the novel, and the many difficulties and challenges of her experience as the wife of the celebrated Tone are sympathetically rendered. Revealingly, she champions Matilda as a truly heroic figure, positioning her as the uncrowned queen of Ireland. At the funeral of Matilda's second husband, Thomas Wilson,[140] the ceremony is laced with regal undertones:

> The poor crowded to it, bewailing the man who had always been ready to give his brains and time to their help, the committees he had worked on were there to a man, some of them hardly able to speak for grief … men from home whose names were dimly familiar to her came to pay respect and sympathy to Matilda, and having done so, they spoke to her and William [Matilda's son], with quiet reverence, of Tone. Katherine Sampson [Matilda's daughter-in-law] standing on William's other side, thought they treated her like a bereaved queen.[141]

Perhaps ventriloquizing Jacob's assessment of Matilda's key role in the history of Irish republicanism, Matilda's sister-in-law, Mary, mutters: "If ever we do win the day … I hope the people will have sense enough to pay some of the honour to *you*": a critique of the occlusion of women in terms of commemoration and remembrance.[142] Furthermore, the novel imbues Matilda with authority as the site of truth about her husband's ideals. This is embodied by Matilda's son William, who, together with his mother, compiles the biography of Tone entitled *Life and Adventures of Theobald Wolfe Tone* (circa 1876). William acknowledges the legitimacy of his mother's voice: "'Of course you knew his mind better than anyone', said William, 'and what you believe is probably the truth.'"[143] This observation is reiterated in the closing line of the novel when Matilda's daughter-in-law, Katherine, observes: "It does not occur to either of them that that may have been partly her own work. With a different sort of wife – who knows?"[144]

---

139 MS 30, Papers of Rosamond Jacob, MS 33107.
140 Matilda married Thomas Wilson, a friend of the family, in 1816, eighteen years after the death of her first husband Theobald Wolfe Tone. Wilson died in 1824.
141 Jacob, *The Rebel's Wife*, p.213.
142 Jacob, *The Rebel's Wife*, p.82.
143 Jacob, *The Rebel's Wife*, p.209.
144 Jacob, *The Rebel's Wife*, p.214.

While *The Rebel's Wife* is primarily a work of fiction, in the Author's Note at the beginning of the book, Jacob is keen to point out its basis in reality:

> Scarcely any of the incidents in this tale are imaginary, except the scene in the theatre in Chapter III, and Matilda's visit to Dublin in 1816. The latter may very possibly have happened.[145]

This ploy echoes that of Irish writer Maria Edgeworth and her fellow nineteenth-century Irish novelists, who regularly prefaced their works with similar statements in order to lend authenticity to their fiction and their research of the subject.[146] This strategy paid off. *The Irish Press* devoted a half page to a review that described *The Rebel's Wife* as written with "loving care" for the family details, while *The Irish Times* recommended it as an "authentic account of his [Tone's] heroic wife".[147] The ideological trend to recuperate forgotten histories in the novels and history books of the period was both driven and celebrated by the republication ethos within the Women Writers' Club, which sought to reconstruct the story of the nationalist struggle with women at center stage. The majority of these texts are almost forgotten, with the notable exception of Dorothy Macardle's historical work. *The Irish Republic* continues to present a dichotomy between those who regard it as a hagiography to the government of de Valera and those for whom it remains "a crucial source" for its reading of politics and events.[148]

Dorothy Macardle (1889–1958) was among the most successful writers involved in the Women Writers' Club. A prolific writer and novelist, she

---

145 The scene in the theatre refers to a discussion between Matilda and her cousin, the Lord Chancellor, Baron Fitzgibbon, who came up to her during the performance, and warned Matilda to use her influence to curb her husband's revolutionary activities. In this scene, Matilda repudiates his warning but remains concerned (pp.29–31). The latter refers to a possible meeting with Matilda and the "Catholic people's leader, Daniel O'Connell, the lawyer from Kerry" on the streets of Dublin (p.205). A tale is told of a Dublin city church that rings its bell for Sunday mass – which was outlawed at the time. The Corporation prosecutes the Church but when O'Connell is retained as a lawyer for the Church, the case is dropped as "the name of O'Connell was enough, and the Corporation had abandoned their case". See Jacob, *The Rebel's Wife*, p.205.
146 Seamus Deane, *A Short History of Irish Literature* (London: Hutchinson, 1986), pp.92–93.
147 "Literary Papers 1–10", MS 30, Papers of Rosamond Jacob, MS 33,107.
148 Eunan O'Halpin, "The Irish Republic" by D. Macardle, reviewed *in Irish Historical Studies*, 31.123 (1999), p.394.

also penned a number of plays for the Abbey and Gate Theatres. As a journalist, she worked as the drama critic for de Valera's paper, *The Irish Press*, in the early 1930s and wrote for the BBC during the Second World War while living in London. Her major works include her first book of fiction, *Earth-Bound: Nine Stories of Ireland* (1924), and the novel *Uneasy Freehold* (1941), which sold over half a million copies. This was later adapted into the Hollywood film *The Uninvited*.[149] Throughout her life Macardle was politically active, first supporting the new political party Fianna Fáil, established by her close friend Eamon de Valera. She was one of the six women elected to the Fianna Fáil executive and was appointed Director of Publicity in 1926.[150] In 1948, she became a founding member of the Irish Association of Civil Liberties, which had its roots in the short-lived Irish Society for Intellectual Freedom.[151] In her later life, until her death in 1959, she turned to international politics, focusing her energies on work with the League of Nations and UNICEF.[152]

Dorothy Macardle was born into the upper-middle-class Catholic Macardle brewing family, and educated at Alexandra College and the National University of Ireland, where she received a BA with first-class honors.[153] As an adult, she returned to teach at Alexandra College where she tutored fellow-club members Edna Fitzhenry, Sheila Richards and Mary Manning. Her friends included Edward Martyn, George Russell (Æ), Charlotte Despard, Countess Markiewicz and Maud Gonne MacBride (with whom she shared a house in 1920). As an active member of Cumann na mBan, Macardle served six months in Mountjoy in 1922 as an anti-treaty activist. There she first met Rosamond Jacob, forming a lifelong and fractious friendship. Throughout her life, she was active in politics and held prominent positions on the committees of the Women Writers' Club and the Irish PEN.

The Irish Republic (1937) is a major historical record of the nationalist struggle and one of the most popular Irish history books of the period.[154] In the title page, a clear and concise description of the book defends its legitimacy as a history book of note that presents a narrative of "the

---

149 Smith, *Dorothy Macardle*, p.102.
150 Smith, *Dorothy Macardle*, p.59.
151 The role of the SIF in Irish literary life is discussed in Chapter One.
152 Smith, *Dorothy Macardle*, p.116.
153 See also Lane, *Dorothy Macardle*.
154 Macardle, *The Irish Republic*.

Anglo-Irish conflict and the partitioning of Ireland, with a detailed account of the period 1916–1923".[155] Although de Valera was the primary advisor to *The Irish Republic*, they disagreed on versions of the story, as is acknowledged in the book:

> Her interpretations and conclusions are her own. They do not represent the doctrines of any party. In many cases, they are not in accord with my views, but her book is an exhaustive chronicle of fact and provides the bases for an independent study of the period and a considered judgement upon it.[156]

In spite of this, they remained friends, and de Valera publicly endorsed the book, praising it highly. When Macardle received the Book of the Year award in 1938, a letter from de Valera was read out that applauded the "great service which Miss Macardle has rendered to the Irish nation".[157] The letter, which was reprinted in *The Irish Times*, commended the author for her timely contribution to historiography: "Had that task been undertaken by one less competent, or postponed for another decade, propagandist myths might have completely overgrown and hidden away the truth for ever."[158] Macardle later bequeathed the royalties of the book to de Valera in her will.[159]

From the outset of *The Irish Republic*, Macardle highlights the equal role of women and men in the 1916 Rising: "About twelve hundred men and women took part in the Rising in Dublin in 1916, and in the country a few hundred more."[160] Shared responsibilities included "studying signalling, first aid and other matters used in war", while her discussion of republicans in prison include the punishments of the women incarcerated in Britain, alongside their male counterparts:

> Mrs Clarke, Madame Gonne MacBride and Countess Markiewicz were in Holloway Prison, and in August Mrs Skeffington joined them there, deported from Ireland as being a person likely to act or about to act in a manner prejudicial to the State.[161]

Invoking the memory of the leader of the Rising, Patrick Pearse, she describes the scene in the General Post Office, prior to surrender:

---

155 Macardle, *The Irish Republic*, title page.
156 Macardle, *The Irish Republic*, p.20.
157 *The Irish Times*, February 4, 1938.
158 *The Irish Times*, February 4, 1938.
159 Stewart, "Ricorso".
160 Macardle, *The Irish Republic*, p.29.
161 Macardle, *The Irish Republic*, p.93.

He told them that without the inspiration and courage the Volunteers could not have held out so long. They deserved, he said, a foremost place in the nation's history. He shook hands with each one before they left.[162]

This determined reminder of the egalitarian ideals of the 1916 revolutionaries deliberately targeted a society that had largely forgotten women's contribution to the birth of the new state. In fact, the role women played in the struggle was increasingly disparaged, with public figures castigating republican women and, in some cases, even blaming them for the Civil War. Notwithstanding Macardle's stark reminders to the contrary, the book was lauded in the Irish national press, with one review praising it as a narrative that "recaptures the spirit of the times, the mixture of idealism and calculation" and is an "indispensable record" of events.[163]

The spirit of keeping the heroic tales of revolutionary times alive was shared by many historians of the period. At a time when the average Irish reader was invested in the story of Ireland and the marketplace flooded with the valor of male revolutionaries, women writers provided an alternative viewpoint: one that gave equal weighting to the supporting efforts and endurance of the wives, sisters, daughters and extended family of these heroic men. This is perhaps best summed up by the playwright Teresa Deevy's insistence that "These sort of plays are badly needed – the best way of keeping alive the real story of Ireland".[164]

---

162 Macardle, *The Irish Republic*, p.163.
163 Nicholas Mansergh, "The Irish Republic: A Documented Chronicle of the Anglo-Irish Conflict and the Partitioning of Ireland, with a Detailed Account of the Period 1916–1923" by D. Macardle, reviewed in *International Journal*, 21.3 (1966).
164 This concerns a letter from Teresa Deevy to Mathew O'Mahony on the subject of his play on Robert Emmet. Mathew O'Mahony Papers, MS 24,900, "Letters to Mathew O'Mahony (with copies of some letters by him), correspondents include many Irish actors, dramatists, and writers, 188 items arranged in alphabetical order of correspondent, c. 1931–1960", National Library of Ireland. Hereafter Mathew O'Mahony Papers.

Censorship and Women Writers: Ethel Mannin, Maura Laverty and Teresa Deevy

Ezra Pound once famously advised Irish government minister Desmond Fitzgerald to keep "condoms and classics" in separate legal systems.[165] Even the most cursory glance at the list of banned books indicates, however, that the Censor Board did not follow Pound's recommendation. Censored material included publications that featured information on birth control and any book they deemed "indecent or obscene".[166] Aldous Huxley's *Point Counter Point* (1928) was the first book listed in the Registrar of Prohibited Publications. This was swiftly followed by Margaret Sanger's *Family Limitations* and Marie Stope's *Wise Parenthood*: both books on sex education, abortion and birth control.[167] Radclyffe Hall's controversial meditation on lesbian relationships, *The Well of Loneliness*, was the thirteenth book on this list, followed by popular British writer and member of the Women Writers' Club Ethel Mannin's autobiography, *Confessions and Impressions*. Mannin was one of three banned authors who won the Book of the Year award; the others being Kate O'Brien and Maura Laverty.[168]

To reiterate, O'Brien was banned twice for her novels *Mary Lavelle* (1936) and *The Land of Spices* (1941), while Laverty was banned for *Never No More: The Story of a Lost Village* (1942), *Alone We Embark* (1943), and *No More than Human* (1944).[169] The response from the Club was three-fold: they awarded the Book of the Year prize to banned writers,

---

165 W. J. McCormack, "Irish Censorship: Some Uncomfortable Revisions", in C. Hutton (ed.), *The Irish Book in the Twentieth Century* (Dublin: Irish Academic Press, 2004), p.85.

166 A list of prohibited books and publications entitled the *Censorship of Publications Acts, 1929 to 1967: Register of Prohibited Publications* can be obtained from the Department of Justice, Equality and Law Reform, Dublin.

167 The Registrar of Prohibited Publications, 1930–1947, Vol 1, is held in a repository at the Film Institute, Smithstown, Dublin.

168 Una Troy was a successful novelist and a member of the Women Writers' Clubs but doesn't feature in the social events held by the club. Her novels did not win any literary prizes but were very successful internationally. Troy's novel, *Mount Prospect*, was banned in 1936 (it was written under the name Elizabeth Connors). Troy also wrote a film, *We Are Seven*, a Hollywood adaptation of her novel *She Didn't Say No* (1957), which was deemed immoral. The Una Troy Papers are held in the repositories of the National Library of Ireland.

169 *No More Than Human* (the 1944 edition) was banned, with an Irish edition reissued in 1945.

spoke out publicly in support of them, and launched a public campaign of protest against censorship through the Council of Action.[170]

As discussed in earlier chapters, censorship was vigorously opposed by the Club. Accordingly, in 1937, when Sheehy Skeffington was invited to talk at the Minerva Club in London, she commended the writer Kate O'Brien for being a banned writer, and promoted it as a "badge of honour", saying, "She also has the distinction of having had one of her books banned in Ireland".[171] Appealing to like-minded intellectuals, she seized this opportunity to promote the Book of the Year award and introduced Nora Connolly O'Brien as a recipient of this prize for her book *Portrait of a Rebel Father*. Teresa Deevy was also particularly vocal in her criticism, questioning the insidious authority of the Censorship Board: "Who are the censors? And by what right do they hold office? And how, in case of proved incompetence, can they be removed?"[172] As a playwright, her work was officially exempt from censorship, though her difficulties in getting work might suggest otherwise. These public interventions were critical for women writers, and point to the collegial and supportive nature of the Club. When Christine Longford was given a damning indictment of her book *Printed Cotton*, she was awarded the runner-up 1936 Book of the Year prize. Similarly, Blanaid Salkeld received second prize in 1936, after a harsh review of her collection of poetry *Hello Eternity* (1933), and again in 1938, when her poetry collection *... the engine is left running* (1937) was turned down by American publishers.[173] Temple Lane received first prize for her collection of poetry *Fisherman's Wake*, a year after a blistering review suggested her novel *The Trains go South* was shallow and somewhat obscene, and condemned her efforts "to depict Irish life in its cheapest, most vulgar, perhaps most repulsive ... aspects".[174] The merest intimation of immorality could have dire implications for book sales and reputation.

---

170 This is discussed in length in Chapter One.
171 The Minerva Club was a residential club established by the Women's Freedom League in London Margaret Ward, *Hanna Sheehy Skeffington: A Life* (Dublin: Attic Press, 1997), p.324.
172 Teresa Deevy, in a letter to the editor of *The Irish Times*, argues against the banning of Sean O'Faolain's "Bird Alone", *The Irish Times*, October 20, 1936.
173 Blanaid Salkeld, "Letters and Poems, 1936–1937", MS 1978-0127R VF Lit, Special Collections 104, Paterno Vault, PENN State University. https://cat.libraries.psu.edu/uhtbin/number_search/57457720.
174 L. K., *The Trains Go South* by Temple Lane, reviewed in *The Irish Monthly*, 67.787 (1939).

Publishers were not immune to the censorship regime, as correspondence between Mannin and Sheehy Skeffington reveal:

> My novel that was to have been called SLEEP AFTER LOVE was all printed and bound, and then the Sunday Times refused an advt [sic]for it, and my publishers panicked, having recently been prosecuted over the James Hadley Chase book they published, and they said this meant that probably no paper wd take an ad and that the libraries might refuse to take the book, so 12000 bindings and jackets and title pages were destroyed and the book is now called CAPTAIN MOONLIGHT – you might recall that not altogether mystical figure in Irish agrarian history ... I thought sleep after love had tenderness and poetry and beauty; but apparently it only suggests pornography to a certain type of mind. The book is certainly not salacious – as you'll see in due course.[175]

Ethel Mannin (1900–1984) was born in London to a working-class family of Irish descent. A successful journalist and novelist and an intrepid traveler, she was considered one of the most industrious authors of the century, producing over one hundred books during her lifetime. According to her biographer, Jonathan Rose, Mannin began her literary career in advertising and moved into writing popular novels, grinding out romantic novels at a guinea per thousand words.[176]

Rose characterizes Mannin as an "anti-Woolf, sweating a living by her pen" to achieve her prolific production of popular novels and by writing for the women's pages of London and provincial newspapers.[177] Her banned novels include *Confessions & Impressions* (1930), *Ragged Banners* (1931), *Common Sense and the Child* (1931), *Cactus* (1935), *Common Sense and Morality* (1941), *Red Rose* (1941) and the aforementioned *Captain Moonlight* (1942).[178] Mannin's affinity with her Irish roots was extremely intense: "Nobody but me knows the nostalgia that's in me! I've no wish to go all Celtic Twilight like Helen Landreth, but it's true I feel at home in Ireland as I never do here. I feel sort of relaxed here."[179] Along with a romantic relationship with W. B. Yeats, she was also close friends with

---

175 Ethel Mannin to Hanna Sheehy Skeffington, August 27, 1942. MS 47, Sheehy Skeffington Papers, MS 33,608/6-7.
176 Jonathan Rose, *The Intellectual Life of the British Working Classes* (New Haven: Yale University Press, 2001), p.171. Hereafter Rose, *The Intellectual Life of the British Working Classes*.
177 Rose, *The Intellectual Life of the British Working Classes*, p.171.
178 These are listed in The Registrar of Prohibited Publications, 1930–1947, Volume 1 is held in a repository at the Film Institute, Smithstown, Dublin.
179 MS 47, Sheehy Skeffington Papers, MS 33,608/6.

Maud Gonne MacBride and Hanna Sheehy Skeffington. In 1940, she bought a cottage in Connemara, where she lived for a year. On returning to it in March 1946, she wrote *Late Have I Loved Thee*, which won the Book of the Year award in 1948.[180]

In the novel, the Englishman and writer Francis Sable converts to Catholicism and later joins the Jesuits, and lives among the Irish poor. Based on the life of Father John Sullivan, the son of the last Lord Lieutenant of Ireland, the novel ostensibly supports the teachings of Catholicism. While this reading arguably accounts for its popularity in Ireland, the archives reveal an entirely different authorial intention:

> Dear Hanna,
> I was delighted to get yr letter, but really dismayed & distressed that you should for a moment imagine that I am reverting to Mother Church! Surely you cannot have read the book – or could not have done when you wrote, for the whole book is an indictment of the Church, as the destroyer of Christianity, & as plea for a return to the ethics of the Sermon on the Mount, which return can never be made thro' the churches, any church or in the given system of society, the whole structure which is opposed to those ethics of love-thy-neighbour and the anarchist ideal of mutual aid as defined by Kroptotkin ... though I could never embrace the Catholic church because of its belief in private property, its anti-socialism, and its "reactionaries" generally ... I am so afraid you will go and write something about the book which might made me "popular" in Ireland, with devout Catholics, but which will embarrass me intensely as someone who can never have any use for orthodoxy, seeing it as a negation of those excellent ethics of that simple socialist Jesus ... the whole point of writing a book (if you're me) is to say what one feels and believes and be damned to everyone![181]

In the novel, the main protagonist, Francis Sable, experiences a revelation on reading the saint's famous lament in *The Confessions of St. Augustine*: "*Too late loved I Thee*".[182] Following this epiphany, he renounces his hedonistic existence and converts to Catholicism to become a Jesuit in Ireland. This takes place following the untimely death of his beloved

---

180 Ethel Mannin, *Late Have I Loved Thee* (London: Jarrold Publishers, Ltd, 1948), p.350. Hereafter Mannin, *Late Have I Loved Thee*. See also Stewart, "Ricorso".
181 MS 47, Sheehy Skeffington Papers, MS 33,608/6.
182 The title of the novel is taken from *The Confessions of St. Augustine* and quoted in Mannin's novel: "Thus it was with Augustine of Hippo; and how else should revelation come? 'Too late loved I Thee, O Though Beauty of ancient days, yet ever new! Too late loved I thee!'" Mannin, *Late Have I Loved Thee*, p.215.

sister Cathryn, who "specially liked 'Too late loved I Thee'". Mannin's intention then was to inspire readers to develop their Christian spirituality through the intellect instead of through the dogma of a hierarchical Church; it echoes with the writings of Kate O'Brien, Helen Waddell and others within the Club.

Although the contemporary reviewer W. Gore Allen commented that the novel offered a "romantic view of life and of religion", he wrought a scalding personal attack on Mannin: "His world [Francis Sable's] is the only one in which Ethel Mannin, as a writer, has ever been at home – a coterie of semi-artistic intellectuals practicing bad morals and professing Left-wing [*sic*] opinions."[183] The denigration of Mannin on the basis of her sexual and political leanings reveals much about the complexities of writing as a woman in a patriarchal society. Her liberal views on free love, equal rights for women and abortion were at odds with the cultural norms of the period. Many of her novels were banned in Ireland, as reiterated above. Roy. F. Foster notes that Mannin was often labeled as a "free spirit", a sexual radical with the reputation of "an apostle of "free love", which later came back to haunt her".[184] It is ironic then that *Late Have I Loved Thee* became one of Ireland's most popular novels of the period, and won first prize. However, not all writers were successfully shielded from public censure. In contrast to Mannin's experience, three of Maura Laverty's books were banned, and one was publicly burned in her hometown of Rathangan, County Kildare. An indignant Dorothy Macardle condemned this as the "outrageous and insulting implications" of censorship and decried the damaging consequences for publishers, authors and the reading public.[185]

Maura Laverty (1907–1966) was born in Rathangan and underwent teacher training at the Brigidine Convent, Carlow. A journalist and broadcaster, children's writer and playwright, Laverty was also well known as a cookery writer and scriptwriter for the television series *Tolka Row*.[186] Her novels, which chronicle the lives of ordinary rural people, are sympathetically narrated with vivid humor and interspersed with anecdotes of rural life as well as instructions on cooking. Caitriona

---

183 W. G. Allen, "The Shires, the Suburbs and the Latin Quarter, Ryder versus Sable", *The Irish Monthly*, 76.900 (1948), p.264.
184 Foster, *W. B. Yeats: A Life*, p.511.
185 Dorothy Macardle to Madeleine Ross, April 24, 1944, Papers of Maura Laverty, unsorted, ACC 4607, National Library of Ireland. Hereafter Laverty Papers.
186 Stewart, "Ricorso".

Clear maintains that "Food is more than a theme that runs through Laverty's writing: it is almost a character".[187] Food, Clear suggests, places women as providers of home and hearth at the very heart of Irish society. Laverty's novels reflect the policies of many social reform movements of the time, such as the Irish Countrywomen's Association and the Irish Housewives Association, which had links through shared membership with the Women Writers' Club.[188] Her writing career underlines the fluid relationship between modernism and traditional cultures that was characteristic of much women's writing. Women wrote in multiple forms, and skillfully grafted the ideals of high-brow avant-garde art into popular culture. The conflation of nostalgia for rural Ireland with modernist art is exemplified in one of Laverty's cookery books, which was published by Longmans, Green and Co. in 1947. In it, the continuity between modernist art, the oral tradition of storytelling and a sensitivity of style that chronicles the values and sentiments of the period, is apparent. Entitled *Maura Laverty's Cookbook*, it features illustrations by the young artist Louis le Brocquy, and a section on nutrition called "Hard Facts" by Sybil le Brocquy. Each chapter begins with a witty sally, such as "The drink we eat – Soups" or "The food we knead – Breads", and equally cheerful illustrations by Louis,[189] and is followed by a cooking anecdote, advice on romance, psychoanalysis or fireside stories handed down from the Famine (see Figure 7). Clearly, the jocundity of the cookbook reflects that of her fictional work and resembles the lighthearted and often carefree protagonists in many of her stories.

Laverty's novels also engage with the Gaelic League idealization of the natural landscape, agriculture and folklore. While her novels tend to endorse the government policies of rationing, neutrality and the celebration of an idyllic rural life, they also critique rural poverty and the patriarchal norms of the period. A contemporary reviewer sums up her style of writing very effectively: "It is artless and yet it is art. There is no stylisation and there is – despite occasional jamming and interlocking – excellent storytelling."[190] Her female characters

---

187 Caitriona Clear, "'I Can Talk About It, Can't I?': The Ireland Maura Laverty Desired, 1942–46", *Women's Studies*, 30.6 (2001), p.827.
188 For example, Rosamond Jacob was actively involved in the Irish Housewives Association; Josephine McNeill was a prominent member of the Irish Countrywomen's Association.
189 Maura Laverty, *Cookbook* (London: Longmans, Green and Co., 1947).
190 This review is in response to the novel *Never No More* but applies equally to *Alone We Embark*. M. Macken, *Never No More* by Maura Laverty, reviewed in *Studies*:

too are often non-conformist women who drive plots brimming with illegitimacy, extra-marital affairs and sexual desires. Therefore, when her second novel, *Alone We Embark* (1943), was banned, many rumors circulated as to the reason. In a letter to Sheehy Skeffington in 1942, Mannin mentioned the "facts of life" passage,[191] most likely the scene depicting the moment when the main protagonist (Mary) commits adultery with her childhood sweetheart Denis:

> [Denis:] "Ah, let me, let me, love! There's a hunger of a lifetime on me. Sure, I can't help it ... I love you so much, Mary." She tried to resist, but woman-pity for male exigency welled up in her, sweeping away will and conscience. With these two watchdogs gone, her freed longing rushed gladly to meet him, and they were lifted together into a beauty that was unbearable, into a delight that was heart-stopping.[192]

On the other hand, Macardle surmised that it was banned because its "values and sympathies" were not in keeping with censorship policy.[193] She considered the novel as simply mirroring life experiences: "Cruelty is shown in it as hideous, compassion and kindness as desirable, the girl's dilemma as tragic and her surrender pitiable. No prejudice, narrowness, nor intolerance will be engendered by *Alone we Embark*."[194] Perhaps more significantly, she deemed the banning of the novel an insult to the intellectual life of the nation:

> This ban, with its outrageous and insulting implications, makes me so angry that I must refrain from writing much more. I will say only this; the realisation that in attaining political freedom Eire has fallen into intellectual tutelage is to many of my generation a disappointment too bitter to find expression in words.[195]

This sentiment expressed the view of many Irish writers, whose disillusionment with the government policies of the 1930s and 1940s was often

---

An Irish Quarterly Review, 31.123 (1942), p.393. Sean O'Faolain made a similar remark about this novel: "Be as critical as you like about this book, its charm is irresistible and lasting." Quoted in Wills, "Women Writers and the Death of Rural Ireland", p.206.
191 Ethel Mannin to Hanna Sheehy Skeffington, September 21, 1942. MS 47 Sheehy Skeffington Papers, MSS 33,608/6.
192 Maura Laverty, *Alone We Embark* (New York: Longmans, Green and Co., 1943), p.132. Hereafter Laverty, *Alone We Embark*.
193 Dorothy Macardle to Madeleine Ross, April 24, 1944, Laverty Papers.
194 Laverty Papers.
195 Laverty Papers.

reflected in their plays, poetry and novels.[196] Macardle also wrote to the Club emphasizing her support for Laverty: "The Women Writers' Club is fortunate in having this opportunity to register its protest again the banning of Maura Laverty's novel, and I am grateful for being allowed to take part, although absent, in this protest."[197]

On the evening of the Book of the Year award, Sybil le Brocquy read out various critiques of the novel written by priests, "all of whom had praised it", to prove that not one of them had hinted it was obscene.[198] Senator Donal O'Sullivan, a guest of the club, paid tribute to the author, and expressed his shock at the book being labeled indecent: "I am astounded that men could find that this book comes within this definition." O'Sullivan then stated his opposition to censorship: "The banning of a book without any appeal was contrary to natural justice, and involved loss of royalties to the author, loss of reputation and fear of discouragement."[199] Sheehy Skeffington's criticism was more direct: "There was hardly an Irish writer, from George Bernard Shaw upwards, who had not been banned by Professor Magennis & Co., and the two universities were in it up to their neck."[200] This decision to publicly support Laverty was a means of elevating her reputation, and she was nominated for her second term as President of the club in 1946.

Two years later, her contemporary, the playwright Teresa Deevy, became the only dramatist to receive the Book of the Year award in 1949 (see Figure 1). Her prize consisted of a copy of Augustus John's paintings in book form, and a copy of *Flowering Shamrock* by Sheila Pim.[201] Deevy (1894–1963) was born in Waterford and educated at the Ursuline Convent in Waterford and at University College Dublin. As a teenager she developed Meniere's disease, which left her profoundly deaf. Her first production, *The Reapers*, was staged by the Abbey Theatre, after which she produced many successful plays including *A Disciple* (1931), *Temporal Powers* (1932), *The King of Spain's Daughter* (1935), *The Wild Goose* (1936) and the highly successful *Katie Roche* (1936), all of which were staged at the Abbey.[202] While the Abbey Theatre rejected her play *Wife to James*

---

196 Terence Brown expresses this view. See Brown, *Ireland*, p.142.
197 Laverty Papers.
198 *The Irish Times*, May 4, 1944.
199 *The Irish Times*, May 4, 1944.
200 *The Irish Times*, May 4, 1944.
201 *The Irish Times*, December 13, 1949.
202 Deevy's plays at the Abbey Theatre were produced by Lennox Robinson, with the exception of *The King of Spain's Daughter*, which was produced by Fred Johnson. Cyril Cusack featured in the first production of *The King of Spain's Daughter* in

Whelan, it was eventually performed at (Daisy) Cogley's fifty-two-seat basement studio in Mount Street in October 1956. The script was lost until a fortuitous discovery by a family member among a few documents. Since then the work has received wide acclaim with a performance in New York by the Mint Theatre in 2010.[203]

Her writing has been described as Chekhovian in style; a view endorsed by Sean O'Faolain. He purported that Deevy's plays concentrated on the complexity of characters and the "vagaries of human nature".[204] Fellow-club member Temple Lane observed that Deevy's dramas expressed a gap between "aspiration and fulfilment", which is articulated not only between the characters but within them.[205] The inability or unwillingness of her characters to conform to the social limits prescribed for them, and their dissident and overtly sexually behavior, flew in the face of the restrictions placed on the women this period. Caoilfhionn Ní Bheacháin explains that Deevy's transgressions are as much off-stage as on, as they appear in the margins of the script, or stage directions portraying dissenting characters: "Mutinous women are the very heroines that feature in the dramatic works of Teresa Deevy."[206] Yet their resilience remains unrewarded and her characters capitulate, resigned to their fate. Indeed, as the eponymous

---

1936 at the Abbey. It played in the Opera House in Cork in 1939. The play *Katie Roche* enjoyed several revivals, and was performed by the touring Abbey Players in London and New York. Ria Mooney featured as an actress in many of Deevy's productions, and directed others. The BBC produced a television production of *Katie Roche* in 1939. For a comprehensive bibliography of Deevy's work, see Martina Ann O'Doherty, "Silver Jubilee Issue: Teresa Deevy and Irish Women Playwrights", *Irish University Review*, 25.1 (1995). Hereafter O' Doherty, "Silver Jubilee Issue". See also Chris Morash, "Irish Theatre", in J. Cleary and C. Connolly (eds), *The Cambridge Companion to Modern Irish Culture* (Cambridge: Cambridge University Press, 2005).

203 *Wife to James Whelan* is a story about the emerging lower classes and business classes of the 1940s, and was turned down by the Abbey Theatre and the Gate Theatre. It has recently been revived and was performed in the Mint Theatre in New York in 2010. O'Doherty, "Silver Jubilee Issue", p.165.

204 John Jordan quoted in Walshe. See Eibhear Walshe, "Lost Dominions: European Catholicism and Irish Nationalism in the Plays of Teresa Deevy", *Irish University Review*, 25.1 (1995), p.134. Hereafter Walshe, "Lost Dominions".

205 Walshe, "Lost Dominions", p.134.

206 Caoilfhionn Ní Bheacháin, "Sexuality, Marriage and Women's Life Narratives in Teresa Deevy's *A Disciple* (1931), *The King of Spain's Daughter* (1935) and *Katie Roche* (1936)", *Estudios Irlandeses*, 7 (2012), p.81, and Caoilfhionn Ní Bheacháin, "'The seeds beneath the snow': Resignation and Resistance in Teresa Deevy's *Wife*

and ultimately thwarted protagonist of *Katie Roche* vents: "the world is a very flat place [bitterly]. It takes everything out of what it gives."[207]

Similarly, in *The King of Spain's Daughter*, the main protagonist, Annie Kinsella, initially defies patriarchal authority, despite the possible punishment by her tyrannical father and, it is implied, the controlling Catholic Church: "If your father heard you were at the crossroad last night – or if the priest heard tell of it – dancin' on the board, an' restin' in the ditch with your check agen mind and your body pressed to me."[208] But the trajectory of her fate, such that she must either marry the dull and conservative Jim or "go to the factory", is disrupted at the end of the play. Although confined to married life with Jim, who "put by two shillin's every week for two hundred weeks", Annie refuses to tolerate this unheroic ending. Instead, she envisions a passionate life with a man who might "cut your throat' in a jealous rage".[209] It is implied rather than stated that Annie *will* marry Jim. This intention is confirmed in a letter from Deevy to Mathew O'Mahony:

> I call King of Spain's Daughter comedy – even though Andrew Malone was not right in thinking Annie ran away. She marries Jim, quite reconciled at the last as she has found passion in his persistent affection, and so can visualise herself as the heroine of a possible tragedy.[210]

Although official censorship did not apply to the theatre, controversial plays could sully a playwright's reputation or result to box office failure. It is likely that the latter influenced Ernest Blythe's decision to exclude Deevy from the Abbey Theatre after he took over as creative director in 1941. In response, she turned to the radio and adapted her plays with some success in Ireland on Radio Éireann (RE) and elsewhere. For example, her plays *The Wild Goose* were broadcast by the BBC from Australia, while *Katie Roche* was broadcast from Sweden.[211]

It is clear that the Book of the Year prize performed a legitimizing function for writers such as Mannin, Deevy and Laverty; helping to restore tarnished reputations, while at the same time publicly challenging

---

to James Whelan", in E. D'hoker, R. Ingelbien and H. Schwall (eds), *Irish Women Writers* (Oxford: Peter Lang, 2011).
207 Eibhear Walshe (ed.), *Selected Plays of Irish Playwright Teresa Deevy, 1894–1963* (New York: Edwin Mellen Press, 2003), p.119. Hereafter Walshe, *Selected Plays*.
208 Walshe, *Selected Plays*, p.32.
209 Walshe, *Selected Plays*, p.35.
210 Mathew O'Mahony Papers.
211 *The Irish Times*, March 14, 1942.

the orthodoxy of censorship. As an instrument of change, it put forward an alternative version of literature that accommodated a specific female locus and a wide corpus of works. In analyzing the books thematically, new light is shed on the philosophy and ethos of the Club in a way that is not obvious at first glance. Common themes are unearthed, some overlapping, as were new ways of thinking about woman writers and their authorial intentions.

Certainly, their united front was inherent to their success and longevity while the reading committee's consistent openness to diverse aesthetic forms and emerging writers underscored the inclusive ethos of the Club. In an uncompromising world, the sustained commitment of the Women Writers' Club to the arts and their belief in the power of the book as a vehicle of ideas, supported the blossoming of Irish women's writing despite the immense national and internal social, political and technological changes all around them. However, the communication of these ideas, and the power of the pen in articulating them, depended on the main publishing houses, and their readers. In the next chapter, the history of print culture is explored, examining the contexts in which women's literature flourished and the importance of the social opportunity is fostering a literary culture.

CHAPTER FOUR

Women Writers in Irish Print Culture, 1930–1960

The evolution of ideas, the exchange of information and the production of texts all take place within a myriad of socio-cultural events and moments. Thus, how literature is made in terms of where ideas originate, who decides what gets published and how work is disseminated is determined largely by literary networks, social opportunities and cultural practices. These and other issues will be broached in this chapter by identifying the types of books that intellectual women read, the publishing outlets they wrote for and their relationship with others in the book trade.

The shaping of a literary culture and the notion of the book as a commodity, what artist Louis le Brocquy called "the thing itself", may be discerned through efforts of the cultural revivalists in the early twentieth century to re-establish an Irish publishing tradition, and more broadly, to "de-anglicize" the Irish economy. The development of the book as an art form in the late nineteenth and early twentieth centuries and the growth of a distinct readership of Irish books encouraged the pool of revivalist writers to publish books on "Irish Paper". This move was prompted by a patriotic impulse to support Irish publishing led by the Irish Arts and Crafts movement and the commitment to the revival of an Irish publishing industry, inspired by the establishment of the private printing press, the Dun Emer.[1] Much has been written about this movement and

---

[1] The Dun Emer was established in 1903 by Elizabeth and Lily Yeats and their patron, Eleanor Gleason. In 1908 this firm was split into two separate firms, and the Yeats sisters established their own printing press, the Cuala Press. The poet W. B. Yeats

of the period that was often hailed as the Irish Renaissance or Celtic Revival. This cultural aspiration was driven by those seeking a national individuality through arts and crafts and resulted in the development of an Irish publishing industry.

Recent scholarship sheds considerable light on the many publishing houses which sprang up during this era. Heavyweights among these included Maunsel & Co. (est. 1905), along with smaller niche printing enterprises such as the Dun Emer (est. 1903), and the Cuala Press (est. 1908). New insights can be garnered from those involved in these ventures including the private memoirs of Edward MacLysaght, a partner in Maunsel & Co. In his journal, he recalls the ideas that drove him to become part of that movement:

> Before I ever took any interest in the political side of nationalism, I was keenly interested in the struggle against the Anglicization of the country and supported any movement which aimed at restoring our center of gravity so to speak to Ireland.[2]

Here, MacLysaght suggests that the development of a completely distinctive "Irish book" was driven by cultural, as opposed to political ideas; though, in reality, many of the writers involved in the Celtic revival were politically inclined. The publishing industry of the late nineteenth and early twentieth-century had branched into more specialist markets. Tony Farmer lists these – "Alexander Thom (printing, directories, and law books), Browne & Nolan (large printing, religious, and general), Fannin (medical equipment and publishing), Eason's (railway bookstalls publishing mainly Catholic prayer-books)"; among others.[3] MacLysaght rightly acknowledged the importance of London publishers to Irish writers with their wide readership and ties to the American market:

> London offered no temptations to writers in Gaelic and the Abbey Theatre existed to produce the work of Irish dramatists in the English Language; but

---

    was literary editor and their younger brother, J. B. Yeats, worked on many of their designs. Gifford Lewis's book *The Yeats Sisters* gives a detailed historical account of this press. See Gifford Lewis, *The Yeats Sisters and The Cuala* (Dublin: Irish Academic Press, 1994), and Ní Bheacháin, *The Dun Emer Press*.

2 MacLysaght, "Master of None".

3 See Tony Farmer, "An Eye to Business: Financial and Market Factors, 1895–1995", in C. Hutton and P. Walsh (eds), *The Oxford History of the Irish Book, Volume V: The Irish Book in English, 1891–2000* (Oxford, Oxford University Press, 2011), pp.209–243. Hereafter Farmer, "Financial and Market Factors".

so far as the Anglo-Irish literary revival was concerned, which was attracting, through the work of Yeats, AE., James Stephens and others, the attention of the whole literary world, its exponents still looked to London as the natural outlet for their books even though they had not so far succumbed as to become exiles themselves.[4]

For lesser-known writers, or those appealing to a distinctive domestic reader, Maunsel was an attractive alternative.[5]

Publishing and the "Irish Book"

George Roberts (1873–1953) founded Maunsel & Co. with the proceeds of a financial contribution of £2,000 from the writer Joseph Maunsel Hone.[6] Roberts, a Belfast man and master printer, moved seamlessly in artistic circles connected to the Abbey Theatre. As a former actor, and one of the original Abbey company, he performed in the Abbey productions of Jonathan Millington Synge's *The Shadow of the Glen* and *The Well of the Saints*. His thespian activities linked him with Lady Augusta Gregory and other playwrights; a connection that he built on to publish a series of plays performed at the Abbey Theatres, including Lady Augusta Gregory's *Kincora*.[7] Alliances with notable writers such as W. B. Yeats, Stephen Gwynn, Seumas O'Sullivan and other key figures further ensured the success of his publishing house. O'Sullivan edited the popular Tower Press Booklet series, although he was never formalized as director.[8] As directors and editors, they had a powerful sway on the type of books and the final content that was published. For example, the Irish shilling Poet's Series edited by O'Sullivan featured poets from Æ's anthology, *New Songs* (1904). *New Songs* had introduced emerging poets to the Irish reading public, including previously unknown women poets such as Susan Mitchell, Dora Sigerson Shorter and Ella Young. Rumors abound that Yeats objected to the influence of Æ's coterie (which included

---

4 MacLysaght, "Master of None".
5 See also Warwick Gould, "Macmillan's Irish List, 1899–1968", in C. Hutton and P. Walsh (eds), *The Oxford History of the Irish Book, Volume V: The Irish Book in English, 1891–2000* (Oxford: Oxford University Press, 2012), p.507.
6 MacLysaght, "Master of None".
7 Roberts would later publish a series of plays performed at the Abbey. Clare Hutton, "'Yogibogeybox in Dawson Chamber': The Beginnings of Maunsel and Company", in C. Hutton (ed.), *The Irish Book in the Twentieth Century* (Dublin: Irish Academic Press 2004), pp.36–46. Hereafter Hutton, "Yogibogeybox".
8 Hutton, "Yogibogeybox".

MacLysaght), prompting him to become more involved with the press.[9] Despite concerted efforts, his maneuvers to replace O'Sullivan with his friend Stephen Gwynn proved unsuccessful. Nonetheless, Yeats's revered reputation and influence ensured publication for his own set, including Lennox Robinson, Patrick Pearse, Padraic Colum, Alice Milligan and Katherine Tynan. Thus, it came as no surprise that Maunsel eventually published the complete works of Yeatsian protegé J. M. Synge, firmly establishing them as a publishing house of note, both at home and abroad.

David Gardiner emphasizes that women writers were crucial to the fortunes of Maunsel, particularly leading up to the 1916 Rising.[10] Bibliographic records list popular books of poetry, which include Dora Sigerson Shorter's *Collected Poems* (1907), Alice Milligan's *Hero Lays* (1909) and Susan Mitchell's *The Living Chalice and Other Poems* (1908).[11] Despite these successes, Maunsel's finances were in ruins by 1916. In a strangely ironic turn of events, their offices were destroyed during the Rising, along with many of their manuscripts. Susan Mitchell famously exclaimed to Æ, "All my books were burned as Maunsells [sic] was burned to the ground, but worse still my agreement with them is *gone!*"[12] More remarkably still, Maunsel's received a sizable compensation for the shelling of their building, while, at the same time, the Rising triggered a rise in book sales.[13]

Indeed, the emotional appeal of the Rising reignited a demand for nationalist books, which ensured adequate funding for a further decade. Mitchell's book was also eventually published. Over the course of twenty-one years, the Maunsel firmly established itself on an international platform as a publisher of the best in Irish writing; producing an average of seventeen titles each year. The eventual closure of the firm in 1926 may be attributed to a multitude of factors. Robert's

---

9 David Gardiner, "The Other Irish Renaissance: The Maunsel Poets", *New Hibernia Review/Irish Éireannach Nua*, 8.1 (2004), p.58. Hereafter Gardiner, "The Other Irish Renaissance".
10 Gardiner claims that the issues of women's suffrage, nationalism and socialism were movements endorsed by many of the writers involved with Maunsel. Gardiner, "The Other Irish Renaissance, p.66.
11 Gardiner, "The Other Irish Renaissance, p.66.
12 This is relayed in Hillary Pyle's biography of Susan Mitchell entitled *Red Headed Rebel*. See Hillary Pyle, *Red-Headed Rebel: Poet and Mystic of the Irish Cultural Renaissance* (Dublin: Woodfield Press, 1998), p.168.
13 Gardiner, "The Other Irish Renaissance", p.62.

awkward personality and lack of business acumen, his numerous literary contretemps with Yeats and James Joyce (he famously refused to print *Dubliners*) and an incompatible editorial team ultimately led to its demise and takeover by the Talbot Press.[14]

The Talbot Press fashioned itself on the prestigious Dent of London and prided itself in presenting "the masterworks of Anglo-Irish Literature".[15] According to John J. Dunne, in his unpublished history of the Talbot Press, it was "destined to be one of the most remarkable publishing enterprises in the history of the state".[16] By the late 1930s, the Talbot Press had published a catalogue of five hundred titles, dominating Irish publishing. Expanding beyond their Dublin base, they opened offices in Belfast and Cork, and established overseas markets in New Zealand, South Africa, Japan and Denmark. Specializing in educational material, and even producing a teacher's magazine, they also traded extensively with India and other territories of the then British Empire.[17] The Talbot Press, an adjunct of the Educational Company of Ireland, was managed by W. G. Lyons with his business partner, William Fitzsimmons. With Lyons at the helm, the Talbot Press also published Irish classics including Maria Edgeworth's *Selections* and Gerald Griffin's *The Collegians*. Lyons was also interested in cultivating the Irish book.[18] This prompted the influential Jesuit priest and bibliographer Stephen J. Brown to refer to Lyons as the "Maecenas of Irish letters" for his commitment to the cultural revival: "He did as much as any fighter for the Irish cause by giving through the publications which he undertook, the

---

14 For more on this, see Gardiner, "The Other Rennaisance", p.61. See also comments from Nicholas Allen and Terence Brown on the business practices of Roberts. Nicholas Allen and Terence Brown, "Publishing after Partition, 1922–39", in C. Hutton and P. Walsh (eds), *The Oxford History of the Irish Book, Volume V: The Irish Book in English, 1891–2000* (Oxford: Oxford University Press, 2001), p.71.

15 John Dunne, "The Educational Company of Ireland and the Talbot Press, 1910–1990", *Long Room: Ireland's Journal for the History of the Book*, 42.34-4 (1997), MS35,134, National Library of Ireland. Hereafter Dunne, "The Educational Company of Ireland".

16 Dunne, "The Educational Company of Ireland".

17 Dunne, "The Educational Company of Ireland". Dunne gives an interesting account of the method of shipment. According to Dunne weekly consignments of copybooks, each weighing a quarter ton, were packaged in wooden crates at a cost of £1 per crate. These were secured by tensioned rope and on delivery, were returned to Dublin for the next consignment.

18 Dunne, "The Educational Company of Ireland".

fullest expression to the national and cultural revival."[19] When he was succeeded by his son Ronald Lyons, he had already built up a network of writers that would provide a wealth of material for the press going forward into the 1960s.

Women artists and writers played a shaping role in this venture. During difficult times, and particularly during the Second World War, the works of literary women were critical to the business. For instance, nineteen reprints of the works of the writer Annie P. Smithson were produced and sold during the period. The fact that poetry and fiction comprised forty percent of titles published between 1938 and 1943, suggests a penchant for intellectual books along with a fondness for nationalist fiction. Smithson's literary milieu included the Irish PEN, with credible links to the Women Writers' Club through her membership of Cumann na mBan and her acquaintance with Rosamond Jacob, and Hanna Sheehy Skeffington.[20] Book publishing data link the Talbot Press with leading members of the Women Writers' Club, and the house published Nora Connolly O'Brien's memoir *Portrait of a Rebel Father* (1935), Edna Fitzhenry's biography *Henry Joy McCracken* (1936), Temple Lane's poetry anthology *Nineteen Sixteen: An Anthology* (1935), and her collection of poems *Fisherman's Wake* (1940).[21] In the early 1960s, the Educational Company was taken over by the Hely Group. The Talbot Press, along with Browne & Nolan, were also succeeded by new entrants to the Irish market in the early 1970s, including Allen Figgis and the largest Irish publishing house to that date, Gill & Macmillan. In strange irony, the pressing materials were inherited by the Three Candles Press and later the Gayfield Press, established in 1937 by Blanaid Salkeld, the founder of the Women Writers' Club.[22]

19 This is referred to in a newspaper article in 1941. *Irish Independent*, March 22, 1941.
20 Annie P. Smithson and Rosamond Jacob were elected to Irish PEN in December 1940. "Minutes Irish PEN", December 13, 1940. There is, however, no record of Smithson's involvement in the Women Writers' Club, although she had associations with Sheehy Skeffington. See MS 47, Sheehy Skeffington Papers, MS 33 607/21.
21 Up to 1939, Lane's books, which were mainly romantic novels, were published by Jerrold in London, although after publication of her collection of poetry *Fisherman's Wake* (Dublin: Talbot Press Limited) in 1940, her novels were published by the Talbot Press. No reason is given. There is little biographical work on Lane although some details are available in digital databases. For more on Lane, see Stewart, "Ricorso".
22 Gardiner, "The Other Irish Renaissance", p.79.

WOMEN WRITERS IN IRISH PRINT CULTURE, 1930–1960

An examination of the two main Irish publishing houses, Maunsel & Co. and the Talbot Press, underscores the significant role of women writers in print culture during the first half of the twentieth century. However, their relationships were not always smooth. Edward MacLysaght referred to authors involved with the Maunsel Press as a "somewhat covetous and difficult lot", while writer Patricia Lynch conversely complained that "most bad things done by authors seem to be the publishers fault".[23] Countless examples of tensions with publishers are evident in the correspondence of literary men and women. Cogent examples include the efforts of Jacob to find a publisher for her debut novel, *Callaghan*.[24] On advice from a friend, she avoided submitting her manuscript to the Talbot Press due to their "cautious approach to finance".[25] Jacob turned instead to Martin Lester, Ltd, who nonetheless insisted she remove "the feminism" in the novel, before agreeing to publish it.[26] The domain of publishing primarily lay within a male-dominated industry and the vagaries of male editors. For women writers, intent on being published, it was necessary to forge a separatist print culture. One way was through the means of private printing presses, such as the Gayfield Press, outlined in Chapter Five. Another was through seeking publication in "little magazines" or periodicals. As forums for mediating the cultural debates of the period, the study of these "little magazines" or periodicals provides a revelatory map of publishing practices of the Irish female avant-garde throughout the early and mid-twentieth century. In fact, Lucy Collins estimates that twenty-five percent of the content of *The Dublin Magazine* was generated by women writers;[27] while Anne Mulhall confirms that women poets were "widely published and often well-regarded in their

---

23 See MacLysaght, "Master of None"; Papers of Rosamond Jacob, MS 32,582/83.
24 Lane, *Rosamond Jacob*, p.144.
25 Lane, *Rosamond Jacob*, p.144.
26 According to Jacob's biographer Leeanne Lane, Jacob took her manuscript to Bulmer Hobson, one of the directors of Martin Lester Publishing, and the book *Callaghan* was published by Lester in 1921. Lane, *Rosamond Jacob*, p.144. *Callaghan* was written by Jacob in 1913 under the pseudonym F. Winthrop. It featured the activities of the suffragette movement in Ireland during this period and deals with themes of nationalism and feminism. Gaelic Irish writer Daniel Corkery reviewed it favorably in 1921 and considered it one of Ireland's best novels. For further details, see Deirdre F. Brady, *Suffragists, New Woman and Nationalists: Representations of Feminism in the Novels of Rosamond Jacob*, unpublished MA thesis (2007), University of Limerick. Hereafter Brady, *Suffragists, New Woman and Nationalists*.
27 Collins, *Poetry by Women in Ireland*, p.39.

day".²⁸ What follows therefore extends on this scholarship as it charts the publishing histories of Blanaid Salkeld, Lorna Reynolds and Christine Longford, illustrating how literary women created a niche for their work as translators and reviewers in "little magazines", and engaged with magazine culture of the period.

Periodicals, "Little Magazines" and "Guns and Roses"

Literary connections through the Women Writers' Club and involvement in cultured city life opened up new opportunities for magazines aimed at a high-brow readership with an Irish and international focus. Salkeld alone contributed several items to Irish periodicals such as *Irish Writing*, *Dublin Magazine* and *The Bell*. Her Irish language skills were in high demand. Examples include a review in *Irish Writing* of Liam Ó Briain's text *Ciumhní Cinn* in 1951²⁹ and Micheál MacLiammóir's collection of essays *Ceo Meala lá Seaca* in 1953.³⁰ The diversity of her work and the internationalization of its content include a study of Anna Akhmatova in 1933,³¹ a translation of the symbolist Russian poet Alexander Blok's *Dialogue about Love, Poetry and Government Service* in 1947,³² and a review of *Seventy Cantos* and *Poems* by Ezra Pound in 1950.³³ Also of note were contributions to the internationally focused *Ireland To-day* (1936–1938) and *Poetry Ireland* (1948–), a sister publication of *Irish Writing* fashioned on its more famous namesake, *Poetry* (Chicago). From 1924 until her death in 1958, her work was published sixty-eight times in the form of poems, reviews and translations.

Contemporaries Christine Longford, Lorna Reynolds and Teresa Deevy were also published in magazines; carving out a niche for women writers as professional translators, reviewers and poets. Longford's

---

28 Anne Mulhall, "'The well-known, old, but still unbeaten track': Women Poets and Irish Periodical Culture in the Mid-Twentieth Century", *Irish University Review*, 42.1 (2012), p.32.
29 Blanaid Salkeld, *Ciumhní Cinn* by Liam Ó Briain, reviewed in *Irish Writing*, 17 (1951).
30 Blanaid Salkeld, *Ceo Meala lá Seaca* by Micheál Mac Liammóir, and *Nuascéalaíocht* edited by Tomás de Bhaldraithe, reviewed in *Irish Writing*, 22 (1953).
31 Blanaid Salkeld, "Anna Akhmatova", *The Dublin Magazine*, viii.4 (1933) (IR 8205 d 4, National Library of Ireland).
32 Blanaid Salkeld, "Dialogue about love, poetry and government service, translated by Blanaid Salkeld", *The Dublin Magazine*, XXII.2 (1947).
33 Blanaid Salkeld, *Seventy Cantos*, poems by E. Pound reviewed in *The Dublin Magazine*, 13 (1950).

classical education at Oxford University was particularly useful for reviewing texts such as *The Helen of Euripides*, translated by Rex Warner, and *Antigone and Eurydice* by Jean Anouilh (1951), and her writing featured twenty-three times in *The Bell*.[34] The *University Review* employed Reynolds to translate Nichola Turchi's text *The Orphic Eschatology of the Monuments in Calabria*, and as a scholar, she regularly reviewed, commented on or submitted poetry to *The Dublin Magazine*.[35] Teresa Deevy also found *The Dublin Magazine* receptive to her two popular plays, *The King of Spain's Daughter* (published in 1936) and *The Disciple* (published in 1937), while *Strange Birth* and *Going Beyond Alma's Glory* were published in *Irish Writing* in 1946 and 1951 respectively.[36] Archival records document the conscientious strategy of reviewing fellow members' books, such as Lorna Reynolds' review of Maura Laverty's novel *Never No More* in *The Dublin Magazine* in 1942, Blanaid Salkeld's review of Sheila Pim's gardening guide *The Flowering Shamrock* in the periodical *Irish Writing* in 1949, and Temple Lane's write-up of the dramatic art of Teresa Deevy in *The Dublin Magazine* in 1946.[37] These reviews typify the unified actions of the group to support each other's work, characteristic of this coterie of professional women writers.

While periodicals were in the main the preserve of an intellectual class, the general reader purchased popular magazines and books influenced by cinema, music and mass-produced books such as Penguin paperbacks. Meaney *et al.* (2013) note the broad availability of British and American books and magazines to the Irish reading public during the early to mid-twentieth century.[38] As cinema became a dominant feature of Irish life and was widely embraced by the general population, American

---

34 Christine Longford, *A Sleep of Prisoners* by Christopher Fry, *The Helen of Euripides* translated by Rex Warner and *Antigone and Eurydice* by Jean Anouilh, reviewed in *The Dublin Magazine*, xvii.8 (1951).

35 Lorna Reynolds, "The Orphic Eschatology of the Monuments in Calabria", *University Review*, 1.9 (1956). Digital repositories, such as "Sources" in the National Library of Ireland, list the complete contributions of Reynolds and her contemporaries.

36 Martina Ann O'Doherty, "Deevy, A Bibliography", *Irish University Review*, 25.1 (1995).

37 Lorna Reynolds, *Never No More* by Maura Laverty, reviewed in *The Dublin Magazine*, XVII.3 (1942); Blanaid Salkeld, *The Flowering Shamrock* by Sheila Pim, reviewed in *Irish Writing*, 8.94 (1949), and Temple Lane, "The Dramatic Art of Teresa Deevy", *The Dublin Magazine*, XXI.4 (1946).

38 Meaney *et al.*, *Reading the Irish Woman*, pp.130–133.

culture influenced contemporary modes of thinking about femininity. Louise Ryan's study of reading material of the period in the magazines *The Modern Girl* and *Ladies Irish Home Journal* presents a picture of typical Irish "modern girls" as "confident, independent and outgoing".[39] According to Ryan, "not all women simply submitted to the dictates of church and state" and were far removed from the images of Irish womanhood fostered by the state. Young women of the period, who "look more like Hollywood stars than Irish Colleens", embraced this new culture, aware of the latest trends in international "Modern Beauty Culture". As previously discussed, Christine Longford's *Printed Cotton* (1935) reflected the optimism of the era and the phenomenon of modern Irish women who live in city "flats" and shop in Grafton Street. So too, women's magazines reflected the preoccupations of the growing middle classes and their principles of freedom, autonomy and sophistication. One such example was the cosmopolitan magazine *Woman's Mirror*, which had close links to prominent members of the Women Writers' Club.[40] The *Woman's Mirror* targeted an affluent upper-middle-class female readership, featuring contributions from writers with exotic names like Yasmina, Minerva and Vera; and articles on traveling, theatre, film, fashion, cosmetics and the opera. For instance, the column entitled "Gossip from Hollywood" featured the Irish actress Maureen O'Sullivan, most famous for her role as Jane in the movie *Tarzan*. Despite the contradictory images of a scantily clad and sexually alluring portrayal of Tarzan's love interest, O'Sullivan is there presented as "untouched and unspoiled by the gay life of Hollywood", thus aligning her with the socially embedded norms of Irish womanhood of the period.[41] Editorials featured elegant women, with photographs of wealthy upper-class women, including the "Countess of Longford" (May 1932) and "Miss Helen Staunton" (pseudonym of Sybil le Brocquy), "the well-known author and playwright" (July 1932).[42] Theatrical woman embodied a heady combination of glitz, decadence and just the right amount of subversion to appeal to the middle-class readers of the magazine. Their status as

---

39 Louise Ryan has written extensively about the rising middle classes in urban areas in Ireland during the 1930s and 1940s. For further analysis see Louise Ryan, "Constructing 'Irishwoman': Modern Girls and Comely Maidens", *Irish Studies Review*, 6.3 (1998), p.265.
40 *Woman's Mirror*, May 28, 1932 (IR 05 W2, National Library of Ireland). Hereafter *Woman's Mirror*.
41 *Woman's Mirror*.
42 *Woman's Mirror*.

privileged, wealthy socialites afforded the necessary leverage to transgress the generally accepted boundaries of "proper" feminine attitude and conduct, while their own brand of movie-star glamour epitomized their particular allure.

Unsurprisingly, many right-wing intellectuals and conservative Catholics expressed unease with the growth in popular reading material; especially where women were concerned.[43] Indeed, for some, the very activity of reading was condemned as harmful to family life. At a parliamentary debate on the expansion of library services in 1947, Dáil Deputy Domhnall Ua Donnchadha warned of the dangers of women reading and recounted his library observations of a "few mothers who became so keen on reading that they kept their children away from school while they themselves read".[44] Though largely ignored by the wider reading public, such extreme attitudes underscore the rigid gender ascriptions of the time. In any event, sales figures from large retailers such as Eason's and Woolworths reveal the consistent popularity of crime, murder mysteries and thrillers during the interwar years, while the books borrowed in rural and urban libraries were mainly ordinary romance genres and "better class fiction", followed by war, travel and biography.[45] Elizabeth Russell uses the phrase "holy crosses, guns and roses" to summarize the reading habits of the Irish Free State in the 1930s:

> Their content was uniform: "guns and roses", shoot-outs at corrals and then happy-ever-after tales, and, when home-produced, an extra-large smattering of soft nationalism and a nod in the direction of the Vatican were added in for good measure.[46]

While Russell's assessment echoes the general consensus of reading trends during the mid-twentieth century, the matter is complicated by the dearth of source evidence. In his study of Irish publishing in the 1920s and 1930s, Frank Shovlin points out that book sales do not

---

43 Frank Shovlin, "From Tucson to Television: Irish Reading, 1939–69", in C. Hutton and P. Walsh (eds), *The Oxford History of the Irish Book, Volume V: The Irish Book in English, 1891–2000* (Oxford: Oxford University Press, 2011), p.137. Hereafter Shovlin, "From Tucson to Television".
44 Shovlin, "From Tucson to Television", p.137.
45 Meaney *et al.*, *Reading the Irish Woman*, p.137.
46 Elizabeth Russell, "Holy crosses, guns and roses: themes in popular reading material", in J. Augustine (ed.), *Ireland in the 1930s: New Perspectives* (Dublin: Four Courts Press, 1999), p.11.

necessarily record the actual number of readers of a text, since the act of reading is a private occupation.⁴⁷ Indeed, a single edition can be read by many different readers, borrowed from libraries and/or passed from person to person. In the Irish context, the history of reading is particularly problematic as many trade figures are inconsistent or even absent. As Frank Shovlin remarks: "Where does one begin?"⁴⁸

'B-Banned': Radical Reading Lists of an Intellectual Woman – Rosamond Jacob⁴⁹

Diaries and letters form critical points of intersection between external and internal spaces of intellectual thought and a useful starting point for constructing a history of reading practices. The personal archives of Rosamond Jacob comprise a jigsaw of personal letters, countless newspaper clippings, plays and unpublished novels, from which it is possible to piece together a more detailed picture of her life and times, and the books she read.

From a young age, Jacob was an avid reader and writer, devoting considerable time to political and artistic concerns. At the age of fifteen, she wrote and compiled a magazine with her brother Tom and his friends: a mixture of stories, poetry and history that reflected their shared interests. Entitled URBS INTACTA (1903/1904), it epitomized the progressive ideas and humanitarian ethos of her Quaker family background. The book jacket stated their intention to donate all subscriptions to fund "Macedonia Refugees and Insurgents", signaling an arguably precocious sensitivity to international strife and the early formation of a radical mindset.⁵⁰ In fact, sympathy for the underdog was axiomatic to Jacob's activism and strikes a regular chord throughout Jacob's texts. Throughout her life she fought tirelessly for women's rights, prisoner's rights and animal rights, and in the latter part of her life, with CND for world peace.

Nicholas Allen's exploration of the reading practices of Jacob during the early 1920s also revealed her keen interests in the occult, anti-vivisection

---

47 Shovlin, "From Tucson to Television, p.129.
48 Shovlin, "From Tucson to Television", p.129.
49 At the end of the year 1941, Rosamond Jacob listed the "Books read 1941". At the top right of the page was the inscription "B-banned" to identify which books were on the censured. Papers of Rosamond Jacob, MS 32,582/98.
50 Papers of Rosamond Jacob, MS 33,122/1–2.

issues and the relatively new science of psychoanalysis.[51] Reading materials from this phase of her life include Forrest Reid's *The Kingdom of Twilight*, which she purchased from Switzers (now Brown Thomas) in Grafton Street, Dublin, and Sigmund Freud's treatise *Totem and Taboo*, which she procured in London's Charing Cross in the 1920s. Other notable titles include D. H. Lawrence's sexually explicit *Lady Chatterley's Lover* and Aldous Huxley's dystopian sci-fi novel *Brave New World*,[52] both of which appear in her 1933 diary under "list of books read", along with a range of esoterica including Arthur Findlay's *On the Edge of the Etheric*, F. Myer's *Most of Human Personality*, and *The Road to Immortality* by Geraldine Cummins.[53]

The reading of literary texts breathes life into the new ideas that affect literary production. In 1924, Jacob penned her experimental novella *Theo and Nix*, a tale recounting the love affair between the androgynous Nix and her inexperienced young lover, Theo. The narrative is clearly influenced by Freud's taboo-breaking psycho-sexual prepositions and rife with explicit erotic scenes. The book was never published. Instead, she rewrote these same characters, albeit in a more sanitized and conventional iteration, into her novel *The Troubled House*.[54] Stories of gallantry and heroic figures typify the reading preferences of the young Jacob; tropes of what Paul Eggert terms the "ancient and enduring pastime", which Jacob later called upon to bring to life in her own writing.[55] Her diaries taxonomize her favorite books under specific categories, such as:

"Men in Fiction" including "Mallory's Launcelot"; and "Austin's Mr. Knightley"; "Women in Fiction" including E. M. Delaware's "The Provincial

---

51 Nicholas Allen, "Reading Revolutions, 1922–39", in C. Hutton and P. Walsh (eds), *The Oxford History of the Irish Book, Volume V: The Irish Book in English, 1891–2000* (Oxford: Oxford University Press, 2011), p.102.

52 Lady Chatterley's Lover was banned until the early 1960s, after which two million copies were sold in Britain. According to Rónán McDonald, notorious novels found a "ready readership" in post-censorship Ireland. See Rónán McDonald, "'Anything about Ireland?': Reading in Ireland, 1969–2000", in C. Hutton and P. Walsh (eds), *The Oxford History of the Irish Book, Volume V: The Irish Book in English, 1891–2000* (Oxford: Oxford University Press, 2011), p.197.

53 Papers of Rosamond Jacob, MS 32,582/74.

54 For further analysis of the novel *Theo and Nix*, see Meaney, "Regendering Modernism"; see also Valerie Traub's work on dissident literature: Valery Traub, *The Renaissance of Lesbianism in Early Modern England* (Cambridge: Cambridge University Press (2002), and Brady, *Suffragists, New Woman and Nationalists*.

55 Paul Eggert, *Work and the Reader in Literary Studies* (Cambridge University Press, 2019). Hereafter Eggert, *Work and the Reader in Literary Studies*.

Lady"; "Men in History", such as Brian Boru and Theodore Wolfe Tone; and "Women in History" like "St. Catherine of Sienna" and "Mary Stuart" (former Queen of Scotland).[56]

Personal daring and revolutionary tendencies are reoccurring tropes in Jacob's books, particularly in her female characters: from the suffragette Frances Morrin in *Callaghan* and the sexually liberated Nix of *The Troubled House*, to the resilient Matilda Tone, wife of the Irish revolutionary Theodore Wolfe Tone.

In 1941, Jacob compiled a comprehensive inventory of the fifty books she had read that year.[57] Entitled "Books read in 1941", the list ranges across a diversity of genres: from a biography of the English dissenter and founder of the Quaker religion, *The Life of George Fox* by Rufus Jones, to literary historiography such as *Writings of E.M. Forster* by Rose Macauley. Her enduring fascination with Forest Reid, as noted above by Allen, appears in the list in the form of his autobiography, *Private Road* (1940). For sheer leisure, she treated herself to Agatha Christie's Poirot mysteries, including *Murder in the Mews* (1937) and *One, Two, Buckle my Shoe* (1940), while on a more sobering note, she engaged with theological discourse, such as C. S. Lewis's contemplation *The Problem of Pain* (1940). Popular novels such as J. M. Barrie's *A Window in Thrums* (1890), *The Marriage Business* by Joan Kennedy (1935) and *Nobody Asked Me* by Mary Burchell (1937) are also listed, along with a trio of titles from the Edwardian novelist Sophie Cole, namely *The Valiant Spinster* (1940), *Mrs. Scarlot's Quaints* (1939) and *London Posy* (1917).[58] Cole (1862–1947), a prolific writer of romance novels, was a particular favorite of upper-middle-class women in the 1930s and 1940s and was the first author to published by the now famous Mills & Boon.[59] Much of Jacob's reading list mirrors that of other middle-brow readers in Ireland and Britain, and demonstrates the fluid relationship between high and low modernism that is typical of the period. It is her inclusion of the "banned books" that sets it apart from regular practice.

56 Papers of Rosamond Jacob, MS 32,582/74.
57 Papers of Rosamond Jacob, MS 32,582/98.
58 Cole published over sixty-five titles with Mills & Boon during her lifetime. For more information, see the Cole Library in the special collections archive of the University of Reading, UK.
59 For further comment on reading practices, see Nicola Humble "Sitting Forward or Sitting Back: Highbrow v. Middlebrow Reading", *Modernist Cultures*, 6.1 (2011).

The more subversive elements of her list are referenced at the top of the page with the explanation "B-banned" and the letter "B" or "b" beside the proscribed title. This annotation is clearly intended for future readers; a code that was not uncommon with diarists of the time. According to Cynthia Huff, diarists often include items such as lists or postcards, or objects of personal interest that provide the key to a writer's processes or preoccupations:

> Diarists did not include bits of lace or newspaper clipping in their journals just because this was a convenient place to store them, but because these extra-textual items are as much as part of the record of personal and historical reconstruction as is the writing.[60]

These extra-textual clues force us to be vigilant – "we must read significance where we may not have known it lay".[61] As a reader, writer and amateur historian since early adulthood, Jacob was deeply cognizant of the importance of archiving papers and documentation. Over the course of her lifetime, she therefore produced two sets of personal diaries numbering 170 in all: one for public viewing; and another for individual reading. As an author, she fully appreciated the power of the pen and was ever mindful of the enduring legacy she wished to leave to future scholars, many of whom have drawn on her diaries to construct a history of the times and her milieu.[62] First logged in her chronological "B" list, and signposted "after this", was the banned anti-war novel *The Impregnable Woman* (1938). This fictional account of the struggle for power between women and men by Erik Linklater is shown as underlined with a "B" beside his name.[63] Other banned books listed include L. A. G. Strong's *Most of the Bay*,[64] Kate O'Brien's *Land of Spices* (1941) and the scientific work *Inequalities of Man* (1932) by John Haldane. Other intriguing titles include *Pain, Sex and Time: A New Outlook on Evolution and the Future of Man* (1939) by Gerald Heard: a philosophical meditation on mysticism and the future of humankind. Indeed, as a lifelong mystic herself, Jacob tended to incorporate elements of the uncanny or otherworldliness into

---

60 Cynthia Huff, "Reading as Revision, Approaches to Reading Manuscript Diaries", *Biography*, 23.3 (2000), p.518. Hereafter Huff, "Reading as Revision".
61 Huff, "Reading as Revision", p.517.
62 Recent examples include Leeann Lane's biography of Rosamond Jacob and Nadia Smith's biography of Dorothy Macardle.
63 Papers of Rosamond Jacob, MS 32,582/98.
64 This is possibly the title of *The Bay* by L. A. G. Strong, published by Gollancz in 1931.

her later novels, most notably *The Rebel's Wife* (1957) and her children's book *The Raven's Glen* (1960).[65]

In 1941, the fifty-three-year-old Jacob was still actively involved in a wide variety of reform organizations. Yet her indefatigable passion for reading in that year was especially instructive: for entertainment, to inform her political views and as an act of support or philanthropy. Despite the difficulties of being a single woman looking after her ill and reportedly contrary flat-mate Helen McGinley, the year proved artistically productive. Noting her achievements in her diary, she listed, "produced 1 3 act play, 4 articles, 2 radio discussions, 1 poem, 1 propaganda talk, revising play", as well as over fifty titles "read in 1941". At this time, she was also a regular visitor of the aging Mrs Mellow. Mother of the late republican Liam Mellows, a former friend and possible lover of Jacob, her "reading & talking" delighted the older lady who Jacobs admired as "very interesting to read for & not a bit deaf".[66]

Unsurprisingly, Jacob's reading practices informed her political thinking. In 1941, for instance, her talk to Women Citizens against Inoculation entailed "a lot of reading up & arrangement".[67] Despite her hectic life, she tended toward a melancholy disposition, and was bitter about the lack of quiet and solitude for writing, complaining: "Not living alone, it's harder to find peaceful time to write."[68] Jacob's disillusionment became even more palpable with the added stresses of paper shortages and wartime rationing. Of the three articles she wrote that year, "only the worst was published". Her drama efforts shared a similar fate: "The main thing I did was the play, '*The Naked Truth*', which is not quite done. I like it, but it will probably get nowhere."[69] Again, her other play, *Conceited*, remained unpublished, revealing her growing frustration: "I wrote the play Conceited for the I.P. Xmas number & then found it had none."[70]

---

65 Jacob, *The Rebel's Wife*, p.205. Jacob was invited to become a member of the Theosophical Society of Ireland by the mystical poet George Russell (Æ). Papers of Rosamond Jacob, MS 33,126.
66 Papers of Rosamond Jacob, MS 32,582/97.
67 Papers of Rosamond Jacob, MS 32,582/97.
68 Papers of Rosamond Jacob, MS 32,582/97.
69 Papers of Rosamond Jacob, MS 32,582/97. The "revising play" refers to a play on Theodore Wolfe Tone, "The Tone Play". The "propaganda talk" appears to be a talk on "the case against inoculation", given at the "Women's Citizen's". It is likely that I.P. stands for *The Irish Press*, a newspaper in which Jacob had previously published.
70 Papers of Rosamond Jacob, MS 32,582/97. For I.P., see previous note.

While a scarcity of publishing opportunities often thwarted Jacob's life as a writer, it is clear that the author drew solace from her activities as a reader. Her reading list is a telling cross-section of the immense variety of books that were actually available to the intellectual class and exemplifies cultural practices within a specific milieu. Interestingly, this list is at odds with public reading lists, and in particular, those promoted to the general Irish reading public during the Book Fair 1941.

The Irish Book Fair

The focus on the book as an emblem of cultural production reveals something surprising about the impact of book fairs on intellectual discourse and the world of the imagination. The exchange of information, and the circulation of ideas, or what Simone Murray refers to as the *making* of the literary, is often mediated through award ceremonies, writers' festivals and book fairs.[71] In his discussion of the history of books, Robert Darnton posits that "By reading and associating with other readers and writers, they [authors] form notions of genre and style and a general sense of the literary enterprise which affects their texts".[72] Thus, trends and fashions emerge through interactions with publishers and writers that, in turn, help shape the literary field. Terry Cochrane notes that the organization of book fairs drives the desire to manage ideas, "whether the motivation derives from a desire for profit or the promotion of certain interpretations of history, politics, literature, and so forth".[73] The organizers of the Irish Book Fair sought to cultivate a distinctive Irish literature, in many ways extending the project that had begun in 1932 when W. B. Yeats founded the Irish Academy of Letters.

The primary motivation for the first Irish Book Fair was the stated desire to promote a specifically "Irish" literature. As honorary secretary of the newly established Friends of the Academy of Letters in 1940 (fund-raising arm of the Academy of Letters), Sean O'Faolain appealed to the committee to support "lectures, or receptions, or awards – however

---

71 Simone Murray, "'Where Did Your Adaptation Begin?': Book Fairs, Screen Festivals and Writers' Weeks as Engine-rooms of Adaptation", in P. Nicklas and O. Lindner (eds), *Adaptation and Cultural Appropriation: Literature, Film, and the Arts* (Berlin: De Gruyter 2012).
72 David Finkelstein and Alistair McCleery, *The Book History Reader* (London: Routledge, 2002), p.11.
73 Terry Cochrane, "Culture against the State", *boundary 2* (1990), p.6.

minute, on investment in the interest of the people" and to advocate for "all work of fine intellectual or poetic quality, written by authors of Irish birth or descent".[74] Within the year, and with the help of O'Faolain's extensive network of friends and alliances in the book trade, the first Irish Book Fair took place with stated purpose of promoting "Books of Irish Interest" and books "the scene of which is laid in Ireland".[75]

The Book Fair was an unexpected triumph, with its series of diverse talks, lectures and exhibitions attracting over six thousand people. Thousands of books lined numerous stalls as the general public poured into the Mansion House. The reception from the media was equally encouraging, with one journalist enthusing, "it's a heartening stocktaking, and an inspiration ... books are the universities of modern days and Ireland still is the land of scholars".[76] Even the usually recalcitrant government joined the celebrations. The event was formally opened by the then Minister of Education, Mr Derry, and presided over by Edward Pakenham (Lord Longford) and other literary luminaries. As one account in *The Independent* reported:

> Every side of the Fair seems to be teeming with important names; even the list of guarantors who have secured the Fair by guarantee against possible losses includes such names as Ethel Mannin, George Bernard Shaw, Rutherford Mayne and Lennox Robinson.[77]

Talks on thematic concerns, including views on drama, censorship, libraries and history, were delivered by well-known writers.[78] Lennox Robinson chaired, and the various panels were presided over by Róisín Walsh, Edmund Curtis and Ernest Blythe, among others. Specific categories included "Drama" (Denis Johnston, Lennox Robinson); "Libraries" (R. J. Hayes); "The Novel" (Elizabeth Bowen); "History" (P. S. O'Hegarty); "Saints & Scholars" (Alice Curtayne); "Poetry" (Austin

---

74 Letter from Sean O'Faolain to Maurice Walsh, January 23, 1940. Maurice Walsh Papers, P/7, 4 (d) Correspondence (1932–1940), *Literary organisations (1938–1940)*, Special Collections, University of Limerick. The registered heading is the Academy of Letters and the address on the letterhead is the Abbey Theatre, Dublin. Hereafter Maurice Walsh Papers.
75 *The Irish Times*, March 15, 1941.
76 *The Irish Independent*, March 24, 1941.
77 *The Irish Independent*, March 19, 1941.
78 Temple Lane and Róisín Walsh were members of the executive. Elizabeth Bowen was an academician with the Academy of Letters, as well as Vice-President of the Friends of the Academy of Letters.

Clarke); "Children's Books" (Patricia Lynch and Winifred M. Letts [Mrs Verschoyle]); and "Book Production" (Colm Ó Lochlainn).[79]

Irish booksellers and publishers took pains to provide attractive, professional displays, earmarking best-selling authors in glass cases along with rare or first editions, paintings, manuscripts, literary curios and special bindings:

> Feverish work was going on to get the exhibits ready. Already the blue and white strand of the Talbot Press had taken shape, the black and gold pyramids of Browne and Nolan were being built up. Completely ready in its alcove was The Sign of the Three Candles.[80]

The Sign of the Three Candles, the printing press established by Colm Ó Lochlainn, hosted a Charles Lamb painting, "Hearing the News". The "first prayer book in Irish", printed in 1608, was also on display. The smaller publishing house of the Gayfield Press displayed its wares under the "wings" of Eason's, as did other regional publishers such as the Quota Press, Dundealgan Press and Waterford-based Carthage Books:[81] prudent alliances that ensured a more extensive distribution channel for their specialist books.[82]

The advocacy of a distinctive Irish literature and the collaborative energies of the various stakeholders involved in the book trade, captured the imagination of both the general population and the media. Róisín Walsh, Chief City Librarian, described the Dublin people's response to the Book Fair as her "most heartening experience in the last twenty years".[83] Meanwhile, Elizabeth Bowen, in her capacity as Vice President of the "Friends of the Academy", lauded "the 'novelists of the nation' as 'its greatest spokesmen'", while Ó Lochlainn underlined the importance of the printing industry as "the third largest in Dublin, coming only after beer and biscuits".[84] For enthusiastic readers and bibliophiles alike, it was a unique opportunity to see the output of an Irish literati at first hand, at a time when the book trade was struggling. Thus, for both writers and publishers, the Fair proved a springboard for the ensuing debates that took place at

---

79 *The Irish Times*, March 8, 1941.
80 *The Irish Independent*, March 19, 1941.
81 *The Irish Independent*, March 19, 1941.
82 For a detailed account of Eason's and the marketplace, see Louis M. Cullen, *Eason & Son: A History* (Dublin: Eason's, 1989).
83 *The Irish Times*, March 24, 1941.
84 *The Irish Times*, March 24. 1941.

the post-Book Fair Irish PEN meeting the following month concerning the positionality of Irish books.

This post-book fair debate, "Authors, Books and Booksellers", which was opened by Róisín Walsh and chaired by Austin Clarke, got off to a lively start. Keenly aware of the attendance of the publishing stakeholders, namely, the mainstream publishing houses of the Talbot Press, Browne & Nolan and smaller presses such as the Gayfield Press, Walsh immediately struck out at publishers of Irish books, bemoaning the undue competition within the book trade and the poor opportunities for Irish books.[85] Calling for the "actual production and publication of Irish books in this country", she was followed by the formidable Hanna Sheehy Skeffington, who criticized Irish authors for being too retiring: "There was a great lack of popular reprints and cheap editions of Irish books. In this way Irish authors suffered from a handicap."[86] Other women speakers at this event included Rosamond Jacob, Blanaid Salkeld (as representative of the Gayfield Press), and Hilda Nolan (as representative of Browne & Nolan). In retaliation, Lyons of the Talbot Press wryly pointed out that Irish books needed special encouragement and hoped the interest shown at the Mansion House Book Fair would not prove "transitory".[87] These debates and discussion took place within a public forum as a means of highlighting the position of the book and the challenges facing the book industry. The social opportunity and commercial possibility afforded by the Book Fair, and the subsequent debates, opened the door to the exchange of ideas and information, and the development of collegial relationships within the literary scene – ones that proved critical to the formation of the "Council of Action" the following year. The collective efforts of those in the book trade – authors, publishers, booksellers and readers – during the event is emblematic of the reciprocal process of communication and the key influence of each agent engaged in the dissemination of the book. Book Fairs and literary events also offer an interesting vantage point for accessing the contribution of writing groups to the print culture of the period – one that challenges received notions of an exclusive homosocial literary scene.

Artistic life, it seems, was developed and perpetuated through periodicals, popular magazines and cultural events. Editorial decisions determined whether a text was published or not, and the question of

---

85 *The Irish Times*, April 1, 1941.
86 *The Irish Times*, March 24. 1941.
87 *The Irish Times*, March 24, 1941.

who or what was published largely rested on a receptive publishing environment and a strategic networking circuit. Communication between those involved in the book trade was a crucial element in fostering writers and their books. Events such as the Irish Book Fair encouraged this process. While exact statistics are difficult to come by, Stephen J. Brown's 1944 article "Ireland in Books, 1944" claimed that an *"Annus Mirabilis* in respect of the publication of books of Irish interest" had developed, with new books coming on stream, aided by smaller presses throughout the country.[88]

One press singled out was the Gayfield Press, set up by Blanaid Salkeld in 1937. Since publishing decisions depended on a decidedly male industry, one way around this was to establish an independent printing press so as to ensure editorial autonomy and artistic independence.

---

[88] S. J. Brown, "Ireland in Books 1944", *The Irish Monthly*, 73.861 (1944).

CHAPTER FIVE

Coterie Culture and Modernist Presses

The Gayfield Press

The formation of a literary culture depends on the overarching relationship between authors, readers, booksellers and publishers and the intellectual, social, political and commercial circumstances that affect textual production. As outlined in previous chapters, the influence of events on the processing of new ideas, the leveraging of connections to open up publishing opportunities and the circulation of a specific female literature through awards and prizes are fundamental components of the story of literary life and the Irish Women Writers' Club. So too, the study of the individual as an agent of change within the broad intellectual history of this period is revelatory. As Alistair McCleary states in his account of the publisher Allen Lane, "If book history emerges from the dynamic interaction of 'the cultural nation' with "the political nation", it must find room in that for the individual actor participating in both these spheres".[1] One actor that deserves particular attention is the founder of the Women Writers' Club, Blanaid Salkeld. Her literary life story epitomizes the significant role of the individual in shaping culture. Whether as an agent of change in introducing readers to new ideas or with an ideological feminist goal of proving that women could publish, Salkeld's private printing press, the Gayfield Press, provides a critical case study for the discussion of Irish modernism, feminism and the influence of coterie culture.

The launch of the Gayfield Press was heralded in the national papers on October 25, 1937 with the publication of its first book, a collection

---

1 Alistair McCleery, "The Return of the Publisher to Book History: The Case of Allen Lane", *Book History*, V (2002), p.179.

of poetry by its founder and owner, Blanaid Salkeld.[2] In an article entitled "Woman Poet", the influential networks of this female writer were underscored: "Blanaid Salkeld is to have a new volume of poetry out shortly, I hear. It is called ... *the engine is left running*. Mrs Salkeld, who has been published in the 'Spectator,' 'London Mercury,' etc., has a poem in the current number of the 'Criterion' edited by T.S. Eliot."[3] This was not the author's first association with the ground-breaking modernist poet and editor: as previously discussed, her poem "in Dublin" had already been published in January 1935 by the Chicago-based periodical *Poetry*, in a special edition issue featuring Irish poetry. Indeed, the association of the Chittagong-born poet with high modernism continued to be cultivated by Salkeld through her network of writers and her press.

Salkeld's public shift from poet, dramatist and *salonnière* to businesswoman or "patron-investor", as Lawrence Rainey might put it, consolidates her avant-garde credentials.[4] In this same October 1937 article, she is extolled as "the hard-working Hon. secretary of the Women Writers' Club, but recently resigned the secretaryship owing to pressure of business ... I gather the *Gayfield Press* intends specialising in limited editions, fine art productions, handwritten MSS, and many things for the connoisseur, as well as ordinary publications".[5] This publicity and conscious promotion of her press was critical in positioning it as a specialist book publisher: a perception that was essential for encouraging revenue streams from wealthy speculators or regular subscriptions.

Ian Chapman's succinct elucidation of the communication of ideas that function through the craft of publishing is useful here: "A business it certainly is – but one which is concerned with the preservation and the communication of the achievements, the thoughts, the visions and the feelings of mankind down the ages."[6] The publications of the Gayfield Press encapsulate this somewhat lofty vision. Echoing what Adrian

---

2 Official documentation hosted by the Company Registration Office confirms Blanaid (Florence) Salkeld's as owner of the Gayfield Press. Company Registrations Office, *Business Name Printout, 19770* (Dublin: Stationery Office, 2013).
3 *The Irish Press*, October 25, 1937.
4 For a useful explanation of the differences between an ordinary book and limited edition see Lawrence Rainey, "The Cultural Economy of Modernism", in M. Levenson (ed.), *The Cambridge Companion to Modernism*, 6th edn (Cambridge: Cambridge University Press, 2003), p.56.
5 *The Irish Press*, October 25, 1937.
6 Ian Chapman, "The Book Business: Art, Craft and Trade", *Journal of the Royal Society of Arts*, 132.5335 (1984).

Johns refers to the "noble gesture" of "private presses",[7] this strictly non-commercial enterprise consistently produced texts and illustrations deemed by Salkeld to be "the best of the Irish artists". Salkeld was quick to set out her unequivocal literary manifesto: "The Gayfield Press publishes entirely at its own discretion – uninfluenced by fashionable tastes, cliques or coteries. It will continue to bring out Limited [sic] and Illustrated Editions [sic] of special interest."[8] While the overall catalogue of the press may read otherwise, its experimental and innovative ethos was evident from the start.

Book Publications

In tandem with their more traditional peers Austin Clarke and Padraic Colum, literary innovators such as Ewart Milne, John Irvine and Sheila Wingfield were published by the Gayfield Press. The appeal of Salkeld's venture doubtless centered around the opportunity to create an audience for their work, and the hope, however optimistic, that publication with a "connoisseur" press might attract the notice of more lucrative and influential American and British publishers. The conjunction of illustrated art and text can be discerned in the prominence of artwork within many of the books, with contributions from contemporary artists such as Cecil Salkeld, Jack B. Yeats and Leslie Owen Baxter.

Private ownership of a press afforded both symbolic agency and a unique platform for cultural expression as it enabled authors to circumvent censorship through limited editions and specialized readership. As Robin Skelton points out, "what censor cares about a circulation of only 300 copies among the literary and artistic set?"[9]

Fergus N. Fitzgerald's work *Sennet for Coriolan* (1941), a philosophical, religious and poetic text, exemplifies this in its stark portrayal of the devastating effect of war on three generations of a German family. Similarly, the left-leaning Milne chose the Gayfield Press to publish his contemporary collection of poetry, *Letter from Ireland* (1940): an anthology featuring a section on his experiences in the Spanish Civil

---

7 Adrian Johns, "The Book of Nature and the Nature of the Book", in David Finkelstein and Alistair McCleery (eds), *The Book History Reader*, 2nd edn (London: Routledge, 2006).

8 This was printed on the back cover of *Forty North Fifty West*.

9 Robin Skelton, "Twentieth-century Irish Literature and the Private Press Tradition: Dun Emer, Cuala and the Dolmen Presses 1902–1963", *Massachusetts Review*, 5.2 (Winter) (1964), p.374.

War. A subversive theme for any Irish writer of note,[10] Milne's clear anti-war sentiments are amplified by the bleak and boldly incisive illustrations of Cecil ffrench Salkeld. Private publications ensured that texts of this nature could fly below the radar of the ever-vigilant censors while at the same time reaching a select audience.

The Gayfield Press list of book publications include the following:

- *... the engine is left running* (1937), a collection of poetry by Blanaid Salkeld. Light brown boards, front illustration by Cecil ffrench Salkeld. (8vo). Limited edition, 250 copies.

- *Towards Irish Nationalism: A Tract offered in awe and reverence to the sublime patience and agonised endurance of the exploited people of Ireland* (1938), by Kathleen Kirwan. Limited edition, 250 copies.

- *Forty North Fifty West* (1938); a collection of poetry by Ewart Milne, including a cover and six original cuts, and a portrait of the author illustrated by Cecil ffrench Salkeld. (8vo). Limited edition, 250 copies.

- *Once Upon a Time ... Being Stories about a fierce Ogre and a small Boy, and a little Princess and a tiny Bird* (circa 1939), by Marcella Ecclesine. This book features four monochrome illustrations by Cecil ffrench Salkeld. (8vo).

- *Letter from Ireland* (1940), the second collection of poetry by Ewart Milne published by the *Gayfield Press*. It was printed on oatmeal cloth, lettered and ruled in red. (9x6).

- *The Fall of the Year* (1940) by Moirin Cheavasa. Printed on boards with green cloth, with the title stamped in gold. (9 x 6). Limited edition, 250 copies.

- *Sennet for Coriolan: A Chorus for Six Voice* (1941) by Fergus N. Fitzgerald. Printed on burgundy cloth boards and stamped with gold, (8 x 6). Limited edition. 250 copies.

- *Lisheen at the Valley Farm and Other stories* (1946) by Patricia Lynch, Helen Staunton [Sybil le Brocquy], and Teresa Deevy. Illustrations for *Lisheen at the Valley* by Beatrice Salkeld. (8vo).

The inaugural publication, *... the engine is left running* (1937), draws

---

10 For a discussion of the response of the Catholic Church to the Irish media coverage of the Spanish Civil War, and list of writers, journalists and the artists deemed as subversive (including those associated with PEN and *Ireland Today*, see Fearghal McGarry, "Irish Newspapers and the Spanish Civil War", *Irish Historical Studies*, 33.129 (2002), p.84.

immediate attention to the modernist tone of the press. Tropes characteristic of the movement such as the use of ellipsis, the drawing of a mechanical train and the open-ended title reflect the cultural impetus of the poet and her press. The "making of a book", to borrow a phrase from Paul Eggert, is "there between the covers and on the page".[11] The collection was produced with a light brown cover, octavo book size, consisting of hard cardboard with a thread binding. Printed on a wooden handpress and using a twelve-point Bodini typeface, the combination of text and illustration captured Salkeld's distinctive aim of linking the aesthetic with the social and political meanings of the poetry.

The first poem of the collection, "Attempt at Commencing", heralded Salkeld's intention to approach poetry "at a slant", thus recycling Emily Dickinson's call to "tell all the truth, but tell it slant" and emphasizing an indebtedness to her poetic foremothers.[12] Themes throughout the book reflect the precise historical juncture in which this collection is set through engagements with contemporary ideas of love, religion, poetry, age, time and the frustrations of artistic production. Fittingly, she sets out her stall as the lonely poet who "New with the new, a poet labours" while "sane men sleep – by the clock": or her expression of the great joy of a spiritual reawakening – when "out of the darkness" the poet finds rehabilitation through art: "Life: this void between being and being, unbelievable there should be a bridge – Art! the bridge – to span it."[13] Additional themes developed in this collection include conceptualizations of nationhood. For many Irish cultural nationalists, the post-revolution realization of the Irish nation proved a profound disappointment, both politically and socially. Salkeld gives emotional expression to this sense of disenchantment in the poem "Shots",[14] through a sharp focus shift to the bleak realities of Dublin city life. Powerful imagery adds richness and depth to the blunt semantics of the poem. Important landmarks such as the Mendicity Institution, where the 1916 revolutionaries fought for freedom, now ring "hollow"; while the "Guinness's barges", emblems of trade and metropolitan prosperity, "export barrels' sequence of revolution" that echo the rampant emigration of the 1930s. Cecil Salkeld's illustration of

---

11 Eggert, *Work and the Reader in Literary Studies*, p.3.
12 Blanaid Salkeld, *... the engine is left running* (Dublin: Gayfield Press, 1937), p.1. Hereafter Salkeld, *... the engine is left running*.
13 Blanaid Salkeld, *... the engine is left running*, p 4.
14 Blanaid Salkeld, *... the engine is left running*, p.32.

a man in a mackintosh and hat, reminiscent of the revolutionary men, shows a head bowed in disappointment at the development of the city, and by implication, the nation.

> You can see through and through the Mendicity Institution
> only in one blank corner
> two blinds are down this morning; further on by Liffey's margin
> barrels to the Guinness's barges barrels barrels are rolled down;
> wind drifts and clouds follow
> I shift from the town
> from this hollow
> Mendicity Institution
> from Liffey with its blanched non-pareils
> the swans. and from the export barrels'
> sequence of revolution
> I depart in confusion.[15]

The images of the boat tied to the pier, circled by the predatory seagulls, a woman wrapped in a shawl and a man leaning despairingly over a wall suggest what Moynagh Sullivan identifies as "the desire to leave, to escape a recurring experience of confinement" as a persistent trope across Salkeld's corpus.[16]

Visual design conjures the essential themes of the poem "Returning".[17] The fusion of text and imagery vivify an atmosphere of remoteness and separateness. A windswept tree; a horse in a paddock, a solitary dwelling; and the bleak backdrop of the "mealy mountains" in a rural setting, compound the isolation of the artist in the pursuit of her trade. While the "illimitable bright speech of the moon", the classical symbol of womanhood, beaming down on the landscape, lights up the isolation felt by the woman poet, it also radiates her sense of optimism.

The title, "Returning", suggests a journey back, perhaps to the inner soul of the poet, wherein the running conceit of a "delinquent moon", which refuses be silenced, continues in "uttering brightness, even as an endless word", while "all matter into spirit blossoms". Here, the reader is again reminded of her cultural milieu within the Women Writers' Club, and the dissidence of women who resist all critical voices by "flooding all sound beside".[18]

---

15 Salkeld, ... *the engine is left running*, p.32.
16 Sullivan, "*The Woman Gardener*", p.54.
17 Salkeld, ... *the engine is left running*, p.6.
18 Salkeld, ... *the engine is left running*, p.9.

The symbiosis of poetic text and illustrations also deserves attention. The front cover depicts a steam engine pulling an array of carriages down a hill (see Figure 11). This illustration, sketched by Cecil ffrench Salkeld, is drawn from a children's story, "The little engine that could", which was popular in the early twentieth century for its themes of empowerment.[19] Also reminiscent of Lois Lensky's 1930s illustration of the popular mantra "I think I can"; the concept is inverted to show the train coming *down* the hill. A more nuanced interpretation aligns this popular motif with Russian cultural images developed in the 1930s to educate the public, and particularly children, about the benefits of technology to contemporary society.[20] Such images became a cultural archetype encouraged by the Stalinist regime of the time as it sought to develop new cultural and social identities. According to Leeann Lane, there existed within a small circle in Dublin a "vogue for all things Russian", albeit expressed mostly at a cultural level.[21] Political ideas forged through membership of the Women Writers' Club and their political (often socialist) members connected Blanaid Salkeld with left-wing intellectuals.[22] Moreover, as a translator of the Russian poets Valery Bryusov and Anna Akhmatova, she was unusually conversant with first-hand Russian intellectual ideas. The 1942 inclusion of Roy McFadden's poem "Russian Summer" in their broadsheet series, along with motifs of modern technology or artifacts (machines, radios, trains) in the compilation of poems, foregrounds Salkeld's familiarity with Russian modernism and her immersion in avant-garde ideals. Jessica Lynn Pannell pinpoints one example in the poem "Apropos for Radio", from ... *the engine is left running*, wherein she suggests the subject of a conversation between the taxi-driver and passenger sounds more like a radio address from a clergyman.[23] Like many members of the Women

---

19 Lois Lenski, an American illustrator and children's writer, was the best-known illustrator of this story in the early twentieth century.
20 Soviet children's books were often adapted from western stories. See "Adventures in the Soviet Imaginary – Children's Books and Graphic Art", Special Collections Research Center, the University of Chicago Library – online exhibition, online, www.lib.uchicago.edu/collex/exhibits/soviet-imaginary/technology/transportation-human-and-machine.
21 Lane, *Rosamond Jacob*, p.243.
22 For example, Rosamond Jacob visited Russia in 1931 as part of an Irish delegation of the Friends of the Soviet Union. Papers of Rosamond Jacob, MS 33,129/1.
23 Jessica L. Pannell, *'Teeming Delight': Irish Poetry 1930–1960*, unpublished PhD thesis (2011), University of Pittsburgh.

Writers' Club, Salkeld keenly embraced radio as a means to promote her verse plays. In a letter to Sybil le Brocquy in 1955, she expresses her delight in having one of her plays produced by the Irish station, Radio Éireann, following an earlier rejection of the piece: "Padraic Fallon called Cecil to 'put a plot' to one of my verse plays, and R.E. would put it on!"[24]

The diversity of book titles provides insights into the creative choice of the editor and her role as mediator of experimental texts. Books aimed at the domestic market include Marcella Ecclesine's children's book ... *Once Upon a Time ... Being Stories about a fierce Ogre and a small Boy, and a little Princess and a tiny Bird* (circa 1938).[25] Possibly a commissioned piece, it consists of two stories: the first dedicated to "Peter", and the second to "Paula". This quarto book on printed card features four monochrome plates by Cecil ffrench Salkeld (see Figure 12). Cecil's artistic training was at Dublin's Metropolitan School of Art, where he studied with contemporaries such as Sean Keating and James Sleator. From there in 1921, he moved to the Kunstakademie in Kassel under Ewald Dulberg, a printmaker and theatrical designer, who had a lasting impression on him. S. B. Kennedy notes that Cecil ffrench Salkeld was inspired by the German *Neue Sachlichkeit* movement or "New Objectivity", which is evident in his paintings.[26] His experience as a publisher stemmed from his partnership with Francis Stuart in the short-lived "little magazine" *To-morrow* in 1924. In this publication, he defined art as "the crystallization of idea into form, which [by means of the senses], is transmuted into idea again",[27] a philosophy that is evident in the Gayfield Press. He took a leading role in the management of the Gayfield Press, printing the broadsheets by hand on the wooden handpress, as a letter from Salkeld to her Austin Clarke testifies: "Cecil will be printing these himself, by hand – and hopes to make a find job of it."[28]

The next publication by the press was Kathleen Kirwan's political tract, *Towards Irish Nationalism: A Tract* (1938).[29] This treatise posits

---

24 Blanaid Salkeld to Sybil le Brocquy, July 29, 1955. Le Brocquy Papers.
25 Marcella Ecclesine, *Once Upon a Time ... Being Stories about a Fierce Ogre and a Small Boy, and a Little Princess and a Tiny Bird* (Dublin: Gayfield Press, circa 1938).
26 S. B. Kennedy, *Irish Art and Modernism, 1880–1950* (Belfast: Institute of Irish Studies, 1991).
27 S. B. Kennedy, "An Incisive Aesthetic", *Irish Arts Review*, 21.2 (2002), p.95.
28 Blanaid Salkeld to Austin Clarke, May 18, 1939.
29 Kathleen Kirwan, *Towards Irish Nationalism: A Tract* (Dublin: Gayfield Press, 1938).

a "philosophy of nationalism" and argues for the right to preserve the cultural values "dating from Druidic times and reasserted in our later Christianity".

Books by the well-known author Moirin Cheavasa commanded the higher price of 7s.6d. and were vital to the survival of the overall venture. In 1940, the Gayfield Press published her collection of poetry and ancient tales entitled *The Fall of the Year: Collected Poems* (1940),[30] which offers that poet's version of the tragic romance between the Irish poets Liadain and Curithir, which was originally written "partly in prose, partly in verse" in the late ninth or early tenth century. The collection also features excerpts from *From the Book of Cait Ni Duibir*, an earlier manuscript called after the symbolic name for Ireland that was originally published by the Three Candles Press in 1920: and the verse play *The Fire-Bringers*, which retells the "oldest version" of the mythical tale *The One Unfaithfulness of Naoise* to the beautiful Deirdre, and is dedicated to the revolutionary Maud Gonne MacBride.[31] Fergus N. Fitzgerald's book delves into the themes of war in *Sennet for Coriolan: A Chorus for Six Voices* (1941).[32] In it, he offers a very unorthodox perspective on war, delineating the lives of three generations of Germans, and laced with intertextual references to Dante Alighieri, T. S. Eliot and Vittorio Alfieri.[33] The final book published by the Gayfield Press was the children's book *Lisheen at the Valley Farm and Other Stories* (1946), a book beautifully illustrated by Beatrice Salkeld, daughter of Cecil Salkeld, featuring fairy tales by Patricia Lynch, Helen Staunton (Sybil le Brocquy) and Teresa Deevy.[34]

Salkeld was candid about the international focus of her press. On the back cover of Milne's book *Forty North Fifty West* (1938), she appeals to writers "at home and abroad" to send manuscripts to the press.[35] In the promotional material for the same publication, she promotes its modernist credentials: "It was enough for him [Milne] to pick up a copy of T.S. Eliot

---

30 Moirin Cheavasa, *The Fall of the Year: Collected Poems* (Dublin: Gayfield Press, 1940). Hereafter Cheavasa, *Fall of the Year*.
31 Cheavasa, *Fall of the Year*.
32 Fergus N. Fitzgerald, *Sennet for Coriolan: A Chorus for Six Voices* (Dublin: Gayfield Press, 1941). Hereafter Fitzgerald, *Sennet for Coriolan*.
33 Fitzgerald, *Sennet for Coriolan*.
34 Patricia Lynch, Helen Staunton and Teresa Deevy, *Lisheen at the Valley Farm and Other Stories* (Dublin: Gayfield Press, 1946).
35 This is outlined in the back cover of Ewart Milne's first book, *Forty North Fifty West* (Dublin: Gayfield Press, 1938). Hereafter Milne, *Forty North Fifty West*.

on a secondhand book-cart, to realise that poetry – even for an able seaman, is the only way out."[36] T. S. Eliot did indeed read the book and praised Salkeld for her statement. In a letter to her friend Sybil le Brocquy, she wrote: "Aiken had a long talk with T. S. Eliot chiefly about my poems! The only phrase he quoted was that he thought my blurb on the jacket <u>very wonderful</u>' [*sic*]", a remark that clearly delighted Salkeld.[37] The description on the cover promotes Milne as a free-spirited patriotic poet with socialist leanings: a writer from a heavily implied Anglo-Irish background who "dodged Trinity to become one of our Wild Geese. A sailor before the mast, and a labourer in American saw-mills."[38] Milne's poetry is informed by his time as a seaman, with striking motifs and association with the sea, as the title suggests.[39] Salkeld's democratic view of modernist poetry, emblematic of the times, is in line with liberal, less elitist modernist women writers such as Marianne Moore (with whom she corresponded) Virginia Woolf and Nancy Cunard.[40]

Milne, who was born in Dublin in 1903, hailed from an Anglo-Irish background and enjoyed a variety of careers as a reviewer, poet, teacher, sailor and journalist.[41] His political affiliations saw him join the republicans in the Spanish Civil War where he served alongside his friend Charles Donnelly as an ambulance driver.[42] By the late 1930s, Milne was living in London and writing for Edward Sheehy's *Ireland Today*: an Irish journal with republican leanings and ambitions to bring an international element to Irish periodical publishing.[43] This comingling of aesthetic and political concerns is reflected in his poetry, and is particularly evident in "Oboe for Yeats". In this poem, Milne echoes Yeats's poem "The Hawk", as "the hawk of the mind", representing the soul that can

---

36 Milne, *Forty North Fifty West*.
37 Underlined text in the original. Blanaid Salkeld to Sybil Le Brocquy, 15 October, 1955. Le Brocquy Papers, MS 24,2321/1.
38 During the 1940s and 1950s, Trinity College Dublin was still considered the doyen of the Protestant Church. Although no longer banned from attending Trinity, Catholics needed special dispensation from their own church to attend.
39 There are many references to the sea in this collection, including the first two poems in *Forty North Fifty West* (1938), which have the titles "Drinking Song" and "The drunken sailor would speak of the sea".
40 Rachel Potter, *Modernism and Democracy: Literary Culture 1900–1930* (Oxford: Oxford University Press (2006), p.2.
41 Gearoid Ó Brien, "Ewart Milne, 1903–1987", *Books Ireland*, III (1987). Hereafter Ó Brien, "Ewart Milne, 1903–1987".
42 Ó Brien, "Ewart Milne, 1903–1987".
43 Blanaid Salkeld contributed to *Ireland Today* on three occasions.

still find expression even within a violent war. Cecil ffrench Salkeld's dark and threatening illustrations (see Figure 13), with war-like symbolism and destructive planes that "wall the sky", foreground the poet and artist's artistic lineage, suggesting a continuation of the quest of Yeats's vision or poetic soul. Likewise, the use of twelve-point Bodini typeset in bold lettering was used to distinguish it from the first publication. The harshness of style compounded the pre-war anxieties felt in Europe and fears of impending war, and resonates with the grotesque fonts of Wyndham Lewis's short-lived magazine *BLAST*, which was published at the beginning of the First World War.

Milne's poetry continued to gain critical attention, and in *Letter from Ireland* (1940), he specifically acknowledged copyright for poems previously published in British journals *New Writing* and *The New English Weekly*, an indication of his rising reputation as a poet. These include "Spring Song", "Sierran Vigil" and "The Poet", respectively. The expert skills and craftsmanship of the Gayfield Press are evident in the production of the volume and include a detailed contents page and smooth paper quality (if a little jagged on the edges). The cover with its back, strip and front, lettered in narrow black horizontal red lettering, and the bellicose language of "war-zone" and "dead" on both the front cover and throughout the text, firmly situate the book within the historical turmoil of the Spanish war, the Second World War and censorship. The list of contents also foregrounds the international dimension of the book, with titles such as "Nachtmusik", "Ave", "Lines for a European Drama" and "Communism would make machines of men". Strongly influenced by Eliot, Milne published sixteen books throughout his long literary career including his epic *Galion* with Liam Miller's Dolmen Press.[44] It is worth noting that the limited edition of *Letter from Ireland* now commands a high price in contemporary online sales. Adding to the current cachet of this volume are illustrations by Cecil ffrench Salkeld: a cover and six original woodcuts, including a portrait of the author, and an original limited print run of "strictly" 250 editions, with the first "1–50" signed by the author.

Distribution for the Gayfield Press was handled by the large bookseller, Eason's & Co. Another method operated through subscriptions. As the back cover of *Forty North Fifty West* urges readers: "If you are not on

---

44 Ó Brien, "Ewart Milne, 1903–1987", and Gustav H. Klaus, "'The Sore Frailty of This Lasting Cause': Some Celtic Versions of Spanish Civil War Poetry", *Irish University Review*, 21.2 (1991), p.279.

our mailing list, please send us your name and address." Visibility in the book trade was obviously critical. Poetry readings and audios (one of which was held in the Woodberry Poetry Room at Harvard University), radio broadcasts, cultivating relationships with booksellers and agents, newspaper reviews, contributions to magazines and Salkeld's network within the Women Writers' Club and the Irish PEN, all afforded crucial links to an existing set of like-minded readers.

Salkeld's immediate circle consisted of a community of male and female writers, activists, publishers and journalists, and was connected to key political and literary figures with international profiles. As discussed in earlier chapters, Sybil le Brocquy organized the Women's International League of Peace and Freedom (Women's International Congress) in 1925, was active in the League of Nations and was one of the founders of the Irish Civil Rights Society. Other friends and affiliates included nationalist figures such as Maud Gonne MacBride and Thomas MacDonagh, Sean O'Faolain, Sheila Pim and Lillian Anderson; and Salkeld maintained lifelong friendships with Austin Clarke and Padraic Colum. Her private correspondence further reveals close personal connections with Mary Colum, Ernie O'Malley, Erica Marx, Sheila Wingfield, Brendan Behan (her grandson-in-law), Teresa Deevy, James Stephens, Pearse Hutchinson, Samuel Beckett, Patrick Kavanagh, Robert Greacen, Jack Sweeney (of the Poetry Room, Harvard), Iseult Gonne and Lennox Robinson. Her extended literary networks were such that her grand-daughter, Beatrice, remarked that her home at 43 Morehampton Road was a place with "so many writers and artists in our house in those days that I couldn't be expected to notice them all".[45] With the press operating from their home, the actual conditions of production were also highly challenging.

Leonard Woolf's recollection of the Hogarth Press, established in the home he shared with Virginia Woolf, encapsulates the adversities facing a small press within the broader book market. He described their efforts as a "mongrel in the business", which suffered from inadequate support and the lack of "sales travellers to take their books round to important booksellers ... to solicit orders before publication".[46] In Woolf's estimation, it was a "depressing business":

---

45 This quotation is in reference to her first meeting with her future husband, Brendan Behan. See Beatrice Behan, *My Life with Brendan* (London: Leslie Frewin, 1973), p.43.

46 Gillian Naylor, *Bloomsbury: The Artists, Authors and Designers by Themselves* (London: Octopus Publishing Group (1990), p.164. Hereafter Naylor, *Bloomsbury*.

We ran it in our spare time on lines invented by myself without staff and without premises, we printed in the larder, bound books in the dining-room, interviewed printers, binders, and authors in a sitting-room. I kept the accounts. Records of sales etc., myself in my own way.[47]

The day-to-day business of publishing requires some elaboration. It requires a variety of skills and knowledge about the activity of publishing. A typical "job" list might involve any combination of the following:

> Telephone, press notices, royalties on prints, designs for cards, card envelopes, tape, tea, stationary, sheet paper for broadside, packing envelopes, labels, exhibition expenses, card blocks, paint brushes, framing and mounting prints, corrugated boards packing, gum, cotton cord, ream white tissues, compliment slips.[48]

Furthermore, the physical processes of printing on the wooden handpress was arduous work, with a range of daily tasks that might include coloring cards, proofing, camping paper and dissing, printing, coloring prints, selling, paging, correcting, setting, rolling (for bookplates), printing books, printing cards, damping (paper) selecting and washing.[49] The substantial costs involved carried no guarantee of returns. As the publisher of the Talbot Press famously explained to an aspiring poet: "It would probably cost £50 or £60 to bring out the book in a form worthy of the poems, and if you could sell 500 copies at 2s or 2s.6d. each, you would make a profitable venture. It is, however, very difficult to sell 500 copies of a volume of poetry."[50] In order to combat these challenges, the Gayfield Press adopted a specific pricing strategy. In essence, this meant charging more for books by well-known authors than those by less-known authors; a policy that attracted negative attention in the national press.

In an article by R. J. entitled "Book for Children" published in *The Irish Independent* on September 24, 1945, the reporter castigated the Gayfield Press, saying that producing and selling "a book less than 40 pages of reading matter on poor paper, and with no more than a thick paper cover seems to me somewhat courageous, even in these days".[51]

---

47 Naylor, *Bloomsbury*, p.164.
48 Cuala Press Archives, Trinity College Dublin, MS11535, Box 1, no. 4–5, October 1938–May 1941.
49 Cuala Press Archives, Trinity College Dublin, MS11535, Creditors' Ledgers, January 1925–1948.
50 Tony Farmer, "Financial and Market Factors", p.223.
51 *The Irish Independent*, September 20, 1945.

This was a direct reference to the children's book *Lisheen at the Valley Farm and Other Stories*,[52] which was retailing at the price of 7s.6d. per unit. As one of the most successful children's writers of the period, Lynch was in a position to command a higher price.[53] In contrast, the works of less known writers, such as Kathleen Kirwan, Marcella Ecclesine and Fergus N. Fitzgerald, were less expensive; the latter priced at the much lower 2s.6d. per unit.[54] Lyon's aforementioned calculation confirmed that, while arguably worthy, a venture predicated exclusively on publishing unknown authors was essentially untenable. Thus, in order to survive in the publishing business, Salkeld was obliged to consider other revenue streams, including the printing of "*belles lettres*, music and fine art, etc." Based on economic imperatives, then, the press embarked on the production of a series of poetry broadsheets, which proved remarkably successful.

Dublin Poets and Artists: The Broadsheet Series

As a cultural innovator, Salkeld was both imaginative and intrepid. She began the production of a series of broadsheets, which included new emerging poets and established poets as part of her aim to promote what she considered representative Irish poetry. In order to do so, she and her son, Cecil, decidedly leveraged their connections in the literary community and sought contributions for their Dublin Poets and Artists broadsheets from their close friends (see Figure 14). These included works from Austin Clarke, as mentioned above, and Colum and Seumas O'Sullivan, along with poems from young up-and-coming talent, including John Irvine, Roy McFadden, Donagh MacDonagh, Robert Greacen and Sheila Wingfield. Contributors were asked to forego

---

52 At the time of printing, paper shortages were rife. Ann Saddlemyer claims that one of the factors that led to the closure of the Cuala Press was the sourcing of special paper for their limited editions. They published their final book in 1945, but continued to publish greetings cards and colored prints until the death of George Yeats in 1968. See Ann Saddlemyer, "The Creation of a Literary Industry", *Éire-Ireland*, 35.3/4 (Fall/Winter) (2000/2001).

53 Other examples include a book by well-known writer Moirin Cheavasa (née Fox). In the same year (1940) that Robert Grave's *No More Ghosts* by Faber was priced at 2s.6d., *The Fall of the Year* by Cheavasa was priced at 7s.6d. See *The Irish Independent*, October 1, 1940.

54 The book *Sennet for Coriolan* was priced at 2s.6d. There is no evidence to suggest that Kirwan or Ecclesine's books were sold in the Irish market and they may have been for private circulation only.

remuneration in this instance. As a letter to Wingfield explains: "We [the Gayfield Press] are not in a position to pay fees – as the scheme is a large one and not a commercial proposition – as you may understand."[55] The bohemian creed of "art for art's sake", espoused by Salkeld, depended on other like-minded altruistic authors and a shared passion for an Irish poetic heritage.

While information on the press is sparse, three private letters from Blanaid Salkeld to Sheila Wingfield ringfence the nature and motivations of the series: "The Gayfield Press intend bringing out a series of Broadsheets – of representative Irish poets. We hope to include with these poems the work of the best Irish artists."[56] A second letter sent one week later mentions listing the poets, Padraic Colum, Seumas O'Sullivan and Austin Clarke, and the "young" poet Donagh MacDonagh:

> We [the Gayfield Press] are getting poems from Padraic Colum, Seumas O Sullivan & Austin Clarke. Also from some young poets – from Don Mac Donagh, anyway. You will have noticed his fine "veterans" in 'The Best Poems of 1938'. It would not matter using matter already published, provided that your permission would be sufficient.[57]

In her third letter, written in mid-June 1939, Salkeld referred to the regional parameters of the project: "Owing to the Dublin nature of our series, it might be no harm (with your permission). But I needn't say, this is only a trifle."[58]

The series was an unqualified success. In 1939, the Gayfield Press published the poem "The Jackdaw" by Padraic Colum with a reproduction of Yeats's hand-colored print "The Saddling Bell". In 1941, Robert Greacen's "The Bird" was published with an accompanying woodcut produced by Leslie Owen Baxter.[59] Maurice J. Craig's "Black Swans" was also published in 1941 with a frontispiece by Sidney Smith. Other broadsheets produced in 1941 include Austin Clarke's verse play *The Straying Student*, featuring an illustration by the modernist artist Mainie Jellet, and Roy McFadden's "Russian Summer" with illustrations by Leslie Owen Baxter (see Figure 15).[60] Two years later, *Two Poems* by Norman G. Reddins and an untitled poem by Emily Hughes were published;

---

55 Salkeld to Wingfield, June 14, 1939. Sheila Wingfield Papers, MS 29,047/34.
56 Salkeld to Wingfield, May 18, 1939. Sheila Wingfield Papers, MS 29,047/34.
57 Salkeld to Wingfield, May 27, 1939. Sheila Wingfield Papers, MS 29,047/34.
58 Salkeld to Wingfield, June 14, 1939. Sheila Wingfield Papers, MS 29,047/34.
59 Stewart, "Ricorso".
60 Stewart, "Ricorso".

both with a frontispiece by Cecil Salkeld.[61] In the same year, 1943, John Irvine's *Two Poems* was also published. The appeal of the broadsheets was such that three hundred copies of each poem or pamphlet had to be printed rather than the usual 250. The press's commitment to advancing the status of Irish poetry by publishing contemporary poets led Liam Miller to enthuse that the printings of Gayfield Press editions, alongside the poetry of Denis Devlin and Brian Coffee, were representative of "Poetry Ireland".[62] Liam Miller's first publication for his Dolmen Press was Thomas Kinsella's chapbook *The Starlit Eye*, which he printed on the wooden press "loaned from Cecil ffrench Salkeld who used it to publish his Gayfield Press series of Dublin poets and artists".[63] Kinsella would eventually acknowledge the centrality of [Blanaid] Salkeld in the discussion of talented women poets of the twentieth century, suggesting that her poetry should be included in a re-edited *New Oxford Book of Irish Verse*: an opinion she would no doubt have relished.[64]

Blanaid Salkeld's Gayfield Press, inspired by her foremothers in the Cuala Press, reclaimed agency for women in the material production of modernist and experimental literature. As an agent of change in opening up readers to new ideas or as an ideological feminist goal proving that women could publish, the Gayfield Press was a platform for political and social expression through poetry. While the nuts and bolts and the high costs of publishing meant that running a private printing press was a difficult and arduous task, the achievements of Blanaid Salkeld and her press were immense.

She succeeded in publishing eight books and a variety of broadsheets despite the scarcity of resources that obtained throughout the Second World War and the prevailing draconian censorship regime. This press is

---

61 These were auctioned by Dublin-based Fine Art Auctioneers and Valuers in 2011. For details, see www.adams.ie/Gayfield-Press-Cecil-Salkeld-A-Collection-of-4-illustrated-Poems-as-follows-i-Craig-Mauice-J-A-Poem-Black-Swans-roy-8vo-D-1941-with-lino-cut-frontis-by-Sidney-Smith-Signed-by-Author-ii-Hughes-Emily-Co?Itemid=&view=lot_detail.

62 T. D. Redshaw, "'The Dolmen Poets': Liam Miller and Poetry Publishing in Ireland", 1951–1961, *Irish University Review*, 42.1 (2012), p.143.

63 Gardiner, "The Other Irish Renaissance", p.79.

64 This is in answer to a question from Michael Smith to Thomas Kinsella. In it, he asks if Kinsella could re-edit *The New Oxford Book of Irish Verse*, whom would he include? Salkeld was mentioned alongside other women poets including Eva Gore-Booth, Juanita Casey, Moira O'Neill and others. For more on this, see Michael Smith, "Thomas Kinsella in Interview with Michael Smith", *Poetry Ireland Review*, 75 (Winter) (2002/2003).

intrinsic to the history of women in print culture in Ireland, reigniting the aims of feminism at a time of uncertainty about the status of women, and highlighting the strategies through which women intervened in the marketplace as publishers, and harnessed their networks and connections to influence the production of cultural texts. The Gayfield Press is situated within prestigious international modernist publishing ventures which were characteristic of the early to mid-twentieth century; including the Hogarth Press, and Irish private printing presses, the Dun Emer and the Cuala Press. However, a number of compelling questions still remain. The decision to set up a private printing press raises issues of intent. Did the Gayfield Press actually fulfill a market need, or was it a merely a form of vanity publishing? Was the Gayfield Press a legitimate response to the constraints of censorship or a noble attempt to foster and patronize free artistic expression? While exhaustive answers to these matters remain purely speculative, perhaps the most revealing clues to her motivations to foster art and a specific tradition of Irish poetry are to be found in the words of the opening poem in her ... *the engine is left running* collection, "Attempt at Commencing":

> Seated
> fire-heated
> over typewriter's shoulder
> I am beholder of a noble art
> the fine intricate design of stark bough and twig.[65]

---

65 Salkeld, ... *the engine is left running*, p.23.

Conclusion

One short newspaper article in the *Dublin Evening Mail* was the catalyst for this book.[1] The report in question centered on the Silver Jubilee of the Women Writers' Club and the impressive list of writers involved in the Club, including those who "are known among reading people in all parts of the English-speaking world and in parts too where no English is spoken at all". To date, this is one of the last reports found in the newspapers of the period and so arguably pinpoints the beginning of its occlusion from cultural history. No memorandum of meetings, history book or autobiography now exists to tell the complete story of this fascinating Club. Yet trace evidence in the archives form a precious seam of information, which can be carefully mined to form a holistic picture of the social, political and literary realm in which these women wrote.

Literature remains a powerful instrument of change, inspiring activism and revealing truths. Progressives within the Women Writers' Club used the power of the pen effectively to inform, educate and entertain their readers, and at the same time as maintaining a space for women's writing in the public sphere. Glittering balls, dinners and "at homes" were key sites of social opportunity, as women writers mingled in influential academic, political and artistic circle, on the fringes of, and close to the corridors of power. This book chronicles their activities – examining the context in which they wrote, the powerful influence of literary networks and their incisive marketing of their creative works. The study is an act of cultural retrieval that alters the literary map of the twentieth century, challenging received assumptions of a stagnant intellectual scene

1 "JOTTINGS by M.A.T.", *The Dublin Evening Mail*, November 26, 1958.

and a decidedly male-oriented literary field. It reveals surprising and compelling insights into book culture that still remain under-researched, and opens the way for future scholarship in the area of Irish women's cultural networks and print histories of the period.

The reconstruction of the history of the Women Writers' Club through the prism of a book history approach has educed significant insights into literary life and to the wider intellectual history of the period. As a paradigm for interrogating print culture per se, it also opens up the field of literary studies to new ways of examining the role of collaborative networks and connections in cultural production, and a blueprint for the act of archival excavation. Examining the trajectory of the book from writer to reader renders the period in a new light, incorporating elements of a narrative that might otherwise be overlooked or ignored. Darnton's communication circuit is useful for an approach that needs to "envision the field as a whole", since in doing so, associations between salon culture, public events, private printing presses, book fairs, literary prizes, symposiums, club memoranda and newspaper reports can be more accurately identified and new histories of the period gleaned.

Over time the Women Writers' Club evolved to become a significant participant and contributor to the development and promotion of Irish literature and to carve out a specific space for the female writer. Its members' novels are heavily invested in highlighting the realities of women's lives in the new nation state and informing the reader of the key role of women in the revolutionary struggle. For many, the conflation of art and politics molded their intellectual stance. They agitated as a powerful collective, lobbying on behalf of the professional women writer, demanding their equal rights to participate as full Irish citizens in the public sphere. The alliance of the Women Writers' Club with various feminist networks represents a new way of thinking about women writers of the period. On one hand, the focus of this cultural group suggests a band of literary women dedicated to the rise of the professional woman; on the other, the women's group commitment to political issues and affiliations with dissident groups was at loggerheads with conventional, discriminatory officialdom. Certainly, the group was ahead of its time in many ways, and the members vouchsafed a shared understanding of the manifest relationship between consumption and book production, the advantageous utility of influential networks and connections and the reputational and financial need for visibility in the public sphere. Their real power may be attributed to their own supportive sorority, and their external links to power centers in government, media and academia. On a world stage, they joined other international grassroots feminist groups to advance emancipatory agendas such as women's rights to contraception, divorce and the right "to earn a living". Their shrewd and meaningful participation in contemporary international relations, particularly that of post-war Europe and South America, was applauded and thoroughly documented in the media reports of the period. In the political field they allied with other women's reform groups to debate the Draft Constitution of 1937, thereby reminding the patriarchal officialdom of the new nation state of Irish women's enduring support and heroic contributions to the new state's formulation, and of the pre-eminence of an intellectual female presence in public life.

In many ways, these women fashioned a writing lifestyle that mirrored those of other European capitals. As for their continental counterparts, the social opportunities afforded by Annual Banquets, poetry readings, café culture and "at homes" events were intrinsic to their success in marketing their writings and were fostered through sympathetic networks and reviews, positive recommendations and intelligent media relations. Furthermore, their involvement in theatrical circles as both playwrights and drama critics, together with a particularly Irish iteration of bohemianism, forged a Dublin metropolis that served as a creative hotbed for new ideas to be formed and tried out. Ready access to centers of influence was crucial for the dissemination of texts and the cultivation of publishing networks, while the Women Writers' Club's astute grasp of the overall book business ensured that any opportunity to promote their works was seized and exploited. This included cross-membership of the internationally minded Irish PEN and high-profile representation at important events such as the Irish Book Fair of 1941, the Post-Fair debate, the International Congress of 1953 and the annual Book of the Year literary awards.

The corpus of book celebrated by the Book of the Year prize presents an alternative canon to the predominantly male-authored works that survive in Irish anthologies and literary histories of the time. As such, it denotes a specific feminist sensibility; and one that ardently championed autonomy, independence and equality for women. In groundbreaking depictions of women's inner and outer worlds, the socially engaged poetry of central figures such as Blanaid Salkeld and Temple Lane openly critiqued patriarchy and the unfettered intrusiveness of the Church; the works of politicized women including Nora Connolly O'Brien, Rosamond Jacob and Edna Fitzhenry questioned grand narratives and commemorated and extolled the sacrifices of nationalist women and their families; while the dramas of playwright Teresa Deevy fashioned a veritable throng of non-conformist female characters who consistently rebelled against Irish cultural mores and the proscriptions of their lives. These thematic concerns form the basis from which a philosophical ethos can be extrapolated. Moreover, since literary prizes were held to confer status on quality writers, the Book of the Year was instigated to award writers whose merit had been proven. During their lifetime, award recipients including Kate O'Brien, Elizabeth Bowen, Helen Waddell, Dorothy Macardle and Patricia Lynch, achieved a high degree of international literary fame. Perhaps more importantly, their various corpuses of work have endured, and remain printed, read, performed, debated and studied to this day. Archival research sheds new light on the role of the Gayfield Press in fostering the publishing careers of young poets such as Wingfield and Milne, and hints at the shifting tides of the avant-garde as writers increasingly looked to Europe for inspiration. Blanaid Salkeld's role in shaping literary modernism in Ireland is now widely acknowledged and her role as a female publisher is of increasing relevance to scholars of literature and history, and to those interested in feminist print culture. Similarly, the burgeoning renaissance of the plays of Teresa Deevy, spearheaded by a New York production of *Wife to James Whelan* in the Mint Theatre in 2010, highlights a growing interest in women playwrights of the era, whose presence has long been occluded in popular history; and Helen Waddell's inspirational *Desert Fathers* is still in print, more than eighty years on, warranting more investigation. Pioneering biographical and historical investigation into Irish cultural history continues to re-evaluate the history of women's writing and opens up new possibilities for thinking about women writers. This book begins the conversation about how we can conceptualize Irish women writers as central participants in the intellectual public sphere, then, and now, and appreciate the web of interrelationship that connect writers with their reading public.

That the Women Writers' Club was a formidable band of women is indisputable, but they did not have an easy time. Against the backdrop of reactionary and discriminatory employment legislation and censorious repression, they pressed ahead in the spirit of solidarity to cultivate supportive and enterprising female networks. While the reasons for the ultimate demise of the group is unclear, it is possible to speculate. By 1960, many of the prominent women involved in the establishment of the Club had passed away; including the formidable founding member, Blanaid Salkeld. External attention had also begun to shift into area of human rights and civil liberties, with the Irish PEN leading the way. In addition, the new world that had opened up post-war enabled a younger generation of women writers such as Edna O'Brien and Mary Lavin to emerge on the scene. While questions could be raised about the exclusion of certain cohorts of women writers, that is for another time. Doubtless, further investigations will reveal more fascinating details of the writing efforts and ethos of Irish women of the period. In the meantime, it is clear that the contribution of female coterie culture to literary life in the mid-twentieth century is beyond dispute.

Their work lives on in the libraries and bookshelves of private collectors, and in the rich argosy of material in the archives of the National Library of Ireland. New histories of the book remain for future scholarship. Our role as narrators is to contribute to this story, following in the footsteps of the redoubtable Kate O'Brien, who once hopefully entrusted to the future women writers of Ireland: "it may be, if we are careful, if we made notes, if we wrote books, that some vestige of the dust we raised might prove to gleam a little for the dustmen who follow us."[2]

---

2 Kate O'Brien, "As to University Life", *University Review*, 1.6 (1955).

Bibliography

Adams, Thomas and Barker, Nicolas, "A New Model for the Study of the Book", in D. Finkelstein, and A. McCleery (eds), *The Book History Reader*, 2nd edn (London: Routledge 2006).
Allen, Nicholas, "Cabaret, Sex and Independence: Publishing in the Early Free State", in M. Fanning and R. Gillespie (eds), *Print Culture and Intellectual Life in Ireland, 1660–1941* (Dublin: Woodfield Press, 2006), pp.186–205.
Allen, Nicholas, *Modernism, Ireland and Civil War* (Cambridge: Cambridge University Press, 2009).
Allen, Nicholas, "Reading Revolutions, 1922–39", in C. Hutton and P. Walsh (eds), *The Oxford History of the Irish Book, Volume V: The Irish Book in English, 1891–2000* (Oxford: Oxford University Press 2011), pp.89–107.
Allen, Nicholas, and Brown, Terence, "Publishing after Partition, 1922–39", in C. Hutton and P. Walsh (eds), *The Oxford History of the Irish Book, Volume V: The Irish Book in English, 1891–2000* (Oxford: Oxford University Press, 2011), pp.70–88.
Allen, W. G., "The Shires, the Suburbs and the Latin Quarter, Ryder versus Sable", *The Irish Monthly*, 76.900 (1948), pp.260–264.
Anon, "Processional", *Motley*, 1.5 (1932), pp.6–7.
Anon, "Bibliography", *Journal of Modern History*, 8.2 (1936), pp.234–272.
Anon, "What Dublin is Reading", *The Irish Times*, March 6, 1937.
Anon, "The Studio", *Trinity News*, May 10, 1956.
Austin Clarke Papers, MS 83, MSS 38,651–38,708, National Library of Ireland.
B. O. C., *Portrait of a Rebel Father* by Nora Connolly O'Brien, reviewed in *The Irish Monthly*, 64.753 (1936), pp.210–211.
Beaumont, Caitriona, "Women, Citizenship and Catholicism in the Irish Free State, 1922–1948", *Women's History Review*, 6.4 (1997), pp.563–585.

Beaumont, Caitriona, "Gender, Citizenship and the State in Ireland, 1922–1990", in S. Brewster, V. Crossman, F. Becket and D. Alderson (eds), *Ireland in Proximity: History, Gender, Space* (London: Routledge, 1999), pp.94–108.

Behan, Beatrice, *My Life with Brendan* (London: Leslie Frewin, 1973).

Binckes, F. and Laing, K. "A Vagabond's Scrutiny: Hannah Lynch in Europe", in E. D'hoker, R. Ingelbien and H. Schwall (eds), Irish Women Writers: New Critical Perspectives (Bern: Peter Lang, 2011).

Bornstein, George, *Material Modernism: The Politics of the Page* (Cambridge: Cambridge University Press, 2001).

Bowen, Elizabeth, *The Death of the Heart* (London: Jonathan Cape, 1938).

Boylan, Patricia, *All Cultivated People: A History of The Arts Club* (Dublin, Buckinghamshire: Colin Smythe, Ltd, 1988).

Brady, Deirdre F., *Suffragists, New Woman and Nationalists: Representations of Feminism in the Novels of Rosamond Jacob*, unpublished MA thesis (2007), University of Limerick.

Brady, Deirdre F., "Modernist Presses and the Gayfield Press", *Bibliologia*, 9 (2014), pp.113–128.

Brady, Deirdre F., "Writers and the International Spirit: Irish PEN in the Post-war Years", *New Hibernia Review*, 21.3 (2017), pp.116–130.

Brady, Deirdre F., "The Road to Cuzco: An Irish woman writer's journey to the 'navel of the world'", *Irish Migration Studies in Latin America*, 9.1 (2018), pp.11–24.

Brown, S. J., "Ireland in Books 1944", *The Irish Monthly*, 73.861 (1944), pp.97–98.

Brown, Terence, *Ireland: A Social and Cultural History 1922–2001* (London: Harper Perennial, 2004).

Carlson Julia, *Banned in Ireland: Censorship & the Irish Writer* (London: Routledge, 1990).

Carson, Niall and Hoey, Paddy, "The Bell and the Blanket: Journals of Republican Dissent", *New Hibernia Review*, 16.1 (2012), pp.73–93.

Chapman, Ian, "The Book Business: Art, Craft and Trade", *Journal of the Royal Society of Arts*, 132.5335 (1984), pp.460–470.

Cheavasa, Moirin, *The Fall of the Year: Collected Poems* (Dublin: Gayfield Press, 1940).

Clay, Catherine, *British Women Writers 1914–1945: Professional Work and Friendship* (Hampshire: Ashgate Publishing Limited, 2006).

Clear, Caitriona, "'I Can Talk About It, Can't I?': The Ireland Maura Laverty Desired, 1942–46", *Women's Studies*, 30.6 (2001), pp.819–835.

Clear, Caitriona, "'The Red Ink of Emotion': Maura Laverty, women's work and Irish society in the 1940s", *Saothar*, 28 (2003), pp.90–97.

Cleary, Joe, "Irish American Modernisms", in J. Cleary (ed.), *Cambridge Companion to Irish Modernism* (Cambridge: Cambridge University Press, 2014).

Cochrane, Terry, "Culture against the State", *boundary 2* (1990), pp.1–68.
Coleman, Ann, "Far from Silent: Nineteenth-Century Irish Women Writers", in N. Kelleher and J. Murphy (eds), *Gender Perspectives in 19th Century Ireland* (Dublin: Irish Academic Press, 1997), pp.203–212.
Collins, Liam, "Jammet's Restaurant: French Revolution", *Sunday Independent*, available at www.independent.ie/life/food-drink/jammets-restaurant-french-revolution-26733154.html.
Collins, Lucy, *Poetry by Women in Ireland: A Critical Anthology 1870–1970* (Liverpool: Liverpool University Press, 2012).
Company Registrations Office, *Business Name Printout, 19770* (Dublin: Stationery Office, 2013).
Connolly O'Brien, Nora, *Portrait of a Rebel Father* (Dublin: Talbot Press, 1935).
Cott, Nancy, *The Grounding of Modern Feminism* (New Haven: Yale University Press, 1987).
Coulter, Riann, "Hibernian Salon des Refusés", *Irish Arts Review*, 20.3 (2003), pp.80–85.
Cowell, John, *No Profit but the Name: The Longfords and the Gate Theatre* (Dublin: O'Brien Press, 1988).
Cronin, Michael, "Projecting the Nation through Sport and Culture: Ireland, Aonach Tailteann and the Irish Free State, 1924–32", *Journal of Contemporary History*, 38.3 (2003), pp.395–411.
Cronin, Michael, "Kate O'Brien and the Erotics of Liberal Catholic Dissent", *Field Day Review*, 6 (2010), pp.28–51.
Cuala Press Archives, Trinity College Dublin, MS 11535.
Cullen, Louis M., *Eason & Son: A History* (Dublin: Eason's, 1989).
Cullingford, Elizabeth E., *Gender and History in Yeats's Love Poetry* (New York: Syracuse University Press, 1996).
Dargan, Ena, *The Road to Cuzco: A Journey from Argentina to Peru* (London: Andrew Melrose Limited, 1950).
Dargan, Ena, *San Martin the Liberator* by J. C. J. Metford, reviewed in *An Irish Quarterly Review*, 40.157 (1951), pp.112–113.
Darnton, Robert, "What is the History of Books?", in D. Finkelstein and A. McCleery (eds), *The Book History Reader*, 2nd edn (London: Routledge, 2006).
Darnton, Robert, "What is the History of Books? Revisited", *Modern Intellectual History*, 4.3 (2007), pp.495–508.
Deane, Seamus, *A Short History of Irish Literature* (London: Hutchinson, 1986).
Department of the Taoiseach Files (1922–1979), S9880, National Archives of Ireland.
Documentary on One, Radio One, June 17, 1400 hrs (2011).
Dowling, Robert M., *Eugene O'Neill: A Literary Reference to his Life and Work* (New York: Facts on File Inc., 2009).

Doyle, Damien, "A Bio-Critical Study of Rosamond Jacob and her Contemporaries", unpublished PhD thesis (2002), Univeristy of Colorado.

Dunne, John, "The Educational Company of Ireland and the Talbot Press, 1910–1990", *Long Room: Ireland's Journal for the History of the Book*, 42.34–4 (1997), MS35,134, National Library of Ireland.

Ecclesine, Marcella, *Once Upon a Time ... Being Stories about a Fierce Ogre and a small Boy, and a Little Princess and a tiny Bird* (Dublin: Gayfield Press, circa 1938).

Eggert, Paul, *Work and the Reader in Literary Studies* (Cambridge: Cambridge University Press, 2019).

Ellmann, Maud, "Shadowing Elizabeth Bowen", *New England Review*, 24.1 (2003), pp.144–163.

Fallon, Brian, *An Age of Innocence: Irish Culture 1930–1960* (London: Palgrave Macmillan, 1998).

Farmer, Tony, "An Eye to Business, Financial and Market Factors, 1895–1995", in C. Hutton and P. Walsh (eds), *The Oxford History of the Irish Book, Volume V: The Irish Book in English, 1891–2000* (Oxford: Oxford University Press, 2011), pp.209–243.

Ferriter, Diarmaid, *Judging Dev* (Dublin: Royal Irish Academy, 2007).

Finkelstein, David and McCleery, Alistair, *The Book History Reader* (London: Routledge, 2002).

Fitzgerald, Fergus N., *Sennet for Coriolan: A Chorus for Six Voices* (Dublin: Gayfield Press, 1941).

Fitzhenry, Edna (comp.), *Nineteen-Sixteen: An Anthology* (Dublin: Browne & Nolan, 1935).

Fitzhenry, Edna, *Henry Joy McCracken* (Dublin: Talbot Press, 1936).

Fogarty, Anne, "'The Influence of Absences': Eavan Boland the Silenced History of Irish Women's Poetry", *Colby Quarterly*, 35.4 (1999), pp.256–274.

Foster, John Wilson, *Irish Novels 1890–1940: New Bearings in Culture and Fiction* (Oxford: Oxford University Press, 2008).

Foster, Roy F., *W. B. Yeats: A Life* (Oxford: Oxford University Press, 2003).

Gardiner, David, "The Other Irish Renaissance: The Maunsel Poets", *New Hibernia Review/Irish Éireannach Nua*, 8.1 (2004), pp.54–79.

Gould, Warwick, "Macmillan's Irish List, 1899–1968", in C. Hutton and P. Walsh (eds), *The Oxford History of the Irish Book: Volume V: The Irish Book in English, 1891–2000* (Oxford: Oxford University Press, 2011), pp.481–510.

Gwynn, Stephen, *Irish Literature and Drama in the English Language: A Short History* (London: Thomas Nelson, 1936).

Hanscombe, Gillian and Smyers, Virginia, *Writing for their Lives: The Modernist Women 1910–1940* (London: The Women's Press, 1987).

Hobson, Bulmer (ed.), *The Gate Theatre Book* (Dublin: Gate Theatre 1934).
Huff, Cynthia, "Reading as Revision, Approaches to Reading Manuscript Diaries", *Biography*, 23.3 (2000), pp.505–523.
Humble, Nicola, "Sitting Forward or Sitting Back: Highbrow v. Middlebrow Reading", *Modernist Cultures*, 6.1 (2011), pp.41–59.
Hutton, Clare (ed.), *The Irish Book in the Twentieth Century* (Dublin: Irish Academic Press, 2004).
Hutton, Clare, "'Yogibogeybox in Dawson Chamber': The Beginnings of Maunsel and Company", in C. Hutton (ed.), *The Irish Book in the Twentieth Century* (Dublin: Irish Academic Press, 2004), pp.36–46.
Hutton, Clare and Walsh, Patrick (eds). *The Oxford History of the Irish Book, Volume V: The Irish Book in English, 1891–2000* (Oxford: Oxford University Press, 2011).
Ingman, Heather, *Irish Women's Fiction: From Edgeworth to Enright* (Dublin: Irish Academic Press, 2013).
Ingman, Heather and Ó Gallchoir, Clíona (eds), *A History of Modern Irish Women's Literature* (Cambridge: Cambridge University Press 2018).
Ireland, Denis (1894-1974): Writer and broadcaster, available at www.newulsterbiography.co.uk/index.php/home/viewPerson/734.
Ireland, Denis, "Scenes from Irish Life: 1941–46", *Dubliner Magazine*, 5 (September–October) (1962), pp.30–31.
Irish Academy of Letters, MS 39, MSS 33,745–33,746, National Library of Ireland.
Irish PEN, *Defending the Freedom of Writers and Readers*, available at www.irishpen.com/the-irish-pen-committee/.
Irish P.E.N. Papers, 1935–2004, National Library of Ireland, Dublin PEN Centre minute books, 1935–2004, MSS 49,143–49,144.
Irish Times Digital Archive, available at www.irishtimes.com/archive.
Jacob, Rosamond, *The Troubled House: A Novel of Dublin in the Twenties* (Dublin: Browne & Nolan, 1938).
Jacob, Rosamond, *The Rebel's Wife* (Tralee: The Kerryman, 1957).
Johns, Adrian, "The Book of Nature and the Nature of the Book", in David Finkelstein and Alistair McCleery (eds), *The Book History Reader*, 2nd edn (London: Routledge, 2006), pp.255–272.
"JOTTINGS by M.A.T.", *Dublin Evening Mail*, November 26, 1958.
Kelly, A. A., "Irish Women Travel Writers: An Overview", *Linen Hall Review*, 10.1 (1993), pp.4–8.
Kennedy, Brian P., *Dreams and Responsibilities: The State and the Arts in Independent Ireland* (Dublin: Criterion Press, 1998).
Kennedy, Róisín, "Experimentalism or Mere Chaos? The White Stag Group and the Reception of Subjective Art in Ireland", in E. Keown and C. Taaffe (eds), *Irish Modernism: Origins, Contexts, Publics* (Oxford: Peter Lang, 2010), pp.179–194.

Kennedy, S. B., *Irish Art and Modernism, 1880–1950* (Belfast: Institute of Irish Studies, 1991).
Kennedy, S. B., "An Incisive Aesthetic", *Irish Arts Review*, 21.2 (2002), pp.90–95.
Kent, Brad, "The Banning of George Bernard Shaw's 'The Adventures of the Black Girl in Her Search for God' and the Decline of the Irish Academy of Letters", *Irish University Review*, 38.2 (2008), pp.274–291.
Klaus, Gustav H., "'The Sore Frailty of This Lasting Cause': Some Celtic Versions of Spanish Civil War Poetry", *Irish University Review*, 21.2 (1991), pp.268–284.
Kirwan, Kathleen, *Towards Irish Nationalism: A Tract* (Dublin: Gayfield Press, 1938).
L. K., *The Trains Go South* by Temple Lane, reviewed in *The Irish Monthly*, 67.787 (1939), p.70.
Laird, Heather, "The 'Placing' and Politics of Bowen in Contemporary Irish Literary and Cultural Criticism", in E. Walshe (ed.), *Irish Writers in their Time: Elizabeth Bowen* (Dublin: Irish Academic Press 2009), pp.193–207.
Lane, Leeann, "'In my mind I build a house': The Quest for Family in the Children's Fiction of Patricia Lynch", *Éire-Ireland*, 44 (2009), pp.169–193.
Lane, Leeann, *Rosamond Jacob: Third Person Singular* (Dublin: University College Dublin, 2010).
Lane, Leeann, *Dorothy Macardle* (Dublin: University College Dublin, 2019).
Lane, Temple, *Fisherman's Wake* (Dublin: Talbot Press, 1940).
Lane, Temple, "The Dramatic Art of Teresa Deevy", *The Dublin Magazine*, XXI.4 (1946), pp.35–24.
Laverty, Maura, *Alone We Embark* (New York: Longmans, Green and Co., 1943).
Laverty, Maura, *Cookbook* (London: Longmans, Green and Co., 1947).
Le Brocquy Papers, MS 24,232, National Library of Ireland.
Lee, Joseph, *Ireland 1912–1985* (Cambridge: Cambridge University Press, 1989).
Lewis, Gifford, *The Yeats Sisters and The Cuala* (Dublin: Irish Academic Press, 1994).
Lewis, Pericles, *Cambridge Introduction to Modernism* (Cambridge: Cambridge University Press, 2007).
Little, P. J., "German reception for PEN", *Irish Independent*, June 13, 1953.
Lomis, Grant, *The Desert Fathers, Translations from the Latin with an introduction by Helen Waddell*, reviewed in *Speculum*, 12.2 (1937), pp.277–278.
Longford, Christine, *Printed Cotton* (London: Methuen, 1935).
Longford, Christine, *A Sleep of Prisoners* by Christopher Fry, *The Helen of Euripides*, translated by Rex Warner and *Antigone and Eurydice* by Jean Anouilh, reviewed in *The Dublin Magazine*, xvii.8 (1951), pp.68–72 (IR 05 b 6, National Library of Ireland).

Luddy, Maria, "A 'Sinister and Retrogressive' Proposal: Irish Women's Opposition to the 1937 Draft Constitution", *Transactions of the Royal Historical Society*, 15 (2005), pp.175–195.

Luddy, Maria, "Sex and the Single Girl in 1920s and 1930s Ireland", *Irish Review*, 35 (2007), pp.79–91.

Lynch, Patricia, *The Turf-cutter's Children* (London: J. M. Dent & Sons, Ltd, 1934).

Lynch, Patricia, *Fiddler's Quest* (London: J. M. Dent & Sons, Ltd, 1941).

Lynch, Patricia, Staunton, Helen and Deevy, Teresa, *Lisheen at the Valley Farm and Other Stories* (Dublin: Gayfield Press 1946).

Macardle, Dorothy, *The Irish Republic* (London: Victor Gollancz, 1938).

MacCarthy, Bridget G., *Women Writers: Their Contribution to the English Novel 1621–1744* (Cork: Cork University Press, 1944).

MacCarthy, Bridget G., *The Female Pen: Women Writers and Novelists, 1621–1818* (Cork: Cork University Press, 1994).

MacCurtain, Margaret, "Poetry of the Spirit, 1900–95, Blanaid Salkeld (1880–1959)", in A. Bourke, S. Kilfeather, M, Luddy, M. MacCurtain, G. Meaney, M. Ni Dhonnchadha, M. O'Dowd, and C. Wills (eds), *The Field Day Anthology of Irish Writing: Irish Women's Writing and Traditions, Volume IV* (New York: New York University Press, 2002), pp.624–625.

Macken, M., *Never No More* by Maura Laverty, reviewed in *Studies: An Irish Quarterly Review*, 31.132 (1942), p.393.

Macken, M. M., *The Road to Cuzco* by Ena Dargan, reviewed in *An Irish Quarterly Review*, 39.154 (1950), pp.232–233.

Mahon, Derek, "MacNeice, the War and the BBC", *Studies on Louis MacNeice*, in J. Genet and W. Hellegouarc'h (eds), *Studies on Louis MacNeice* (Caen: centre de publications de l'Université de Caen, 1988), pp.63–77.

Mannin, Ethel, *Late Have I Loved Thee* (London: Jarrolds Publishers, Ltd, 1948).

Mansergh, Nicholas, "The Irish Republic: A Documented Chronicle of the Anglo-Irish Conflict and the Partitioning of Ireland, with a Detailed Account of the Period 1916–1923" by D. Macardle, reviewed in *International Journal*, 21.3 (1966), pp.390–391.

Mathew O'Mahony Papers, MS 24,900, National Library of Ireland.

Matthews, Kelly, *The Bell Magazine and Representations of Irish Identity* (Dublin: Four Courts Press, Ltd K., 2012).

Maurice Walsh Papers, P/7, 4 (d) Correspondence (1932–1940), *Literary organisations (1938–1940)*, Special Collections, University of Limerick.

MacLysaght, Edward, unpublished memoirs, "Master of None", MS 41,750, National Library of Ireland.

McCleery, Alistair, "The Return of the Publisher to Book History: The Case of Allen Lane", *Book History*, V (2002), pp.161–185.

McCormack, W. J., "Irish Censorship: Some Uncomfortable Revisions", in C. Hutton (ed.), *The Irish Book in the Twentieth Century* (Dublin: Irish Academic Press, 2004).

McDonald, Rónán, "'Anything about Ireland?': Reading in Ireland, 1969–2000", in C. Hutton and P. Walsh (eds), *The Oxford History of the Irish Book, Volume V: The Irish Book in English, 1891–2000* (Oxford: Oxford University Press, 2011), pp.180–208.

McFayden, Donald, *Vespasian and Some of His Contemporaries* by Christine Longford, reviewed in *The Classical Journal*, 24.8 (1929), pp.617–618.

McGarry, Fearghal. "Irish Newspapers and the Spanish Civil War", *Irish Historical Studies*, 33.129 (2002), pp.68–90.

McKenzie, Donald F., "History of the Book", in P. Davison (ed.), *The Book Encompassed: Studies in Twentieth Century Bibliography* (Cambridge: Cambridge University Press, 1992), pp.290–301.

McNeill, Josephine, Papers of Josephine McNeill, P234, Descriptive Catalogue, UCD Archives (Dublin: University College Dublin, 2009).

Meaney, Gerardine, "Regendering Modernism: The Woman Artist in Irish Women's Fiction", *Women: A Cultural Review*, 15.1 (2004), pp.67–82.

Meaney, Gerardine, *Gender, Ireland, and Cultural Change: Race, Sex and Nation* (London: Routledge, 2010).

Meaney, Gerardine, "Fiction, 1922–1960", in H. Ingman and C. Ó Gallchoir (eds), *A History of Modern Irish Women's Literature* (Cambridge: Cambridge University Press 2018), pp.187–203.

Meaney, Gerardine, O'Dowd, Mary and Whelan, Bernadette *Reading the Irish Woman: Studies in Cultural Encounter and Exchange, 1714–1960* (Liverpool: Liverpool University Press, 2013).

Miller, Carol, "'Geneva – the key to equality': Inter-war Feminists and the League of Nations", *Women's History Review*, 3.2 (1994), pp.219–245.

Milne, Ewart, *Forty North Fifty West* (Dublin: Gayfield Press, 1938).

Mitchell, Geraldine, *Deeds Not Words: The Life and Work of Muriel Gahan* (Dublin: Townhouse, 1997).

Mentxaka, Aintzane L., "Orpheo, Eurydice, and Co.", *SQS Journal of Queer Studies in Finland*, 2 (2006), pp.116–121.

Mentxaka, Aintzane L., *Kate O'Brien and the Fiction of Identity: Sex, Art and Politics in "Mary Lavelle" and other Writings* (North Carolina: McFarland, 2011).

Morash, Chris, "Irish Theatre", in J. Cleary and C. Connolly (eds)., *The Cambridge Companion to Modern Irish Culture* (Cambridge: Cambridge University Press, 2005), pp.322–338.

Motley (1932–1934), MS 2H70 IR 391941, National Library of Ireland.

Mulhall, Anne, "'The well-known, old, but still unbeaten track': Women Poets and Irish Periodical Culture in the Mid-Twentieth Century", *Irish University Review*, 42.1 (2012), pp.32–52.

Murray, Simone, "'Books of Integrity' The Women's Press, Kitchen Table Press and Dilemmas of Feminist Publishing", *European Journal of Women's Studies*, 5.2 (1998), pp.171–193.

Murray, Simone, "The Cuala Press: Women, publishing, and the conflicted genealogies of feminist publishing", *Women Studies International Forum*, 27 (2004), pp.489–506.

Murray, Simone, "'Where Did Your Adaptation Begin?': Book Fairs, Screen Festivals and Writers' Weeks as Engine-rooms of Adaptation", in P. Nicklas and O. Lindner (eds), *Adaptation and Cultural Appropriation: Literature, Film, and the Arts* (Berlin: De Gruyter 2012), pp.57–69.

N. A., *Concord of Harp: An Irish PEN Anthology of Poetry* (Dublin: Talbot Press, 1952).

National Archives of Ireland, Department of the Taoiseach Files (1922–1979), S9880.

Naylor, Gillian, *Bloomsbury: The Artists, Authors and Designers by Themselves* (London: Octopus Publishing Group, 1990).

Neill, Olivia, *The Lost Decade of "Ulster's Darling" Helen Waddell: A Biography* by D. Felicitas Corrigan, reviewed in *Fortnight*, 235, March 10–23 (1986), pp.20–23.

Ní Bheacháin, Caoilfhionn, "'The seeds beneath the snow': Resignation and Resistance in Teresa Deevy's *Wife to James Whelan*", in E. D'hoker, R. Ingelbien and H. Schwall (eds), *Irish Women Writers* (Oxford: Peter Lang, 2011), pp.91–110.

Ní Bheacháin, Caoilfhionn, "Sexuality, Marriage and Women's Life Narratives in Teresa Deevy's *A Disciple* (1931), *The King of Spain's Daughter* (1935) and *Katie Roche* (1936)", *Estudios Irlandeses*, 7 (2012), pp.79–91.

Ní Bheacháin, Caoilfhionn, *The Dun Emer Press*, Modernist Archive Publishing Project (MAPP), available at www.modernistarchives.com/business/the-dun-emer-press.

Ní Bheacháin, Caoilfhionn, "'It was then I knew life': Political Critique and Moral Debate in Teresa Deevy's Temporal Powers (1932)", *Irish University Review*, 50.2 (2020), pp.337–355.

Ó Brien, Gearoid, "Ewart Milne, 1903–1987", *Books Ireland*, 111 (1987), p.34.

Ó Drisceoil, Donal, "'The best banned in the land': Censorship and Irish Writing since 1950", *Yearbook of English Studies*, 35 (2005), pp.146–160.

Ó Faracháin, Róbaird, "Henry Joy McCracken" by Edna Fitzhenry, reviewed in *The Irish Monthly*, 64.761 (1936), pp.781–782.

O'Brien, Kate, *That Lady* (London: William Heinemann, 1946).
O'Brien, Kate, *The Flower of May* (London: William Heinemann, 1953).
O'Brien, Kate, "As to University Life", *University Review*, 1.6 (1955), pp.3–11.
O'Callaghan, Margaret, "Women and Politics in Independent Ireland, 1921–68", in A. Bourke, S. Kilfeather, M. Luddy, M. MacCurtain, G. Meaney, M. Ni Dhonnchadha, M. O'Dowd and C. Wills (eds), *The Field Day Anthology of Irish Writing: Irish Women's Writing and Traditions, Volume IV* (New York: New York University Press, 2002), pp.120–134.
O'Doherty, Martina Ann, "Silver Jubilee Issue: Teresa Deevy and Irish Women Playwrights", *Irish University Review*, 25.1 (1995), pp.163–170.
O'Donnell, Peadar, "And, Again, Publishing in Ireland", *The Bell*, 18.10 (1953), p.581.
O'Faolain, Sean, "The Bell: A Survey of Irish Life", *The Bell*, October 1 (1940).
O'Faolain, Sean, *Vive Moi!: An Autobiography* (London: Sinclair-Stephenson, 1993).
O'Halpin, Eunan, "The Irish Republic" by D. Macardle, reviewed *in Irish Historical Studies*, 31.123 (1999), pp.389–394.
O'Regan, Danae, "Representations and Attitudes of Republican Women in the Novels of Annie M. P. Smithson (1873–1948) and Rosamond Jacob (1888–1960)", in L. Ryan and M. Ward (eds), *Irish Women and Nationalism, Soldiers, New Women and Wicked Hags* (Dublin: Irish Academic Press, 2003), pp.81–95.
Orzoff, Andrea, "Writing Across the Wall: The German PEN Clubs and East–West Dialogue, 1964–1968", *German History*, 33.2 (2015), pp.232–254.
Oxford English Dictionary (2019), Definition of *coterie* in English, available at https://en.oxforddictionaries.com/d'finition/coterie.
Pannell, Jessica L., "'*Teeming Delight*': Irish Poetry 1930–1960, unpublished PhD thesis (2011), University of Pittsburgh.
Papers of Rosamond Jacob MS 30 (1878–1960), MSS 33,107–33,146: MS 32,582, National Library of Ireland.
Papers of Maura Laverty, unsorted, ACC 4607, National Library of Ireland.
Papers of Patricia Lynch and R. M. Fox, MS 79, MSS 34,923–34,931; 40,248–40,419, National Library of Ireland.
Paseta, Senia, "Women and Civil Society: Feminist Responses to the Irish Constitution of 1937", in J. Harris (ed.), *Civil Society in British History: Ideas, Identities, Institutions* (Oxford: Oxford University Press, 2003), pp.213–229.
Perrick, Penny, *Something to Hide: The Life of Sheila Wingfield, Viscountess Powerscourt* (Dublin: Lilliput Press, 2007).

Perriton, Linda, "Forgotten Feminists: The Federation of British Professional and Business Women, 1933–1969", *Women's History Review*, 16.1 (2007), pp.79–97.

Perriton, Linda, "The Education of Women for Citizenship: The National Federation of Women's Institutes and the British Federation of Business and Professional Women 1930–1959", *Gender and Education*, 21.1 (2009), pp, 81–95.

Piesse, Amanda, "Fictionalizing Families", in V. Coughlan and K. O'Sullivan (eds), *Irish Children's Literature and Culture: New Perspectives on Contemporary Writing* (New York: Routledge, 2011), pp.85–98.

Pihl, Liz, "'A Muzzle Made in Ireland': Irish Censorship and Signe Toksvig", *Studies: An Irish Quarterly Review*, 88.352 (1999), pp.448–457.

Pilkington, Lionel, *Theatre and the State in Twentieth Century Ireland: Cultivating the People* (London: Routledge, 2001).

Pomfret, J., *The Rise of the United Irishmen, 1791–94* by Rosamond Jacob, reviewed in *American Historical Review*, 44.1 (1938), pp.108–109.

Potter, Rachel, *Modernism and Democracy: Literary Culture 1900–1930* (Oxford: Oxford University Press, 2006).

Potter, Rachel, "Modernist Rights: International PEN 1921–1936", *Critical Quarterly* 55.2 (2013), pp.66–80.

Pyle, Hillary, *Red-Headed Rebel: Poet and Mystic of the Irish Cultural Renaissance* (Dublin: Woodfield Press, 1998).

Quinn, Justin, *The Cambridge Introduction to Modern Irish Poetry: 1800–2000* (Cambridge: Cambridge University Press, 2008).

Radway, Janice, "A Feeling for Books: The Book-of-the-Month-Club, Literary Taste and Middle-class Desire", in D. Finkelstein and A. McCleery (eds), *The Book History Reader*, 2nd edn (London: Routledge 2006), pp.469–481.

Rainey, Lawrence, "The Cultural Economy of Modernism", in M. Levenson (ed.), *The Cambridge Companion to Modernism*, 6th edn (Cambridge: Cambridge University Press, 2003), pp.33–69.

Redshaw, T. D., "'The Dolmen Poets': Liam Miller and Poetry Publishing in Ireland", 1951–1961, *Irish University Review*, 42 (2012), pp.141–154.

Registrar of Prohibited Publications, 1930–1947, Censorship of Publications Acts, 1929–1967.

Reynolds, Lorna, *Never No More* by Maura Laverty, reviewed in *The Dublin Magazine*, XVII.3 (1942), pp.49–50.

Reynolds, Lorna, "Thirty Years of Irish Letters", *Studies: An Irish Quarterly Review*, 40.160 (1951), pp.457–468.

Reynolds, Lorna, "The Orphic Eschatology of the Monuments in Calabria", *University Review*, 1.9 (1956), pp.19–27.

Reynolds, Lorna, *Kate O'Brien: A Literary Portrait* (Buckinghamshire: Colin Smythe, Ltd, 1987).

Richardson, Caleb, "'They are not worthy of themselves': The Tailor and Ansty Debates of 1942", *Éire-Ireland*, 42.3/4 (2007), pp.148–172.

Roberts, Henry L., "Recent Books on International Relations", in *Foreign Affairs: An American Quarterly Review*, 29.104 (1951), p.335.

Rose, Jonathan, *The Intellectual Life of the British Working Classes* (New Haven: Yale University Press, 2001).

Russell, Elizabeth, "Holy crosses, guns and roses: themes in popular reading material", in J. Augustine (ed.), *Ireland in the 1930s: New Perspectives* (Dublin: Four Courts Press, 1999).

Ryan, John, *Remembering How We Stood: Bohemian Dublin at the Mid-century* (Dublin: Gill and Macmillan, 1975).

Ryan, Louise, "Leaving Home: Irish Press debates about female employment, domesticity and emigration to Britain in the 1930s", *Women's History Review*, 12.3 (2003), pp.387–406.

Ryan, Louise, "Constructing 'Irishwoman': Modern Girls and Comely Maidens", *Irish Studies Review*, 6.3 (1998), pp.263-272.

Ryan, Louise, *Gender, Identity and The Irish Press 1922–1937: Embodying the Nation* (New York: Edwin Mellen Press, 2002).

Saddlemyer, Ann, "The Creation of a Literary Industry", *Éire-Ireland*, 35.3/4 (Fall/Winter) (2000/2001), pp.34–47.

Salkeld, Blanaid, "Anna Akhmatova", *The Dublin Magazine*, VIII.4 (1933), pp.51–55.

Salkeld, Blanaid, "Footnote on Mutability", *Motley*, 11 (1933), p.6.

Salkeld, Blanaid, "Letters and Poems, 1936–1937", MS 1978-0127R VF Lit, Special Collections 104, Paterno Vault, PENN State University.

Salkeld, Blanaid, *... the engine is left running* (Dublin: Gayfield Press 1937).

Salkeld, Blanaid, "Dialogue about love, poetry and government service", translated by Blanaid Salkeld, *The Dublin Magazine*, XXII.2 (1947), pp.18–27.

Salkeld, Blanaid, *The Flowering Shamrock* by Sheila Pim, reviewed in *Irish Writing*, 8.94 (1949).

Salkeld, Blanaid, *Seventy Cantos*, poems by E. Pound reviewed in *The Dublin Magazine*, 13 (1950), pp.61–64.

Salkeld, Blanaid, *Ciumhní Cinn* by Liam Ó Briain, reviewed in *Irish Writing*, 17 (1951), pp.65–67.

Salkeld, Blanaid, *Ceo Meala lá Seaca* by Micheál Mac Liammóir, and *Nuascéalaíocht* edited by Tomás de Bhaldraithe, reviewed in *Irish Writing*, 22 (1953), p.72.

Schreibman, Susan, "Irish Women Poets 1929–1959: Some Foremothers", *Colby Quarterly*, 37.4 (2001), pp.309–326.

Sheehy Skeffington, Andrée, *Skeff: A Life of Owen Sheehy Skeffington 1909–1970* (Dublin: Lilliput Press, 1991).

Sheehy Skeffington Papers, MS 47, MSS 33,603–33,635, National Library of Ireland.
Sheehy Skeffington Papers (Additional), MS 82, MSS 40,460–40,563; 41,176–41,245, National Library of Ireland.
Sheila Wingfield Papers, MS 107, MSS 29,047–29,062; 25,559–25,616, National Library of Ireland.
Shovlin, Frank, *The Irish Literary Periodical 1923–1958* (Oxford: Clarendon Press, 2003).
Shovlin, Frank, "From Tucson to Television: Irish Reading, 1939–69", in C. Hutton and P. Walsh (eds), *The Oxford History of the Irish Book, Volume V: The Irish Book in English, 1891–2000* (Oxford: Oxford University Press, 2011), pp.129–148.
Showalter, Elaine, *A Jury of Her Peers: American Women Writers from Anne Bradstreet to Annie Proulx* (London: Virago Press, 2009).
Skelton, Robin, "Twentieth-century Irish Literature and the Private Press Tradition: Dun Emer, Cuala and the Dolmen Presses 1902–1963", *Massachusetts Review*, 5.2 (Winter) (1964), pp.368–377.
Smith, Michael, "Thomas Kinsella in interview with Michael Smith", *Poetry Ireland Review*, 75 (Winter) (2002/2003), pp.108–119.
Smith, Nadia, *Dorothy Macardle: A Life* (Dublin: Woodfield Press 2007).
Steele, Karen, *Women, Press, and Politics during the Irish Revival* (Syracuse: Syracuse University Press, 2007).
Stewart, Bruce, "Ricorso, A Knowledge of Irish Literature", MS, Ulster University, available at www.ricorsco.net.
Sullivan, Moynagh, "'The Woman Gardener': Transnationalism, Gender, Sexuality, and the Poetry of Blanaid Salkeld", *Irish University Review*, 42.1 (2012), pp.53–71.
Traub, Valery, *The Renaissance of Lesbianism in Early Modern England* (Cambridge: Cambridge University Press, 2002).
Travis, Trysh, "The Women in Print Movement: History and Implications", *Book History*, 11 (2008), pp.275–300.
Una Troy Papers, MS 56, MSS 35,683–35,699, National Library of Ireland.
Valiulis, Maryann, "The Politics of Gender in the Irish Free State, 1922–1937", *Women's History Review*, 20.4 (2011), pp.569–578.
Waddell, Helen, *The Desert Fathers* (London: Constable, 1936).
Walshe, Eibhear, "Lost Dominions: European Catholicism and Irish Nationalism in the Plays of Teresa Deevy", *Irish University Review*, 25.1 (1995), pp.133–142.
Walshe, Eibhear (ed.), *Selected Plays of Irish Playwright Teresa Deevy, 1894–1963* (New York: Edwin Mellen Press, 2003).
Walshe, Eibhear, *Kate O'Brien: A Writing Life* (Dublin: Irish Academic Press, 2006).

Walshe, Eibhear, "A Time for Hard Writers", in E. Walshe (ed.), *Elizabeth Bowen* (Dublin: Irish Academic Press, 2009).
Ward, Margaret, *Hanna Sheehy Skeffington: A Life* (Dublin: Attic Press, 1997).
Weintraub, Stanley, *Shaw's People: Victoria to Churchill* (Pennsylvania: Pennsylvania University Press, 1996).
Wilford, R. A., "The PEN Club, 1930–50", *Journal of Contemporary History*, 14.1 (1979), pp.99–116.
Wills, Clair, "The Aesthetics of Irish Neutrality during the Second World War", *Boundary*, 2.31.1 (2004), pp.119–145.
Wills, Clair, "Women Writers and the Death of Rural Ireland", *Éire-Ireland*, 41.1&2 (2006), pp.205–209.
Wills, Clair, "Neutrality and Popular Culture", *The Art of Popular Culture: From "The Meeting of the Waters" to Riverdance*, Series 1 [podcast] (2008), available at www.ucd.ie/scholarcast/scholarcast5.html.
Woman's Mirror, May 28, 1932 (IR 05 W2, National Library of Ireland).
Women in Modern Irish Culture database at https://warwick.ac.uk/fac/arts/history/irishwomenwriters/database/#!/people/-340794009, AHRC/University College Dublin/University of Warwick.
Zuelow, Eric G. E., *Making Ireland Irish: Tourism and National Identity Since the Irish Civil War* (Syracuse: Syracuse University Press, 2008), pp.57–58.

Index

Aalto, Alvar 17
the Academy of Letters 15, 18, 23, 24–34, 52, 143
   criticism of membership bias 28–31
   domination of male role 32–34, 56–57
   opposition from Catholic Church 25–27
Adams, Thomas 10, 78
Akhmatova, Anna 86, 134, 155
Alfieri, Vittorio 157
Aligheri, Dante 157
Allen, Nicholas 21n21, 138–139, 140
Allen, W. Gore 119
Ammons, Elizabeth 57
Anderson, Lillian 160
Archdale, Betty 64n44
Arts Club *see* United Dublin Arts Club

Bannard, Madame Daisy "Toto" 20–21
Barker, Nicholas 10, 78
Barrie, J. M. 140
Baxter, Leslie Owen 151, 163
Beckett, Samuel 21, 160
Behan, Brendan 160

Behn, Aphra 74
The Bell 134, 135
Belloc Lowndes, Marie 90
Bennet, Louise 109
Bennett, Louie 62n38, 63, 64–65
Berlin, Isaiah 99
Betjeman, John 101
Binckes, Faith 98
Blok, Alexander 86, 134
Blythe, Ernest 124, 144
Book of the Year 9–10, 19, 34, 68–69, 77–125, 169, 170
Bowen, Elizabeth 7–8, 10–11, 29–30, 33, 38, 70–71, 80, 99–101, 144–145, 170
   Death of the Heart 77, 99–101
   The Heat of the Day 100
   on Irish neutrality 41–42, 43
Boylan, Patricia 19, 21
Brendin Publishing 11
Brown, Stephen J. 131–132, 147
Brown, Terence 40
Browne & Nolan (publishing house) 128, 132, 146
Bryusov, Valery 155
Buchan, John 99
Bullock, Shan 25
Burchell, Mary 140
Byrne, Eithne 63, 79, 80

Campbell, Joseph 48–49
Carney, Frank 88
Carthage Books 145
Cary, Joyce 49
Casement Award 31
Cattaui, Georges 96
Cavanagh, Ernest 5
Cavanagh-MacDowell, Maeve 55, 75, 79, 80
Cecil, David 99
censorship 8, 11, 43–48, 49, 50–51, 115–125
Chamson, Andre 50
Chapman, Ian 150
Cheavasa, Moirin 152, 157
Clark, Lia 55
Clarke, Austin 5, 22, 23, 25, 46, 48–49, 75–76, 82, 93, 144–145, 146, 151, 156, 160, 162, 163
Clear, Caitriona 119–120
Clive, Kitty 56–57n13
Cochrane, Terry 143
Coffee, Brian 164
Coghill, Rhoda 48–49
Cogley's Club 20–21, 123
Cogley's Studio 15–16
Cole, Sophie 140n58
Collins, Lucy 6–7, 80, 133
Colum, Mary 160
Colum, Padraic 22, 23, 24, 25, 32, 48–49, 130, 151, 160, 162, 163
communication theory 4
Connolly, Cyril 99
Connolly, James 80, 95, 105
Connolly O'Brien, Nora 7–8, 63, 79, 80–81, 95, 108, 169–170
Portrait of a Rebel Father 105–106, 116, 132
The Unbroken Tradition 105
Conyers, Dorothy 80–81
Corkery, Daniel 28
Country Store (St Stephen's Green) 16–17, 74

Cowell, John 102
Craig, Maurice J. 163
Crommelin, May, *Over the Andes from Chile to Peru* 96
Cross, Eric, *Tailor and Ansty* 44–45
Cuala Press 127–128n1, 162n52, 164, 165
Cullingford, Elizabeth Butler 33
Cummins, Geraldine 139
Cunard, Nancy 158
Curtayne, Alice 144–145
Curtis, Edmund 144

Dargan, Ena 84, 95–99
The Holy Ghost 95–96
The Road to Cuzco 95–99
Darnton, Robert 3, 143, 168
Davidson, Ethel G. 55n6, 67, 73, 76
political activism 65–66
Davidson, Lilian 35, 59, 62
Dawson Scott, Amy 37
Day, Dorothy (Dora McAuliffe) 37, 75
Day-Lewis, Cecil 31n73, 32, 38, 47n137
De Valera, Eamon 31, 39, 51
drafting of Irish Constitution 62–66
Deevy, Teresa 7–8, 9–10, 33, 63, 75, 84, 114n163, 116, 122–124, 134–135, 152, 157, 160, 169–170
The Disciple 135
Katie Roche 122–123, 124
The King of Spain's Daughter 122–123n201, 124, 135
The Reapers 122
Wife to James Whelan 21, 123, 170
The Wild Goose 122, 124
Despard, Charlotte 112
Devenport O'Neill, Mary 33, 48–49
Devlin, Denis 164
Dickinson, Emily 153
Dolmen Press 159, 164

Donnelly, Charles 158
Dowling, Robert M. 29
The Dublin Magazine 16, 133–134, 135
Dublin Poets and Artists broadsheets 162–165
Dulberg, Ewald 156
Dun Emer Press 127–128n1, 165
Duncan, Ellen 22
Dundealgan Press 145
Dunne, John J. 131
Dunsany, Lord 32

Eason publishers 128, 145
Ecclesine, Marcella 162
  Once Upon a Time 152, 156
Edgeworth, Maria 111
  Selections 131
the Educational Company of Ireland 131–132
Edwards, Hilton 72n88
Eggert, Paul 139, 153
Eliot, T. S. 34, 86, 157, 157–158
Ellerman, Winnifred "Bryher" 11
Ellmann, Maud 100
Ellmann, Richard 22
Elvery, Beatrice 22
English, James 32
Ervine, St John 25
Evans, Edith 39

Fannin publishing 128
Farmer, Tony 128
Farrell, Brian 22
ffrench-Mullen, Madeleine 62n38, 75
Findlay, Arthur 139
Fitzgerald, Desmond 101, 115
Fitzgerald, Fergus N., *Sennet for Coriolan* 151, 152, 157, 162
Fitzgerald, Mabel 101
Fitzhenry, Edna 10, 67n70, 106–108, 112, 169–170
  Henry Joy McCracken 81–82, 89, 105, 106–108, 132
  Nineteen Sixteen: An Anthology 83, 106–108
Fitzmaurice, George, *Country Dressmaker* 85
Fitzsimmons, William 131
Fogarty, Anne 5, 88
Forster, E. M. 101
Foster, Roy F. 28, 119
Fox, R. M. 5, 92
Franks, Cynthia 55
French, Percy 16
Freud, Sigmund 139

Gaffney, Gertrude 37
Gahan, Muriel 16–17n5
Galsworthy, John 38
Gannon, Fr P. J. 25–26, 28
Gardiner, David 130
Gayfield Press 11–12, 20, 67, 73n96, 85–86, 132, 133, 145, 147, 149–162, 170
  poetry broadsheets 162–165
Gibbon, Monk 30
Gill & Macmillan 132
Gleason, Eleanor 127n1
Gogarty, Oliver St John 23, 25, 28, 93n63
Gonne, Iseult 42, 160
Gonne MacBride, Maud 18, 41–42, 112, 117–118, 157, 160
  A Servant of the Queen 71
Greacen, Robert 160, 162, 163
Gregory, Lady Augusta 18, 22, 33, 37, 129
Gregory Medal 31–32
Griffin, Gerald, *The Collegians* 131
Grimshaw, Beatrice, *Strange South Seas* 96
Gunn, Neil 50
Gwynn, Stephen 23, 29–30, 32, 48–49, 129–130

Hackett, Francis 22, 27, 37
Haldane, John 141
Hall, Radclyffe, *The Well of Loneliness* 115
Hanscombe, Gillian 12–13
Harmsworth Award 31
Haugh, Irene 54, 55
Hayden, Professor Mary 62, 68, 108
Hayes, R. J. 144–145
Hays, Mary 107–108
Heard, Gerald 141
Herberts, Jean *see* Lane, Temple
Higgins, F. R. 25, 28
Hinkson, Pamela, *Indian Harvest* 96
Hobson, Bulmer 37, 102
Hogarth Press 11, 160–161, 165
Hone, Evie 47
Hoult, Norah 37, 44, 75
Huff, Cynthia 141
Hughes, Emily 163–164
Hutchinson, Pearse 160
Hutton, Clare 6
Huxley, Aldous 139
  Point Counter Point 115
Hyde, Douglas 28, 32, 37

Ibsen, Henrik, *A Doll's House* 87
ICA (Irish Countrywoman's Association) 16–17n5
Ingman, Heather 6, 104
International PEN 8–9, 36–38
  International Congress (Dublin 1953) 48–52
Ireland, Denis 37, 39–41n113, 42
Irish Academy of Letters 5–6, 8
Irish Book Fair 10–11, 47–48, 68, 143–147, 168
Irish literary scene
  "at homes" 5, 16, 37, 38, 40–41, 47, 73–76, 85, 167, 169
  censorship 8, 11, 43–48, 49, 50–51
  changes after creation of "new state" 15–16, 20–21

coterie and club culture 15–21, 167–171
dichotomy between tradition and modernity 16–17
mid-twentieth-century 1–13
notion of "Irishness" 28–29
relationship with politics and human rights 36–44, 53–54
republican narrative 105–114
seen as cut off from European contemporary intellectualism 8–9
women writers in culture 127–147
Irish PEN 5–6n16, 8–9, 15, 19, 34, 35–48, 52
  International Congress (1953) 48–52, 169
  relationship with politics and human rights 36–44, 51–52
Irish Society for Intellectual Freedom (SIF) 20, 45–46, 112
Irish Women Workers' Union 53, 60, 62
Irish Writing 134, 135
Irvine, John 151, 162, 164

Jacob, Rosamond 5, 6, 10, 11, 19, 20n19, 56, 58, 62, 108–110, 132, 133, 133n26, 146, 169–170
  The House Divided/The Troubled House 82, 83, 95, 105, 108–109, 139
  The Raven's Glen 141–142
  reading lists 138–143
  The Rebel's Wife 58, 70, 74, 109–110, 111, 141–142
  relationships and networks 70, 74, 75n103, 112
  The Rise of the United Irishmen 105, 108–109
  on wartime censorship 43–46
Jameson, Storm 50
Jammet, Louis 18n14

Jammet's Restaurant (Nassau Street) 18n14–19
Jellett, Mainie 17, 47, 62, 68, 83, 163
Johns, Adrian 150–151
Johnston, Denis 22, 41, 72n88, 75–76, 144–145
Jones, Rufus 140
Joyce, James 28, 130–131

Kavanagh, Patrick 23, 73, 160
  The Green Fool 89
Keating, Sean 156
Keats, John 85
Kelly, Anna 54
Kelly, C. E. 75–76
Kelly, Charlie 24n34
Kennedy, Joan 140
Kennedy, S. B. 156
Kent, Brad 26–27
Kettle, Mary Sheehy 55, 62n38, 75
Kiely, Benedict 27, 37
Kingsmill, Hugh 24
Kingston, Lucy 109
Kinsella, Thomas 164
Kirwan, Kathleen 162
  Towards Irish Nationalism 152, 156–157
Koestler, Arthur 50

Laing, Kathryn 98
Lamb, Henry 101
Lane, Allen 149
Lane, Hugh 22
Lane, Leeann 6, 58, 155
Lane, Temple 7–8, 22, 37, 52, 67, 68, 77, 84, 86, 135, 169
  Curlews 88
  Fisherman's Wake 88, 116, 132
  Friday's Well 88
  The Trains Go South 88, 116
Laverty, Maura 7–8, 9–10, 17, 37, 46, 58, 74, 84, 104, 115, 119–122, 124–125

Alone We Embark 68, 71, 115, 121
Lift up our Gates 68
Never No More 115, 135
No More than Human 115n168
Lavin, Mary 33, 73n96, 171
Lawrence, D. H. 139n52
Lawrence, T. E. 29
Le Brocquy, Louis 24, 47, 68, 120, 127
Le Brocquy, Sybil 20n19, 22, 23–24, 43, 47, 55, 62, 120, 122, 152, 157
  relationships and networks 68–70, 74–75, 160
Lensky, Lois 155n19
Leslie, Mary Isabel *see* Lane, Temple
Lesueur, Winifred 64
Letts, Winifred M. (Mrs Verschoyle) 6–7, 16, 24, 48–49, 54, 55, 63, 67, 68, 80, 83, 145
  The Dean's Tree 81
  Pomomos Island 81
Leventhal, A. J. (Con) 21, 75–76
Lewis, C. S. 140
Lincoln Chambers 19
Linklater, Eric 141
literary prizes 1, 31–33
  see also Irish Book of the Year
literature, role in society 3–4
Lomis, Grant 89
London PEN 39–40
Longford, Lady Christine 7–8, 10, 18–19, 22, 33, 62, 80, 81, 83, 84, 101–104, 134–135
  A Biography of Dublin 101–102
  Country Places 101–102
  Making Conversation 101
  Printed Cotton 101–104, 116, 136
  Vespasian and Some of his Contemporaries 101
Longford, Lord (Edward Pakenham) 18–19, 34, 37, 40, 72n88, 101, 102, 144
Luddy, Maria 61–62

Lynch, Patricia 5, 7–8, 17, 33, 55, 58, 62, 74, 75, 83, 84, 92–95, 133, 144–145, 170
   Fiddler's Quest 94–95
   Lisheen at the Valley Farm 152, 157, 162
   The Turf-Cutter's Donkey 93
Lynd, Robert 106
Lyons, Ronald 48, 132
Lyons, W. G. 131–132, 146, 162

Mac Nie, Issa 24
Macardle, Dorothy 6, 7–8, 16–17n5, 20n19, 22, 33, 37, 52, 54, 55, 58n18, 93, 109, 170
   independence determined by class 58n18
   The Irish Republic 105, 108, 111–114
   political activism 62, 63–64, 119, 121
   reading committee 79
   relationships and networks 67–68, 69–70
Macauley, Rose 140
MacBride, Maud Gonne 9
MacCarthy, Bridget G. 8, 13, 91, 104
MacCurtain, Margaret 87–88
MacDonagh, Thomas 160
Mackenzie, Compton 50
MacLiammóir, Micheál 71–72n88, 80, 134
MacLysaght, Edward 5, 128–130, 133
MacManus, Francis 32
MacNamara, Brinsley 25, 26
MacNeice, Louis 42
MacNeill, Eoin 32
magazines and periodicals 10, 133, 134–138
Malone, Andrew E. 35, 37, 76
Mannin, Ethel 9–11, 19, 75, 84, 117–119, 124–125, 144
   Cactus 117
   Captain Moonlight 117
   Common Sense and the Child 117
   Common Sense and Morality 117
   Confessions and Impressions 115
   Late Have I Loved Thee 118–119
   Ragged Banners 117
   Red Rose 117
Manning, Mary 17, 72n88, 112
Markiewicz, Count Casimir 22
Markiewicz, Countess Constance 22, 112
Martin, Kingsley 47n127
Martyn, Edward 112
Marx, Erica 160
Masefield, John 31, 38
Masugi, Shizue 50
Maunsel & Co. 10, 128–131, 133
Maurois, Andre 49
Maxwell, Constantia 33
Mayne, Rutherford (Samuel John Waddell) 22, 37, 89, 144
McAuliffe, Dorothy 74
McCall, Seamus 37, 75–76
McCarthy, Desmond 37, 38, 39
McCracken, Mary-Ann 109
McCreary, Alistair 149
McDonagh, Donagh 12, 162, 163
McFadden, Roy 12, 155, 162, 163
McGinley, Helen 142
McGuinness, Norah 17
McKenzie, Donald F. 3–4, 84
McLeod, Caitriona 83
   Robert Emmet 81, 105
McNeill, James 75–76, 79–80
McNeill, Josephine 55, 75–76, 79–80, 82, 83, 99
Meaney, Gerardine 2, 6, 56, 66, 72, 135
Mentxaka, Aintzane Legarreta 72
Meredith, Owen 37
Miller, Carol 61
Miller, Liam 159, 164
Milligan, Alice 25, 33, 37, 130
Milne, Ewart 12, 151–152, 158–159, 170

Forty North Fifty West 152, 157–160
Letter from Ireland 151–152, 159
Mitchell, Margaret, *Gone with the Wind* 44
Mitchell, Susan 22–23, 129–130
Moloney, Helena 56, 109
Mooney, Ria 55
Moore, Marianne 85, 158
Morell, Lady Otteline 101
Morton, May 39–40
Motley magazine 16, 102
Mulhall, Anne 133–134
Murphy, Dervla 96
Murray, Simone 143
Murray, T. C. 25
 Spring Horizon 44
Myer, F. 139

National Library Reading Rooms 19
Nevinson, Henry 40
Ní Bheacháin, Caoilfhoinn 123
Ni Grada, Mairead 83
Nolan, Hilda 146

Ó Briain, Liam 134
Ó Gallchoir, Clíona 6, 104
Ó Lochlainn, Colm 144–145
O'Brien, Dermod 22
O'Brien, Edna 171
O'Brien, Flann 37, 73
O'Brien, Kate 7–8, 23, 29–30, 37, 46, 67, 71–72, 84, 90–92, 115–116, 119, 170, 171
 The Flower of May 91–92
 The Land of Spices 44–45, 92, 115, 141
 Mary Lavelle 92, 115
 That Lady 77, 90–92
O'Casey, Sean 28, 44, 46
O'Connor, Frank 25, 44
O'Donnell, Peadar 25, 34, 39–40, 44, 49
O'Donovan, Michael 25

O'Dowd, Mary 6
O'Faolain, Sean 10, 25, 26n47, 34, 35–36, 37, 44, 46–47, 123, 143–144, 160
O'Farrelly, Professor Agnes 16, 59, 62, 68
O'Flaherty, Liam 21, 25, 26n47, 46
O'Growney Award 31, 32
O'Hegarty, P. S. 28–29, 144–145
O'Kelly, Phyllis 51
O'Kelly, Sean T. 51
O'Leary, Margaret 32–33n79
O'Mahony, Mathew 114n163, 124
O'Malley, Ernie 160
O'Neill, Eugene 29n63
Orpen, William 22
O'Sullivan, Senator Donal 122
O'Sullivan, Seumas 20, 25, 37, 48–49, 129, 130, 162, 163

Pannell, Jessica L. 155
Pearse, Patrick 113–114, 130
PEN network *see* International PEN; Irish PEN
Piesse, Amanda 93
Pim, Sheila 37, 96n77, 160
 The Flowering Shamrock 122, 135
Potter, Rachel 36
Pound, Ezra 85, 86, 115, 134
printing presses 127–147, 168
 private 1, 11, 133, 147, 151–152, 168
publishers, interaction with writers 10
publishing histories 1

Quinn, Justin 85
Quota Press 145

Rainey, Lawrence 150
reading committees 1, 78–84
 decision-making process 80
Reddin, Kenneth 35, 40, 75–76
Reddins, Norman J. 163–164

Reid, Forrest 25, 37, 139, 140
Reynolds, Lorna 2, 7–8, 67, 68, 71–72, 77, 86, 91, 134–135
Richards, Sheila 72n88, 112
Rivers, Elizabeth 17
Robert's Café (Dublin) 18, 35
Roberts, George 129–131
Roberts, Henry L. 99
Robinson, Lennox 10–11, 22, 23, 25, 32–33, 80, 130, 144–145, 160
Rose, Jonathan 117
Ross, Madeleine 20n19, 67
Russell, Bertrand 101
Russell, Elizabeth 137
Russell, George (Æ) 19n17, 22, 23, 25, 30, 32, 112, 128–129
  New Songs 129–130
Ryan, John 23
Ryan, Louise 136

Salkeld, Beatrice 152, 157, 160
Salkeld, Blanaid 6–8, 11–12, 18, 20, 33, 37, 48–49, 53, 55, 93, 147, 169
  ... the engine is left running 85–86, 87–88, 116, 152–153, 165
  background 84–85
  Experiment in Error 85–86
  The Fox's Covert 85–86
  Hello Eternity! 84–85, 86, 116
  poetry 84–87
  political activism 62
  reading committee 79, 80–81
  relationships and networks 67n70, 69–70, 72–73, 160
  Scarecrow over the Corn 86
  shift from artist to businesswoman 150–162
  "Terenure" 87n39
  "The Woman Gardener" 85
  see also Gayfield Press; Women Writers' Club
Salkeld, Cecil ffrench 12, 37, 85, 151, 152, 153–154, 156, 162

Sand, George 74
Sanger, Margaret, *Family Limitations* 115
Sayers, Peig 32–33n79
Schriebman, Susan 86, 88
Scott, Patrick 17
Sears, David 35, 93n63
Shaw, George Bernard 10–11, 23, 24, 32, 93n63, 144
Sheehy, Edward 158
Sheehy Cruise O'Brien, Kathleen 55, 63
Sheehy Skeffington, Hanna 5, 7–8, 9, 18, 37, 45–46, 54, 55, 56, 58n21, 75, 109, 116, 117, 117–118, 132, 146
  drafting of Irish Constitution 62n38
  Geneva Conference (1936) 60–61
  reading committee 79, 80–81
Sheehy Skeffington, Owen 71n87
Shepard, Graham 42
Shovlin, Frank 137–138
Sigerson Shorter, Dora 129–130
Skelton, Robin 151
Sleator, James 156
Smith, Sidney 163
Smith, Stevie 50
Smithson, Annie P. 37, 73n96, 132
Smyers, Virginia 12–13
Smyllie, Bertie 24n34, 42–43
Solomon, Estella 22
Somerville, Edith 25, 33
Soroptomists Club 59
Staunton, Helen *see* Le Brocquy, Sybil
Stephens, James 24, 25, 129, 160
Stope, Marie, *Wise Parenthood* 115
Strachey, Lytton 101
Strong, L. A. G. 141
Stuart, Francis 25, 41–42, 156
Sullivan, Moynagh 85, 154
Swanzy, Mary 17
Sweeney, Jack 160

Swift, Jonathan 55, 68
Synge, John Millington 129, 130

Tagore, Rabindranath 85
Talbot Press 10, 20, 48, 105, 106,
    131–133, 146, 161
Thom, Alexander 128
Three Candles Press 132, 145, 157
Toksvig, Signe 27
    Eve's Doctor 44
Tone, Matilda 109–110n139, 140
Tone, Theobald Wolfe 19, 70,
    105n118, 107n128, 109, 110, 140
Travis, Trysh 4
Troy, Una 115n167
Turchi, Nichola 135
Tynan, Katherine 33, 130
Tynan, Kathryn 96

United Dublin Arts Club 15, 19,
    22–24n35
    membership 23–24
Ustinov, Peter 50

Venture Club 59n25

Waddell, Helen 7–8, 33, 38, 81, 84,
    89–90, 119, 170
    Desert Fathers 82, 89–90, 170
    Peter Abelard: A Novel 89
Waddell, Hugh 89
Walshe, Maurice 37, 38, 96
Walsh, Patrick 6
Walsh, Róisín 75n105, 144, 145, 146
Watts, Richard 47n127
Waugh, Evelyn 101
Weaver, Harriet 11
Weintraub, Stanley 29
Wellesley, Dorothy 33

Wells, H. G. 37–38
Whelan, Bernadette 6
White Stag Group 17–18, 47–48
Wilford, R. A. 36
Wills, Clair 41, 42
Wingfield, Sheila 5, 6–7, 12, 73, 86,
    151, 160, 162–163, 170
Wollstonecraft, Mary 107–108
Women Writers' Club 1–2, 19, 52,
    167–171
    appeals for professional status for
        women 58–59
    engagement with drafting of Irish
        Constitution 58–66, 169
    feminism 60–66
    foundation 7–8, 17–18, 53–54
    political activism 57–66, 115–116
    relationships and networks 67–76
    social and political context 2–3, 9,
        17–18, 53–56, 55–57, 78
    see also Book of the Year
Women's International League for
    Peace (WILFP) 19
Women's Social and Political League
    (WSPL) 68–69
Woolf, Leonard 11, 160–161
Woolf, Virginia 11, 33, 91, 99, 158,
    160–161
    A Room of One's Own 104

Yeats, Elizabeth 127n1
Yeats, Jack B. 22, 75–76, 93, 151
Yeats, Lily 127n1
Yeats, W. B. 8, 19, 22, 23, 24, 26n48,
    33, 35, 85, 101, 117–118, 143
    Maunsel printing 127–128, 129–130
    promotion and fundraising of
        Academy of Letters 30–32
Young, Ella 129–130

www.ingramcontent.com/pod-product-compliance
Lightning Source LLC
Chambersburg PA
CBHW071410300426
44114CB00016B/2247